Editor Dr. T S M MacLean

A JUST GOD AND A SAVIOUR

(and other sermons and addresses)

R A FINLAYSON

Published in 2002 by:
Knox Press
15 North Bank Street
Edinburgh EH1 2LS

ISBN 0 9514599 4 5

Cover design by D W MacLeod
Cover photo of Lochcarron courtesy of
Alex Ingram ABIPP AMPA ARPS
Typeset by D W MacLeod
Printed by Lewis Recordings, Inverness

Foreword

R A Finlayson was Professor of Systematic Theology at the Free Church of Scotland College in Edinburgh from 1946 to 1966. It was a barren time in British evangelicalism. Dr Martyn Lloyd-Jones and Rev John Stott were beginning to exercise memorable ministries and Dr F F Bruce was beginning to lay the foundations and plot the course for conservative Biblical Studies. But in theology proper, little was being done. Evangelicals lived in an intellectual fortress, content to be identified with the single doctrine of inerrancy, treating the incarnation, the atonement and the trinity as in-house mysteries on which everything had already been said and leaving the work of the Holy Spirit to be defined by experience rather than by doctrinal formulation. There was reverence a-plenty, but little academic rigour. We were still at the stage where scholarship was an enemy and every scientist who became a Christian was liable to be paraded as a trophy.

It would be too much to say that in the 1940s and 50s Finlayson was the only evangelical Systematic Theologian working in Britain, but it would not be all that far off the truth. James Orr had died in 1913 and Jim Packer heralded his arrival on the theological scene with the publication of *Fundamentalism and the Word of God* in 1958. There wasn't much in between. Finlayson was ploughing a lonely furrow and the loneliness was often exacerbated by the opposition of those who should have been his friends.

A major part of his contribution was made in the class-room where he gave successive generations of students a grounding in Christian doctrine not matched anywhere else in the United Kingdom. But he also worked tirelessly outside the class-room, not least through the *Monthly Record,* where his editorials focused the sharp light of Christian principles on the public questions of the day. The article, "The Bible and the Nation", sets forth brilliantly the political theology which guided those twenty years of first-class Christian journalism.

In addition to lecturing and writing Finlayson also preached tirelessly and some readers will instantly recognise such sermons as "The Three Men of Calvary". Like much of the material published here, it is only an outline and inevitably conveys a very inadequate impression of Finlayson as a preacher. We miss the inflection of the voice, the spare, yet energetic figure, the reverent authority of the body language, the angelic smile (such a contrast to the acerbic prose of the *Monthly Record*) and the piercing blue eyes, half glint, half gleam. But Alexander Stewart's *Tree of Promise* consists only of outlines, as does McCheyne's *Basket of Fragments* and Hodge's *Princeton Sermons*. We would love to have the flesh as well as the bones, but the bones are better than nothing.

The remaining dimension to Finlayson was his work in the wider evangelical world beyond the Free Church. This extra-denominational activity wasn't always counted to him for righteousness, but it was invaluable to struggling students in the various Christian Unions and even more so to the struggling ministers whom Finlayson gathered into the Scottish Tyndale Fellowship. These men (in those days there were no women ministers) were working valiantly as biblical expositors, but they often had little idea of "the analogy of the faith" and Finlayson's thorough and comprehensive vision of the whole field of Christian doctrine gave them an indispensable context for their preaching. At such gatherings, the speaker welcomed questions, but the queries were raised at the interrogator's risk. Anything that verged on stupidity would be dealt with ruthlessly.

Part of the value of this connection is historical. It provides us with one of our few documentary sources for the state of Scottish evangelicalism after the War. As such it will serve as an enduring reminder of the issues they were facing, the topics they were exploring, the assumptions they were making and the world they were living in.

But this is no mere monument. It is a living repository of Christian truth. Some of it I heard long ago. That didn't surprise me. What did surprise me was how much of it I myself had preached. I obviously learned more than I knew. Could there be any better tribute to a great teacher?

Donald Macleod
Edinburgh, June 2002

Introduction

This collection of Sermons by the late Professor R A Finlayson (1895-1989) is a sequel to those published by Christian Focus in 1996 under the title *Reformed Theological Writings*. Earlier published books and lectures of his include the Campbell Morgan Memorial lecture *The Holiness of God* (1955), *The Cross in the Experience of our Lord* (1955). 'Contemporary ideas of Inspiration' in *Revelation and the Bible* (ed. C F H Henry 1959), and *God's Light on Man's Destiny* (n.d.).

The previous collection of sermons in *Reformed Theological Writings* was chosen because of the clarity of thought evident in them, which would appeal to readers worldwide, and not merely to those within the theological community of the Free Church of Scotland. This sequel has the same aim.

The sermons in the book as a whole have been divided into eight groups, beginning naturally with a group entitled *GOD*. And the first sermon begins "God is, and is knowable", which is the foundation of the whole book.

In the second group entitled *THE CROSS*, the exposition begins with *The Suffering Servant* in Isaiah 52-53, passes through chapters such as *The Three Men of Calvary*, and ends with a chapter on *The Sacraments*.

The third group entitled *THE RESURRECTION*, initially considers this, first as a physical fact following the crucifixion of the Messiah, then as a message of the existence of real ties between heaven and earth which cannot be broken, and finally as an experience which provides peace, purpose and power to the believer.

In the fourth group which deals with the Apostle Paul, the introductory chapter is entitled *Paul, the Most Companionable of Men*. Among the twenty-six names of Paul's friends listed in Romans 16, at least seven were women, who toiled at duties, the faithful carrying out of which were both observed and praised by Paul himself.

The fifth group deals with *THE CHURCH*, that Temple of which Christ is both the Foundation and Chief Corner Stone. It is also described as an organism of which He is the Head, and of which she is the Bride.

In the sixth group entitled *The Quest of the Individual Soul* the subject of Salvation is illustrated both from the point of view of God pursuing the soul and taking it home, and also of the soul of man, in turmoil, being brought to see the light, and wending its own way home under Providence.

The seventh group deals with sermons which did not fit easily into any of the preceding sections, but were still of an expository nature. It includes Professor Finlayson's first publshed paper *The Mystery of Folded Wings*, written when he was aged 33, which provides an indication of the good things that were to follow. It deals partly with the consequences of overwork in man.

Finally there is a small group of sermons on the devil. It is short because it is wise to spend as little time as possible on this subject, since it is known that it may lead to unnecessary temptation. But to ignore it completely is to ignore one aspect of the truth, and so two sermons on this subject have been included.

The Editor wishes to acknowledge help received in different ways from Rev. and Mrs. Hugh Ferrier, Dr. I R Macdonald, Rev Professor J L Mackay, Mr D W MacLeod and Rev. Professor J A Macleod, and finally Rev W B Graham for his care and consideration in checking the text.

Tom MacLean
Perth, March 2002

Contents

7 Bible Sermons

8 The Devil

Group 1
God

GOD

God is. That is the greatest affirmation that mortal man can make. It is said of Dr John Duncan, Rabbi Duncan of Aberdeen, that he danced with delight on the Brig of Dee on the night when he was convinced that there was a God.

To the fundamental statement 'God is', we add three more words, 'and is knowable'. These two affirmations of faith form the foundation and inspiration of all religion. But the Christian religion is distinctive in that it affirms that God is known only in his self-revelation. God is like the sun in the heavens which reveals and communicates itself as it shines. Thus God reveals himself and communicates himself as he shines. And to know him we must stand in his self-revelation, and respond to his self-giving.

The story is told that there was some discussion among the birds of the forest as to the reality of the sun in the sky. To all it was no problem except to the owl which is a bird of the night and seldom ventures out in daylight. One day the other birds persuaded the owl to come out into the light of day and see for herself. The owl with much hesitation agreed. But as it came out it closed its eyes tight, looked around, and then hooted, 'Where is the sun?'

The fool says in his heart, 'There is no God'; he closes his eyes and dismisses God with these words.

True, God has more than one firmament in which he shines, but to gain intimacy and certainty of knowledge, that is, to know him as a personal God, it is his self-revelation in the Bible that matters most to us. The Bible is given, not to prove the existence of God, but to reveal him at work, to let his light shine as he speaks and acts.

There is thus but one kind of revelation that makes God personal to us – his revelation as a Saviour. And this is given only in the Bible. There we can see him at work creating and saving, creating that he may save.

In the light of the Bible's revelation we can assert certain facts about God – his being, his character, his activities.

1. God is a Spirit in his being (or nature)

While this fact forces itself upon our attention from the opening pages of Scripture, it was Christ who formulated most clearly that definition of God as he spoke to the woman of Samaria at the well of

Sychar: 'God is a Spirit and they that worship him must worship him in spirit and in truth.'

We can claim that God is *pure Spirit* in the sense that he is not part Spirit and part physical as man is. As pure Spirit he has no parts, no body, no limbs, no passions. For that reason he has no physical presence. He is visible only to spirit. When the Bible speaks of God having eyes, ears, hands, feet, it is to convey to us the sense perceptions that these organs convey to us – hearing, feeling, seeing and even tasting.

But we assert that this implies no sort of imperfection in God. Spirit is not a limited, restricted form of existence. It is the perfect unit of existence. The body that man possesses is, in many ways, a restriction, limiting his experience in many directions as to time and place.

But when we say that God is infinite Spirit we pass completely out of the realm of our own experience. We are limited as to time and space, as to knowledge and power.

God is essentially unlimited, as every element of his nature is unlimited. Time as past or present or future does not exist for him. He dwells in an eternal present. This may be the meaning of his revelation to Moses at the bush as the 'I am'. His infinity as to time we call his eternity, his infinity as to space we call his omnipresence, his infinity as to knowledge we call his omniscience.

The infinity of God also means that he is transcendent above the universe. This emphasises his detachment from his creation as himself uncreated and self-existent – the fire that burnt in the bush, and yet the bush was not consumed; the fire that owed nothing to its environment, but was self-fed. God is thus external to the world, the sovereign Creator and Judge.

But we apply another quality to the infinite Spirit that is God: it is his immanence. By this we mean that as infinite Spirit he is within all things, acting from within outwards, from the centre of every atom, and from the innerward springs of life and thought, of feeling and will, a conscious sequence of cause and effects. As God says to Isaiah the prophet (57:15), 'I dwell in the high and holy place; with him also that is of a contrite heart and a humble spirit', or as Paul said to the men of Athens (Acts 17:24-28): 'God that made the world and all things therein....dwelleth not in temples made with hands....seeing he giveth to all life and breath and all things....and is not far from any one of us....for in him we live and move and have our being.'

As infinite Spirit he is transcendent....above all, and immanent....within all: within the smallest atom of matter and the whole material universe. It is all an atom to God for whom our dimensions of small and great do not exist.

2. God is a person – (His character)

Here we are on more familiar ground, inasmuch as man, bearing God's image, is a person. The personality of man unifies all his faculties and functioning – his thinking, and feeling and willing – so that he can act responsibly and intelligently. His person is the whole of him.

Christ spoke to God in terms that were possible only in person to person relationship. From our own personality we can deduce something of what personality must mean in God. It means *self-consciousness*. The animal creation is endowed with consciousness; only man has self-consciousness. He can reflect on himself. God has perfect and complete knowledge of himself.

Personality also means *rationality*. God is supreme mind and therefore possesses infinite intelligence and wisdom.

Einstein attained to this conception of God, though the prophets of his race would have brought him much further. 'My religion,' says Einstein 'consists of a humble admiration of the illimitable superior spirit who reveals himself in the slight details we are able to perceive with our frail and feeble minds. That deeply emotional conviction of the presence of a superior reasoning power, which is revealed in the comprehensible universe, forms my idea of God.'

But person in God, as in man, means *emotion*: heart as well as mind in the highest order imaginable. He takes the tenderest emotion known to mankind – that of a mother to her infant child, and he envisages a situation in which that tie may break: 'Can a mother forget her sucking child that she should not have compassion on the son of her womb?: yea they may forget, yet will I not forget thee' (Isa. 49:15).

Person implies moral character in God. *Moral character* with a sense of moral values. It is in virtue of God's possession of moral values that we can attribute to him moral qualities that can be attributed to character in the lower plane: justice, righteousness, love and compassion. And the infinite God is in each of these attributes, and each is a full manifestation of God in the situation in which it is exercised. While God is more than the sum of all his attributes, it must be true that there is never more of one attribute than of another: more love than of justice, more mercy than truth. God in the full plenitude of his nature is in each. And if there be one attribute of God's character that is all pervading or all comprehensive, it is his holiness. It is the heart of all that God is and is predicated of all his other attributes, holy love, holy compassion, holy wisdom, holy justice. It finds some exemplification in the faculty of light. The natural spectrum contains within it all seven colours, as in the rainbow, but when the sun shines without obstacle or interruption all the colours blend into white light. So all God's attributes in operation blend into the radiance of his holiness.

Our conclusion must be that without personality in God there could be no religion. An abstract ideal, however beautiful, could not inspire a religion that would command the entire commitment of rational beings. The worship of a personal God means that we are entering into a personal relationship with him, and that we can respond to his fellow-ship in reverence, love and obedience.

God is a fellowship

Here we depart from analogies in human personality. Not only can God enter into fellowship, but he is a fellowship in his own very substance. He could not be God without this fellowship. This is what we mean by a Trinity. The word itself is not in Scripture, but the reality of it underlies the whole of biblical revelation, and the fact of it dawned upon the consciousness of the church quite gradually as she pondered the substance of the revelation given to her. Thus she came to accept God as one in three persons. It is true that 'person' is not the ideal term to use, but we cannot find a better.

'Person' suggests to us an individual who thinks or acts independently of all other persons. But this is not what we mean by the word 'Trinity'. Though Father, Son and Spirit can be distinguished as three persons, they are not three individuals with independent life and rights. They exist in such a unity of thought, and will, and life that they constitute one God. There is thus perfect equality between all three persons, as well as perfect unity. But they operate differently, and it is only in their operations that we recognise them as ordered persons. The first person, i.e. the Father, plans or purposes; the second person, i.e. the Son, reveals the plan; and the third person, i.e. the Spirit, applies it so as to make it effective. Or as it is sometimes stated, thought is of the Father, word or hypostasis is of the Son, and action is of the Spirit. These are, of course, only attempts to summarise what must ever remain to us a mystery, but a mystery none the less that sheds light on other mysteries.

(i)   It means, for example, that God is by very nature self-revealing and self-communing, and that this communion was possible within the Godhead from all eternity, the Father communicating himself to the Son, and the Father and Son communicating to the Spirit.

(ii)   It means that wherever God enters he creates a fellowship patterned on his own: the church, the home, the family are all reflections of that fellowship that is in God.

(iii)   It means that because there is diversity in God's manifestations and operations, his manysidedness is reflected in all his creation: in the being of man, in the whole of animate and inanimate creation, in the entire universe, giving scope for the researches of those who are tracing the footsteps of the Creator in his creation.

(iv)   It means God was never quiescent – dormant as we might say – he was eternally throbbing with life and love and self-giving – the living God. If there were not a fellowship of this kind, he would have been living for the eternal ages, when there was no creation, aloof and alone. Such a God is to us inconceivable, a being alone in an empty universe. He could not be a God of love, since love is self-communication to another and there cannot be love without an object to love. Such a God could scarcely be said to be alive. But it is the eternal, living God that we are in touch with.

So the Christian conception of God is not an impersonal being who is alone and aloof, but a fellowship, three equal persons in the blessedness of deity, not needing anyone or anything from without to perfect that blessedness, and not needing a created universe to add to it. But when God created a rational universe it was to extend his fellowship with his rational creatures. Thus he created man – made in his image and after his likeness – to respond to that fellowship and extend and enlarge human spiritual life to new and inexhaustible levels.

3.   God in his activities

(i) God in creation

God's relation to creation can be conceived of as physical and moral. Matter is not evil – it is the creation of God. Creation is the visible expression of God's wisdom in planning, and God's power in executing.

It has to be remembered that power in God is altogether different from our conception of power as we find it in man. Man's power is largely the intelligent use of power that is already existing, such as water, steam and electricity. God's power is not dependent on existing material. It is creative. It brings into existence what did not exist before.

The biblical revelation regarding the creation of the universe in general and of this world in particular indicates three distinguishable factors:

(a)   The free exercise of God's will was the causative element in creation and the fontal source of all that is. Creation was a free and intelligent act based on infinite wisdom and goodness.

(b)   The second factor is God's word. God's will found realisation in a word. 'Let there be' was the divine fiat that caused his will to be expressed and become visible as it was. From it creation took its form and pattern.

(c)   The third factor in creation is God's Spirit. The creative word became operational through a Spirit. 'The Spirit of God brooded over the face of the deep.' The figure is of the mother dove sitting on her eggs, so that through the warmth and vitality of her body life might emerge.

It is not difficult for us to see here the Trinity and each of the three persons – the purpose of the Father to create, the revelation of the Son to work out the pattern in God's mind, and the power of the Spirit to execute it.

The three material elements introduced into this operation are light, energy, and matter, and in that order are recognisable today as the three phases of the same reality. It is indeed a commonplace in the laboratory of the physicist to turn matter into energy and energy into light. God operated in the reverse order, light generating energy and energy generating matter. So the divine command, 'Let there be light', was setting in motion the creative energy of God. Sir James Jeans in *The Mysterious Universe* asserts that the whole story of the creation of the universe can be told with perfect accuracy in the six words, 'God said, Let there be Light'.

In this the triune God was at work so that we can say that creation is from the Father, through the Son, by the Holy Spirit.

(ii) God in redemption

The moral creation was marred through the intrusion of moral evil. Man claimed his right to determine for himself what was good and what was evil; that is the meaning of eating of the tree of the knowledge of good and evil. And man's self determination means his disavowance of God's right to direct him. And so sin entered through man's choice and the whole creation was marred.

It was then that the purpose of God's heart to redeem a fallen race came into operation. It was the product of his wisdom and grace. And God the Son became sponsor for the restoration of a lost race and the recreation of a ruined humanity. It is for him a matter of putting away sin. He does not deal with evil by refusing to recognise its existence or by extenuating its guilt or by minimising its consequences. He deals with it openly so that it is seen for what it really is, and he dealt with it as it deserved. This is what happened historically at Calvary. God sent his messenger, His own Son, on a task that only God could meet, and the Holy Spirit upheld the sin-bearing Saviour in life and in death. And so God – all three persons – was in Christ reconciling the world unto himself.

There on Calvary the great moral issues were brought into the open for the entire moral universe to behold. The sin that devised it – its malice. The sin that wrought it – its cruelty. The sin that needed it – its guilt. But that is in the forefront. In the background there was the righteousness that demanded it in its rectitude, the love that offered it in its sacrifice, the fidelity and patience that crowned it in its devotion and self-sacrifice.

To stand at Calvary in penitence and faith is to be reconciled with God in dealing with sin in the here and the hereafter. Whatever the eternal future may unveil in suffering and pain as the desert of sin, it is but a drop in the bucket of moral and spiritual suffering compared to the anguish in the soul of the Son of God as He drank the cup of divine wrath for sin that was not His own. And the Holy Spirit unveils it before our gaze, and bids us to look upon Him whom we have pierced and sorrow for Him. Thus the fountain of our penitence is broken open and we mourn as one mourns after an only child, as a mother mourns for her first-born..

(iii) God in the experience of the Christian life

There God is working, restoring, recreating, reconciling. This is particularly the department of the Spirit's operation, and I think He is called the Holy Spirit because it is His task to communicate the holiness of God to the souls of men. In this he quickens a regenerate soul to cooperate with Him and make the soul willing in a day of His power. This cooperation is made through faith, the gift of the Spirit of God to the new-born soul. Thus the divine Spirit puts the sinner's station right with God in justification. Then the sinner's position is made regular by adoption as a child into the family of God. And then his condition is put right, so that in regeneration he feels and acts as a child. And then his life and character are put right in sanctification.

And little by little, these become real to the quickened soul. The love of the Father that reached him, the mercy of the Son that redeemed him, and the grace of the Spirit that regenerates and sanctifies him. And with words, love and praise the Christian traces his salvation to Father, Son and Spirit, one God, Saviour and lord, and recognises that his life is now hid with Christ in God.

That is the Christian's God. His greatness calls for our adoration. His majesty calls for our surrender. His goodness calls for our fortitude and love.

'How great is the God we adore'

THE NAMES OF GOD

The biblical significance of a name is likely to be unknown to most of us. For us a name is merely a means of distinguishing one person from another, a tag that distinguishes Tom from Dick, and Dick from Harry. But the names tell us nothing else about Tom, Dick or Harry.

In the Bible it is far different. In biblical usage names are a fitting introduction to the persons who bear them. And as children grew into manhood and their characters became formed and significant, there was another name added. Thus the disciples of Jesus were renamed after their incorporation into his travelling fellowship; Simon was called Peter to point to certain elements in his character as a witness to Christ.

This is more strikingly seen in the Old Testament where names were laden with deep personal significance - Collected Sermonsicance, sometimes indicating what the bearer was, or what it was fondly hoped he would become. Names were, therefore, descriptions of the bearer, pointers to character.

In some such way was the name of God used; it was a disclosure of His nature, or character, or activity. And since the biblical revelation of God is progressive, the names of God form a progressive revelation of His nature and character. This lends absorbing significance to God's names; it is part of the divine revelation.

It will be noticed, too, that the names of God are disclosed to meet certain situations His people may be in. A name becomes meaningful because of the personal situation in which it is given. It is designed to reveal or emphasize the sufficiency of God to meet that situation, the adequacy of God to fit into that situation in which His trusting servants may find themselves. That lent added significance of the divine name to those to whom it was disclosed – it had a personal relationship, a personal relevance, a personal adequacy. We shall notice this fact as we go along – the name of God revealed to persons in a relationship in which the name was meaningful to them.

1 El, Eloah, Elohim

This is the general name of deity, and it is always translated 'God' in the English Bible. *El* was its simple form and it is used extra-biblically

– used by pagans and polytheists. It is used of the biblical deity mainly in poetry.

Eloah is a further extension of the name, expressive perhaps of personality. The Muslims have preserved it in the name Allah. We cannot forget that the Jews and Muslims had a common father in Abraham, and to that extent a common revelation.

Elohim is, however, the common name for God in the Bible, used between 2000 and 3000 times. It is a plural form of Eloah. There is considerable discussion as to why it should be a plural form with a singular verb. Some would say it signifies the plural of majesty, i.e. the sovereign 'we'. Others think it may be a vestigial remnant of polytheism, but for this there is no proof. Christians often accept it as a subtle disclosure of the plurality of persons in the Godhead; subtle because the doctrine of the Trinity was not to be disclosed to man till the ministry of Christ began. But it served at least to signify the unity of God and at the same time suggest that it was not a single unity – it was a complex unity, a plurality in a unity.

The name stands pre-eminently for the power, the all-prevailing force of deity. It is significant that it appeared in the opening verse of Genesis: 'In the beginning God created....' Here God is revealed in creative energy and power. All creation is a forth-putting of the creative power of Elohim. It is significant that the plural Elohim is the creative agent, since creation implies the manifoldness of God, the manysidedness of his nature and power.

It is here that the physical scientist finds scope for his investigations – unlimited scope we would say, for there is unlimited manysidedness in God, unlimited variety that can impress itself upon his creation, manifold ways in which His works can be investigated and followed out. It is this that gives breadth and depth to the field of exploration and investigation – it is the work of Elohim.

2. Yahweh – translated Jehovah

This is the specific name of God, as Elohim was the generic name; the God of nature and the God of revelation. It is a pastoral name that bears on His relationship to His people. It occurs nearly 7000 times in the Bible. It is thought to proclaim the self-existence of God – to reveal God as the only one who has self-existence.

When Moses asked for a revelation of God that would convince the children of Israel that he was His messenger, God gave the name: 'I am' – I exist – I have an independent, autonomous existence. Then Moses asked for a further explication of this cryptic name, and the reply was, 'I am that I am.' I am equals I am. I can be compared only to myself, to no other being. Self-consistent as well as self-existent. And that was the conception of God that Moses was given in the symbolism of the burning bush; a fire that was self-fed, that owed nothing to its surroundings, for the bush was not consumed. It is the personal name of God, a name that reveals His independent self-existence – independent of all His creation – a name that reveals His nature and character.

When God entered into a covenant with His people to save, it was the name Jehovah He used as indicative of this relationship. Of Abraham, Isaac and Jacob, God said, 'By my name Jehovah was I not known to them' (Exod. 6:2-3). That is, they were not conscious of this covenant relationship to their God – it was now being invested with new meaning. He became the God of revelation. This was a new revelation by means of which God was now identifying Himself with the history of Israel, with the national happenings of their lives. And since that time Israel walked in the light of that revealing name. The self-existing God – the author and giver of life – was their God – quickening, sustaining, reviving and upholding. So henceforth God was acting in a new relationship – saving, delivering, sealing the people as His.

It is significant that Elohim is the name used by non-Israelites – by believers in God outside the Jewish race, or before the Jewish race had any separate identity. Jehovah is the name used by the Israelites as signifying that covenant relationship. In the book of Job, at the beginning and ending is the name Jehovah used. When Job and his friends speak, it is Elohim they use.

3. Adonai, or Lord

Adonai is again a plural form occurring some 350 times; the singular Adon is not often used. The word Adonai expresses, of course, authority in God's relationship to His people, but not an arbitrary authority – rather the authority of ownership combined with paternal love. When it was first revealed to Abraham it proclaimed God's sovereignty over all events – the God who was in control of affairs and fulfilled His purposes.

This is seen in the vision of the young prophet Isaiah; when King Uzziah died, he 'saw the Lord on his throne, Adonai and Lord, high and lifted up' – the earthly throne vacant, the heavenly throne occupied by one who controlled all events.

This name in particular was applied to Christ and was accepted by Him: 'Ye call me Master and Lord, and ye say well, for so I am,' He said to His disciples. It was pre-eminently the name applied to Him after His resurrection: 'We have seen the Lord.' His triumph over death and the grave proclaimed His supreme Lordship.

These are the three basic names of God; all others are extensions of these three. The basic names reveal the creative energy of God, His self-existence that places Him outside His creation (His transcendence), and His Lordship that brings Him into His creation as sovereign ruler and disposer of all things (his immanence).

His other names are extensions of these three – given in special situations to present and apply the sufficiency of God to meet the situation in hand. The life of Abraham is a good example of this. Abraham's progress is punctuated by fresh revelations of God; these were the milestones on his pilgrim way leading him on to his destination.

4. God-Almighty – El Shaddai

The Authorised Version translation of El Shaddai is not a good translation. The root word 'shad' is connected with maternal sustenance and is translated here and there as 'breasts' and 'teats'. The significance of it is that it is a particular, tender word implying sufficiency – the all-sufficiency of God is the most adequate presentation.

Its first appearance is again in the life of Abraham. At a critical period in Abraham's life, when the path ahead was dark and inscrutable, God said to him: 'I am El Shaddai, walk before me, and be thou whole hearted' (Gen. 17:1). It was the all-sufficiency of God for the situation that confronted Abraham.

'The God that is enough' is the most fitting translation. It is the revelation of a God who is completely adequate to the situation you are in, who fits into the situation so perfectly that there is no intrusion on your personality, no outrage – all so natural because it is supernatural, like mother and child.

5. Jehovah-Jireh

In the Old Testament this name is associated with a place (Gen. 22:14), but it was a place that revealed the certainty of the divine provision – and the faithfulness of God towards them that trust Him. It was associated with Abraham's supreme testing on Mount Moriah when he was about to sacrifice his son Isaac, and at the critical moment God stepped in and made provision for this sacrifice – provision by the substitution of His own lamb for the sacrifice.

While El Shaddai proclaims that God is adequate for every situation, Jehovah-Jireh proclaims that God promises to provide what is needed – He pledges His faithfulness to meet the need. And so He links His sufficiency to us with a promise.

6. Jehovah-Shalom – The Lord give Peace

This was the name given to Gideon when he was being called to be Leader of the Israelite forces against the Midianites. He felt his own inadequacy for the task and his mind was troubled; he was engulfed with bewilderment and fear. And in his perplexity he set up an altar of worship and there he found the new name Jehovah-Shalom – the God who gives peace.

It is perhaps significant that it was at the altar of worship that this disclosure was given. But it never faded out. Shalom became the peculiar Jewish greeting, and one can see the force of it. The Jews were relatively a small country surrounded by foes. The threat of war was never far away, but the great yearning of the Jewish heart was for peace, for the Jews were essentially a peace-loving people. That disclosure that their God was Jehovah-Shalom – the God that gives peace was very meaningful to them. But for us the name will ever be associated with the altar – the altar of Calvary.

7. Jehovah Tsidkenu – the Lord our Righteousness

It is to Jeremiah the prophet that this name is communicated. The prophet was dismayed and appalled at the unrighteousness around him. Even God's prophets were not immune from the general declension of standards and morals. And over the welter of declension and depravity Jeremiah sees one arising who shall restore equity, raise the moral standards, and 'A King who shall reign and prosper and shall execute judgment and justice in the earth'. And, according to Jeremiah, He shall be called 'Jehovah Tsidkenu', the Lord our Righteousness.

If we accept the probability that it was a vision of Messiah – of Christ – that Jeremiah had, we can see the far reaching significance of the new name – 'The Lord our Righteousness.' The one who came to declare the righteousness that God demands, and who himself is the righteousness that God provides. In any case the name has been taken over by the New Testament, especially by Paul in Romans, for there we have an unfolding of the fact that the righteousness God demands, God provides.

8. God as Father

This is the designation most sparingly employed in the Old Testament, though the most frequent one in the New. Yet it has its root in the Old.

It was used in the creative sense – God is Father in the sense that He is our Creator, our Maker, our Provider. This though sparingly used is a biblical conception – other religions had not risen to the vision of God being our Father in the sense that He had made us and therefore had claims upon us. The prophet Isaiah (64:8) used it in that sense.

The description Father is also used of God's relationship to Israel as a nation. It signified His covenant relationship with His people. In this connection it did not seem to have later on a personal sense. No Israelite was likely to address God as 'My Father'. He was rather the Father of the nation, of the covenant people of Israel. It was the New Testament that brought out the wealth of meaning in this name. On the lips of Christ it was a relationship such as no other human being ever bore. He was eternal Father to an eternal Son. But Christ taught His disciples to use it for themselves as 'our Father'. And the message of the resurrection bases it in His relationship to God: 'Go and tell my disciples, behold I ascend unto my Father and your Father, my God and your God' (John 20:17). There He bases our sonship on His Sonship – though of a different order, the one is the root of the other. And 'Father' seems to sum up the wealth of all the divine names and gather them all together in a personal relationship. But it is exclusively the privilege of those who are joined by faith to Jesus Christ, and is based on worship. As Paul says: 'Ye are the children of God by faith in Jesus Christ' (Gal. 3:26).

Conclusion

One can thus see how the name of God stood for God Himself– His character, His nature, His person. So when a person worshipped he is said to have called on the name of the Lord, in all that He is, in faithfulness, mercy and love. And departure from God was spoken of as 'forgetting the name of the Lord'. 'To take the name of the Lord in vain' was to despise His character, to dishonour His majesty. So the name of the Lord became the sheet anchor of faith – the pledge of His faithfulness: 'The name of the LORD is a strong tower; the righteous runneth into it and is safe' (Prov. 18:10).

This connotation of Christ's name was taken over in the New Testament. To believe on the name of the Lord Jesus is to shelter behind what He is. To gather together in His name is to worship Him for what He is, and found a community of worshippers in what He is. To be hated of all men for His name's sake is to trust the kind of God who is revealed in His people. The Jewish rulers forbad Peter and John 'to speak at all nor teach in the name of Jesus' (Acts 4:18) – to proclaim His saving power and unfold the riches of His character, but the Church members became known as all those who called upon the name of Christ – hence Christians.

THE STAINLESS PURITY OF GOD'S CHARACTER

Holiness exposes and condemns sin. Sin is the absence of holiness. The purity of God was an abiding consciousness of many Old Testament prophets. Habakkuk speaks for them all when he declares (Hab 1:13) 'Thou art of purer eyes than to behold evil, and canst not look upon iniquity'. The thought is that the holiness of God creates in Him such a revulsion against sin that He cannot look upon it: it is so alien to His holy nature that He stands at an infinite distance from it; it is in such disharmony with His character that He cannot allow it into His presence. He destroys it with the breath of His mouth. There is no other way of assessing sin than of viewing it in the light of God's purity.

The fact and the nature of sin cannot be understood unless it is seen at the font from which it sprang, as shown to us historically in Genesis 3. Apart from this view of it, our notions about it will be haphazard and confused. To many it is just a misfortune, or an animal instinct, or a breach of social convention, or a symptom of neurosis. But the Bible presents it as arising not from man's physical relation to the brute creation, but from his spiritual relationship to God. Man's relation to God was ethical – a relation of person to Person. It was because of this that man was taken into covenant with God, and that he was acquainted with the terms of entering that covenant, and the promises of blessing that would flow from it in the abiding fellowship of God and development in all spiritual progress.

Thus the possibility of sin is involved in the constitution of man's nature as a free moral agent.

While the origin of sin in the universe is not revealed to us, we can see from Genesis 3 that it entered into man's experience from without. It is significant that man had been warned of God of the existence of evil in the spiritual realm as soon as he had been created. And it is evident that this power of evil had access to man – he was not sheltered from it because he was a free moral agent with right of choice. He was permitted by his maker to have an experience of God, and he was forbidden to have an experience of evil. That is why he was forbidden to eat of the tree of the knowledge of good and evil.

But because man has God's image, he was a special target for assault from the powers of evil. An attack on man was an attack on God whose image he bore.

While God made it clear to man that happiness lay in an experience of good, and that an experience of evil would bring sorrow and death, there came a whisper to him from without: 'Has God said?' It was the injection of doubts into man's mind. Following on that came the powerful denial: 'Ye shall not surely die.' Then the insinuation that God was acting in a factious and unfair manner in depriving man of this experience of evil, 'for He knows that the day ye eat ye shall be as gods.'

This was aimed at breeding distrust – that God was withholding from man something that would develop him. For the promise was 'Ye shall know good and evil', and so be like God – an offer of emerging quickly as divine. And man believed the base scandal, pride and ambition took hold of him, then unbelief.

Unlike the Last Adam who 'thought equality with God not a thing to be snatched at', the first Adam snatched at the very possibility. In that act of disillusionment fostered by unbelief and distrust, sin entered. Sin was therefore an act of rebellion and deliberate defiance.

And so it immediately acted Godwards, Selfwards and Racewards.

Godwards

It affected man's relation to God. That went wrong first.

(1)   Godwards, man became a rebel. He exercised the freedom given to him to put his own will against the will of God. He became a creature in revolt.

(2)   Man then became a fugutive. He hid himself from God, a prey to guilt, fear and shame.

(3)   Man then became an exile. 'God drove out the man' is the Biblical record. But that was the logical sequel to rebellion and estrangement – separation.

Selfwards

In man's inner self all the centres of life were affected, mind, conscience, heart, will. The mind became clouded with ignorance, the conscience laden with guilt, the heart estranged and hateful, and the will caught in bondage and impotence. And these elements are recognisable still: – guilt describes our position, corruption describes our condition and impotence describes our powers.

That is what we mean by total corruption – sin affected man in all his parts.

Racewards

Adam's sin entered the stream of our humanity. When the fountain head was polluted it sent its polluted streams throughout the race. This was because of man's corporate oneness in the sight of God. When God created man there were two possible conditions of creation.

(1)   as isolated units – like the angels where each would bear the full and final responsibility for himself.

(2)   as a racial unity in which God could deal with man not on an individual basis, but on a collective basis. The race became linked together through all its generations. This meant that when the head was sick all the members were diseased. Sin could thus flow through all the channels of social, racial unity. So when Adam fell he dragged the race down with him – he made us into a rebel race.

So Adam became the head of a race in revolt and every one born into the race inherits a rebel nature, acts in defiance of God and does not wish to do otherwise. So we see that sin cannot be isolated: it is never a man's private affair. And so we are by nature children of wrath.

In case we may harbour a grievance and make the collectiveness of the human family into an infringement of our personal freedom and responsibility, let us pause to recollect that it was this collectiveness – this unity of the race – through which we fell into sin that made it possible that we could be saved by a new Head and Representative. As by one man came sin, by One came deliverance. Christ took over the Headship of a new race.

Thus it is that the O. T. throughout, dealing as it does with the deepest problems of the human heart, is occupied with the expression of sin in its many forms. God's first question to fallen Adam was 'Where art thou?, and the rest of the O. T. is occupied with the answer, showing to fallen man where he is in relation to his God.

It is significant that the first question of the N. T. is 'Where is he that is born King of the Jews?' – the searchlight is directed on man's Saviour.

And the question addressed to Adam in the hour of his banishment failed to get any adequate answer until the cry was heard from the darkness of Calvary 'My God, my God, why hast thou forsaken me?' There, in the darkness, was where man was, and this is where his Representative and Sinbearer had to go to reach him.

We can follow the blood – red trail of sacrifice right through the O. T. telling of the reality of sin and of the soul's need to find deliverance. The altar dripping with the blood of sacrifice bore testimony to the deep consciousness of both sin and the need to find forgiveness that belonged to the people who were in touch with God.

As the offerer laid his hands on the head of the animal, he laid down, as it were, all his feelings of guilt and shame and despair, on the head of the victim whose blood was now to flow for him and appear in the sight of God for him.

That these sacrifices were often repeated and were of many kinds only served to testify to the abiding consciousness of sin and the many ways in which it loaded the quickened consciousness of a penitent sinner. Thus the sacrifices were of the various kinds to meet with the varied feelings aroused by conviction of sin.

There were five offerings, each with its own significance for the offerer:

1. The trespass offering – seeking forgiveness for a trespass, an act of sin.

2. The sin offering – seeking propitiation and pardon from a state of guilt

3. The peace offering – where a sinner whose offering had been given was now seeking a restored relationship which had been disrupted by the sense of sin.

4. The meal offering – giving a sense of acceptance.

5. The burnt offering – often called a whole burntoffering, where the received and restored sinner accepts the ownership of sin and yields himself in devotion and obedience.

It is noteworthy that while the sacrifices of blood set forth the fact of sinbearing and especially its guilt for the person, they also set out the violence of sin: the animals were slain before the altar in a public exhibition of the violence of sin.

Thus through the entire O. T. as the character of sin is more fully revealed, there is a deepening sense of sin and therefore a heart – rending cry for the one sacrifice that was for ever to put away sin. And it was this consciousness that God could deal in justice and mercy with sin that led to one of the most heart-moving visions of God as Micah gives it: (7:18-20) 'Who is a God like unto thee, that pardoneth iniquity, and passeth by the transgressions of the remnant of his heritage?; he retaineth not his anger for ever, because he delighteth in mercy. He will turn again, he will have compassion upon us; he will subdue our iniquities; and thou wilt cast all their sins into the depths of the sea. Thou wilt perform the truth to Jacob, and the mercy to Abraham, which thou hast sworn unto our fathers from the days of old'.

This is God dealing with sin in a God–like way.

THE HOLINESS OF GOD

A Call to Gratitude

We owe both the word and the thought of holiness distinctly to revelation. It is only the Bible that speaks of the holiness of God, and the Bible speaks of God as the only Holy One. 'There is none holy but the Lord' is a declaration that excludes every created being from the possession of essential holiness. This, indeed, seems the root idea of holiness, that it belongs to a Being who is separate and different from all that is not Himself. God's holiness, therefore, constitutes His distinction and separateness from all that is created. This, as we have said, is essentially a Biblical revelation of God. It does not enter into man's own conception of God. The gods of the heathen, for example, were not credited with holiness. They may have been conceived of as possessing justice, wisdom, power, mercy, but not holiness. It is thus left to the Bible to reveal to us the holiness of God, and the conception is interwoven with all its history; it is the foundation strand of all its legislation, the inspiration of all its poetry, and the standard and touchstone of all its values. Moreover, the Bible calls us not merely to a recognition and acknowledgment of the holiness of God, but to gratitude upon the remembrance of it. 'Give thanks upon remembrance of His holiness' is an injunction more than once repeated in the Book. A mere man remembering perfect holiness with gratitude! A sinner seeking access to God and remembering His holiness with a thankful heart! How can it be done?

1. Our Gratitude is invoked by the recognition that the Holiness of God is the condition of our reverence and worship. If God were not holy, He could not become a true and rightful object of our worship. That is to say, we could not give Him the reverence and worship of our souls without doing violence to our own spiritual natures. That is why pagan worship is so degrading to the human spirit: holiness is not an attribute of the pagan gods. Were God all else, and not holy, we could not yield Him the worship of our spirits. Were He almighty merely, we might cringe before Him and tremble in His presence, but that is not worship. Were He all-wise merely, we could come before Him with deference and admiration, to learn but not to worship. Were He all-merciful merely, we might approach

Him with confidence and hope, but not in the spirit of true worship. It is only in perfect holiness that the spirit of man finds a fit object of reverence and adoration. It is not surprising, therefore, that everything connected with the ancient Temple and its worship – the altar, the priests, the sacrifice, the oil, the bread, the vessels – were designated holy. Similarly, all the manifestations that God, in Old Testament times, had made of Himself as the Object of our worship were associated with His holiness, such as His holy Name, His holy Day, His holy Habitation, His holy Word. Nor does the holiness of God receive less emphasis in the New Testament, however much men may speak to the contrary. Christ is the Holiness of God incarnate. The glory of Christ's Life was the outshining of His holiness; His Death was the most adequate vindication of the Divine holiness that the moral universe had ever seen. The sacrifice of Calvary indicated that it was only as holiness did its work that mercy could flow savingly to the sinner. And so in the Bible throughout, worship ever has in view the holiness of God. The Israelites on the shore of the Red Sea worshipped God, saying: 'Who is like unto Thee, O Lord; who is like unto Thee, glorious in holiness?' The Psalmist had the holiness of God in view when he cried 'Exalt ye the Lord our God and worship at His footstool; holy is He.' The Song of Moses and the Lamb, sung by the sea of glass, has this note likewise: 'Who shall not fear Thee, O Lord, and glorify Thy name? For Thou only art holy.' And the 'living creatures' of John's Apocalypse rest not day nor night, saying: 'Holy, holy, holy is the Lord God Almighty.' Thus we see that it is the holiness of God that calls forth the worship of His saints, alike in the Old Testament and the New, alike on Earth and in Heaven. And because God is holy, and holiness is the expression of His perfection and the very essence of His nature, so the human spirit, unfettered and emancipated, can bow before Him in worship and adoration. Since man must worship, shall we not rejoice we have a God worthy of our worship, and shall we not thank Him upon every remembrance of His holiness?

2. Our gratitude is further invoked in understanding that the Holiness of God is the sheet-anchor of our Faith. Though faith might perhaps stretch out to a God that was not revealed as holy, it could not long retain its hold. Faith might shelter for a while under the wings of mercy, but its foothold there were insecure if the

foundations of mercy were not laid in holiness. The truth is that God would not be a fit object of trust, if He bestowed mercy without respect to holiness. Such mercy would bestow no security for the soul of man, and faith could no longer live. This is as true in the wider field of the Divine operations as it is in the realm of a man's soul. As we could not hope for personal peace and security from operations that did not proceed from the holiness of God, so we can entertain no hope for the world if perfect holiness is not behind its varying fortunes.If God is not holy, there is no ground for faith in the ultimate triumph of truth and righteousness on earth. When we look abroad on the world as it has been in every age and see the conflict of good and evil, of light and darkness, of truth and falsehood, what hope can we cherish that it will end in the triumph of righteousness? In our own day we see the same fierce conflict – more grimly terrible, perhaps, than ever it has been. Wickedness seems in the ascendancy and truth is fallen in the streets. The forces of evil are giving battle and the final issue would be very uncertain, did we not believe that the God of the whole earth is holy. We believe that right will triumph, that truth will prevail, that righteousness will be established, and hate and tyranny overthrown. How much cause have we, then, to thank God upon every remembrance of His Holiness.

3. Our gratitude is called forth by the knowledge that the Holiness of God is the ground of the most Blessed Hope of the Christian Life. Scripture everywhere indicates that believers are called to holiness, and the hope of their calling lies in the holiness of God. If God were not holy they could never entertain a good hope that they would ever be holy. How much this must mean to the soul torn in awful conflict as evil strives with good and the old nature seeks dominion over the new. At such times the victory might seem to lie with evil, and we cry in an intensity of agony: 'O wretched man that I am! Who shall save me from this body of death?' Certainly the struggle seems unequal, and we feel we are no match for that trinity of evil – the world, the flesh, and the devil – arrayed against us. When we are trying to assess the probabilities of victory, let us recall this one factor that is decisive – the holiness of God. Because God is holy, His destiny for us is holy, His operations in us are holy, as truly as His requirements of us are holy. 'Be ye holy, as I am

holy' is much more than a command from God to us. Like all the commands of God to His people, it conceals a promise. It is a promise that holiness is the destiny of God's people, and that the Holy Spirit of God is conforming them daily to that destiny. It is more; it indicates that God Himself is the standard of our holiness and that to be like Him implies that we are to share His holiness. Thus God's nature is both the standard of our holiness and the pledge of its attainment. What cause for gratitude the struggling people of God, therefore, have when they remember His holiness – the standard and the pledge of theirs.

Thus we learn that Holiness, the word that the seraphs utter with veiled faces, the word in which all God's perfections centre, is man's incentive to draw nigh to God in the humility and brokenness of worship, man's highest encouragement amidst the unequal struggles of this life, and man's highest glory in the eternity to come. Let us take hold of this hope and comfort in troublous days, and thank God upon every remembrance of His holiness.

A JUST GOD AND A SAVIOUR

When we speak of the justice of God we must guard against the misconception that God's justice can be set in isolation, or be separated from His other attributes. Failure to observe this has led often to a misrepresentation of God as harsh,vindictive, and even cruel. In other words, justice is represented as the opposite of love, as the antithesis of mercy. Theology, in other days, unwittingly lent colour to this by coining the phrase: 'The hands of His justice were tied by the cords of His mercy'. This suggests a tension in the being and character of God in which one attribute sought pre-eminence over another. This is so untrue as to constitute a gross misrepresentation of God. The whole of God's nature operates in every act of His power, and justice is a revelation of God as He is.

What, then, is the justice of God? It is His holy nature maintaining itself against any and every violation of His holiness, and operating in perfect harmony with all the perfections that constitute Him divine. We must, therefore, get rid of this foolish distinction being commonly made between 'the God of the Old Testament' and 'the God and Father of Jesus'.

In order to see this in its true perspective we must look at the justice of God in several contexts. We will look at it manifested in four particular situations: in the Moral Order, in Moral Personality, in Redemptive Activity and in Human Destiny.

The Justice of God as it is seen in the Administration of the Moral Order

There is a moral universe under the administration of God, and this world is part of it, but only part. But the world has this centrality, that it became, as it were, a platform on which God revealed the meaning and implications of deep moral issues, particularly the issue of sin and spiritual rebellion, and how in justice and love, in compassion and righteousness, in mercy and truth, He would deal with it. God owes it to the whole of the moral universe, as well as to His own nature, that He acts justly and righteously. For that reason when the world became involved in sin, and the human family became a race in revolt, it must be expected that God would give a special manifestation of His justice; of the holiness that is the architectural plan to which He built the universe, the justice that maintains harmony and order and stability in the moral order, and that is the sheet-anchor of the universe, keeping it from chaos and despair.

To those who try to see God's administration on the broad and wide pattern of human affairs, I think it will become evident that it is permeated through and through with fundamental justice that will 'justify the ways of God to men'. We admit that it may not always appear to be so. Take the complex pattern of nature and natural law, for an example. When we view natural and moral evil in the world, we are ready to conclude that nature as such is indifferent to pain, and suffering, and evil among her offspring.

We agree that it seems so, but we point out that nature itself has been upset and unbalanced by the entrance of something from without: moral evil. Nature is not what God designed it to be; it is an abnormal and frustrated creation of which we are part. An alien force has entered that is antagonistic to God's order, and for that reason creation or nature is not a true expression of the mind and will of God. This is true at both ends of the dimensional scale. Many of the micro–organisms that so afflict us – bacteria and viruses – could well be the degeneration of forces that were originally designed for our good. Degeneration has been at work, not only on the larger pattern of moral behaviour, but down to the smallest of living cells, turning the benign malignant, and the beneficent harmfully virulent. Nevertheless, on the whole, nature may be said to be well–disposed towards men, and towards life in general, insofar as we are willing to cooperate with it. Christ has taught us to see a Heavenly Father in the regular forces of nature. He makes His sun to shine, and His rain to water the earth. His voice is heard in the thunder, and His footsteps in the storm. This means that God is not only above nature, but that He operates in and through nature. And He uses nature to fulfil His purpose and often to execute His justice. He does not, however, meet the challenge and affront to His justice always or often in one fell stroke of judgment. Instead He is using it to discipline and educate His moral creation to see and experience evil in all its consequences, and He promises to impart strength to His moral creatures to overcome it. It is God's world, but it is also man's world, and God respects man's position and trusteeship. Man must put right what is wrong in himself and his environment, but he can do it only in the strength and by the wisdom of his Creator and his God. This strength is what we call grace.

This explains, perhaps, why God does not immediately exterminate a sinful and runaway world. He is fulfilling a higher purpose of restoration and re-creation, so that where nature has failed, grace undertakes the task of a new creation. Notwithstanding this, there are, as it were, outbursts of divine justice and righteousness in the order of the moral world. When evil threatens the stability and safety of the race, God steps in by an act of justice, which is also mercy, and cuts the diseased part away. This form of surgery has been seen again and again in the history of our race from the Flood onwards. There is a solidarity of the human family such that one member can bring moral disease and death to the whole, and a God of justice and love intervenes, and uses nature itself to overthrow the evil.

This happened of old with the Cities of the Plain, when they were consumed by 'a fire from heaven', probably the result of the ignition of the bitumen and sulphur in which the area abounded, caused perhaps by a spark of lightning. But because it was nature, it was nonetheless God, God working through nature, and employing natural forces already there.

There are other times on record, however, when it happened by human intervention at the express command of God. The destruction of the ancient Canaanites is a case in point. Today it is quoted as the classic example of the cruelty of the God of the Old Testament. Viewed aright, it was an act of deep surgery, since the Canaanites are now recognised as the poisoned source of the foulest diseases in the ancient world. Medical research in recent times has traced the scourge of venereal disease in the ancient civilisation to the gross immorality of the Canaanite tribes. It was vital that the Israelites, from whom the Holy Seed was to spring, should be kept free from this contamination. Hence the command of God. A quotation from the medical source employed on this research will put it in its proper context: 'If they had been allowed to remain, they would have corrupted the whole world....You will know what your God did? He picked a lance out of Egypt, took the Israelites across the desert, and used them as His instrument to cut the cancer out of the heart of the world'. 'Behold the goodness and severity of God'. In more modern times there is the case of San Francisco which was destroyed by earthquake and tidal wave in 1906. Situated on the coast between America and the East, it became a moral cesspool into which the filth of the ancient East poured itself, till it became a source of contamination for the whole of America. To quote the words of someone close to the Administration Centre of the United States: 'It was the major headache of all the politicians, and none of them knew how to deal with it'. In one fearful night God did it. First the earthquake, and then the tidal wave that swept the corrupt city into the Pacific. And then to quote my source again, 'the politicians agreed it was the only way it could be done'. Behold again 'the goodness and severity of God'.

In ordinary cases it is left to human government as God's representatives to purge out the evil, and if it fails it has forfeited its place of trust under God. For example God has ordered that a murderer be not allowed to live (Num. 35:16 onwards). He is a cancerous cell in the body of human society, and it requires surgery to remove it. It is false mercy to fail to do this, since, like all malignant cells, it eats more and more into the vitals of the social life of a people, cheapening human life and all its values.

While there seems now, as always, a protracted civil war between man and God for the right of sovereignty, it will not remain so for ever. God's holy justice ensures that there will be but one sovereign in the moral universe, and for that reason we know that moral evil will be finally and completely overthrown.

We see this manifestation of Justice, on a smaller canvas, in Moral Personality.

No individual breaks the divine law with continuing impunity. It is so in the realm of the body, as well as in the moral and spiritual life. The wages of sin is death, and sin pays its wages unfailingly and unceasingly. And sin most frequently pays its wages in kind, in the same kind in which the sin had been committed. This, of course, is the real meaning of wages, payment in kind. This is brought to light in the well–known characters in the Bible. There is the case of Jacob. He deceived his aged and blind father, and he deceived him concerning a favourite son Esau, and used the skin of a slain animal to give colour to the deception. And God was silent. Then in God's time the wages became due. Jacob, in old age, was deceived by his own sons, deceived regarding a favourite son, Joseph, and the blood of a slain animal was used to give flavour to the deception. Other examples abound. In this realm, there are no favourites with God. No one can opt out of the harvest he has sown:'for as a man sows, so shall he reap; he that soweth to the flesh, shall of the flesh reap corruption'. There is no sickly sentimentality in the love of God that we should make use of it to further our own selfish ends. 'Whom the Lord loveth He chasteneth, and scourgeth every son whom He receives'. (Heb.12:6). Christ wept over Jerusalem: it was a touching expression of His compassion. And then He pronounced its doom: an expression of the just severity of God.

We can also see the Justice of God in His Redemptive Activity

When God took in hand the redemption of a fallen race, He acted as God must act. His entire nature and character are involved in it, and it is in this sphere, perhaps, that He gives the fullest disclosure of His nature. It is a matter of putting away sin. He does not deal with moral evil by refusing to recognise its existence, or by extenuating its guilt, or minimising its consequences. He deals with it realistically. It must be thrust into the open to be seen for what it really is, and dealt with as it deserves.

This is what happened historically at Calvary. There the moral issues were brought into the open for the entire moral universe to behold. There is the sin that planned it: its malice. There is the sin that wrought it: its cruelty. There is the sin that needed it: its guilt. But there is also the righteousness that demanded it: its rectitude.

There is the love that offered it: its sacrifice. And there is the fidelity and patience that endured it: its devotion and self-denial. When we visit Calvary we see that justice runs through all that happened there: not man's, but God's. The entire procedure is under God's control. It was God's plan, and underlying it all is the justice that demanded it.

Yet never did the moral universe behold the blending together of such justice and love, such righteousness and mercy, such compassion and truth. Someone has said of this scene that the background of God's sacrifice was His justice, and the foreground was His love. And only when the divine justice makes the background resplendent in the beauty of holiness, will the foreground of Calvary glow in the white radiance of a love that passes knowledge.

To stand at Calvary, thus, is to be reconciled with God's dealing with sin in the here and hereafter. Whatever the eternal future may unveil in suffering and pain, as the desert of sin, it is but a drop in the bucket of moral and spiritual suffering, compared to the anguish in the soul of the Son of God as He drank the cup of divine wrath for sin that was not His own.

But the atonement and reconciliation of the Cross does not mean that God lets sinners off easily. God's redeemed people know this. Sin is not less sinful or odious when seen in the lives of those who have found mercy. Amos of old had this message to proclaim from God to the Israel of his day: 'You only have I known of all the families of the earth, therefore will I punish you for all your iniquities' (Amos 3:2). Thus it is that judgment begins at the house of God (1 Pet. 4:17). This finds its starkest revelation in the history of the Jewish people, chosen and loved of God of all people in the world, cast off because of their unbelief and rejection of their Messiah Jesus, yet not destroyed, but kept separate from the nations among whom they are scattered, for a time of restoration and blessing still to come. Once again, 'Behold the goodness and severity of God'.

Once more, let us see the Justice of God in Human Destiny

Moral evil is a spiritual reality, and as such it is not, and cannot be annihilated.

It is not subject to death like physical evil, which dies with the dissolution of the body. It carries its life, in all its characteristic actions, beyond death, and so, at the last, there are only two categories recognised, the righteous and the wicked. They are categories of moral character. There is injustice to none; every man goes 'to his own place', the place for which he is fitted morally and spiritually. At the Judgment Seat of Christ, we receive *back* – that is the force of the word – the things done in the body, whether it be good or bad (2 Cor. 5:10).

Thus there is wrath in God:it is the counterpart of His love. It is another evidence that God cares, and how much He cares. It makes the wrath of God against sin all the more terrible when it is recognised to be the unavoidable wrath of a Being who is infinitely loving in His nature. In Biblical terms, it is 'the wrath of the Lamb', of meekness despised, of love rejected, of mercy trampled underfoot.

We cannot minimise the Biblical emphasis on the holy justice of God. It is because God is just as well as loving that Jesus was sent. It is because God is holy justice as well as holy love that an atonement is provided. It is because God is just as well as loving that destiny is based on character, and that all things work together for good to them that love Him, and to eternal disadvantage for those who refuse and reject Him. It is because of His holy and just love that the Biblical distinction between the redeemed of God and the enemies of God, shall never be abolished.

But there is a wonderful note of hope to strike. It is the holy justice of God that fills life with purpose and hope. It puts the distinctions between right and wrong upon eternal foundations. It gives moral quality to human living, and it justifies and maintains the moral meaning and impulse of life. It also accounts for the moral element that cannot be eliminated from our destiny. Holiness tells man what his highest glory is to be, and what his darkest doom: on the one hand to be made partakers of the divine holiness, on the other to be repelled by it into eternal antagonism.

REGENERATION

Regeneration is a necessity for two reasons, the nature of sin and the nature of God. It presupposes that sin has so marred our natures in the totality of its parts that there is no soundness in us. The foundations of our nature have been so marred that life cannot begin anew without new foundations being laid. If there had been a part of our complex natures of which it could be said that sin had not touched it, a new beginning could be made from that point. But we are spiritually dead in trespasses and sins, and the old creation had to be set aside and a new creation made.

Then again if God was not the perfectly Holy One, He might be pleased with less than a perfectly holy nature. But He claims for us a holiness equal in quality to His own: 'Be ye holy as I am holy, saith the Lord.' For this a very radical change must take place in man, and this change is compared in Scripture to a quickening of those who are dead, and a resurrection of those who are in their graves. The New Testament word for what happens is regeneration, involving a new birth, a new life, a new disposition and character. A patched up remedy for our state would not be acceptable to God or saving for ourselves.

1. What is Regeneration?

This regeneration, by which a person is made completely new, is an act of the creative Spirit of God by which the soul of man is endowed with spiritual life. With it comes a new principle of living, and of thinking, new appetites, new desires, new hopes and longings.

In its Nature it is Divine: that is, it is animated by the same principle as animates the life of God. And so we are said to be 'partakers of the Divine Nature'. This does not mean that God gives us a part of His own nature, for if He did, we would become Divine. And, in any case, God is a Spirit and His nature is not divisible. But it does mean that we are animated in all our parts by a Divine spirit, by a life that operates on the same moral principles as the life of God.

In its Quality, it is eternal. That is to say, it is not earth-born, it is of the essence of eternity, and the principle that animates it is the principle of eternal beings. This does not mean that it is merely immortal. It is not its duration that is different, it is its very quality, as if a tidal wave from the ocean of Eternity entered the life of man. It is thus heir to all the fullness and richness of the life of eternity.

In its Character, it is holy as God is holy. It partakes of the moral purity of God, and cannot be contaminated by sin. This explains why it can remain clean and holy in the midst of an ocean of uncleanness. 'That which is born of God cannot sin.'

2. How does Regeneration take Place?

The agent is the Holy Spirit, the Author and Giver of life. He is the Creative Spirit of God and the only One who can kindle this spark of Divine life in the soul. He was the Agent in the first Creation, and to Him is entrusted the Second Creation.

Where is it given? It is implanted in the hidden depths of the soul and spirit in such a way that it will touch the springs of life and affect the entire being of man. It must be as radical, at least, as the first life given to man, and its seat is equally indefinable.

How is it given? We cannot tell. It is instantaneous and man is not conscious of its happening. Thus, we think, it is implanted in the sub-conscious, in the hidden depths of the being of man, by the Spirit of God who has access to every part of us, and searcheth the deep things of the spirit of man.

3. How does Regeneration Develop?

Seeing the person is not conscious of the act of implanting the life, it may be possible for it to lie dormant in the unconscious life. But, sooner or later, the person becomes fully conscious of its presence and power. As it rises up into the consciousness, we feel a new principle of holy life operating within.

At this stage the man may be said to be truly 'Born Again'; regeneration has come to birth in his consciousness. An eye is opened in the soul, and he sees God, an ear is opened and he hears God's call, and a response is created within the soul. This is faith. Faith is therefore the responsive faculty of the new-born soul, and it responds to the call of God as a child responds to his mother's voice. Thus the Word of God calls the soul to consciousness, and we obey its summons. Scripture speaks of it, therefore, as the life-giving Word by which we are begotten into a living hope. Now it must be carefully noted that though this is the Divine order and sequence, it is not at all the order of our experience. No child can give a reasoned account of its own birth, and the new-born soul can only talk of its conscious experience. He is conscious of hearing the call and responding, of seeing the light and believing, of being given the offer and accepting. But God was operating before this consciousness came. Until the new life was imparted by God there was no eye to see, no ear to hear, no hand to accept. But the New Birth constituted our first conscious experience of having passed from death unto life, and so it may be said to mark the beginning of our Christian state.

And the New Birth asserts itself in the life and produces what we call Conversion – a turning of the entire life Godwards. That is the most conspicuous and spectacular of the effects of Regeneration. In Conversion, however, we are conscious agents and we cooperate with the Spirit of God. It is Regeneration that empowers us for this cooperation: our minds are enlightened, our wills renewed, and our whole being goes willingly over to God as the God of our Salvation.

Before we leave this section, we must note that, in the experience of the soul, regeneration, new birth, and conversion may be all one – one big tumultuous upheaval as a result of which, though once blind, we now see. It is not possible, therefore, for the Christian to mark these progressive steps in his own case, but little by little God enables him to see that the Spirit of God was there before we became fully conscious of His work.

4. Some of the Implications of Regeneration

The first of these is that God cannot be reconciled to the old nature, and they that are in the flesh cannot please God. The old nature can never be taught to obey God.

Then the change wrought by regeneration does not destroy the human personality. There is no change in the substance of the soul. The faculties of the soul are all there as before, but they now operate after a new principle. Thus it is a new spirit that is given to the man, not a new faculty or part that had not been there before. The human personality is intact and undamaged, the same but different.

But the quickening of regeneration permeates the whole being of man. It is not a change in one faculty, but it extends its influence to the whole being and life of man, giving light to the mind, conviction to the conscience, cleansing to the heart, power to the will, and life to the soul. Even the body is affected by it, as its impact is felt in our outer natures bringing a new vitality.

The most serious implication of regeneration, however, is that there are now two natures in the Christian, the old and the new. We may well express surprise why the good Lord did not eradicate the old when He implanted the new: but He did not. Furthermore the old is not changed, not even improved and refined. But the new comes in to supplant it, to dominate it and finally to subdue it. Thus when the new asserts itself, and the old resists, there is conflict. There will remain an unceasing antagonism between the corrupt and the holy natures; and the Christian is acutely conscious of this conflict from the start. But in the conflict, the man himself is on the side of the new. Christ has won over my will, my inclinations, my personality, and so the renewed self is all on the side of holiness in this conflict. Thus it is that my personality is not split – I am not two persons, though I have two natures. I am a redeemed person, and I am as a person on the Lord's side. It does not result in a split personality; rather is the personality unified, integrated, pulled together, to present a united front against the common foe.

But for this very reason what is done in obedience to the inclinations of the old nature, is the responsibility of the person. We cannot shelter under the excuse that 'it was the old man that did it', as if the 'old man' was not ours at all, and we had no responsibility for its actions. The person is one, and it is to the person that praise or blame attaches. Thus it is that from 2 Cor. 5:10 'we must all appear before the Judgment Seat of God and get back the things done in the body, whether it be good or bad'. Confession of sin thus becomes us as long as we are in the body, and no one is free from sin until the old nature is completely put off at death. Yet that does not relieve us of our duty to 'put off the old man with its affections and lusts' and to (Eph. 4:24) 'put on the new man which after God is created in righteousness and true holiness'. And this we shall be enabled to do, as the work of sanctification proceeds within the soul, and we catch the vision of what God would have us be.

THE WISDOM AND GRACE OF GOD IN DIVINE ELECTION

It was an old Professor of Philosophy who was heard to observe rather wistfully at the close of a lecture that it was not always easy to do justice to both God and man. Theologians also have not been unaware of this difficulty, and our theological systems are, in the main, distinguished by their tendency to place the main emphasis on the one side or the other. The two principles operating in apparent conflict are the sovereignty of God and the autonomy of man.

This appears markedly in a discussion of the Biblical doctrine of election. The Bible itself does not attempt to rationalise the dogma of election: it seldom or never attempts to rationalise any of the apparently conflicting doctrines. It is content to place them side by side in unrelieved tension as parallel expressions of the one reality: at one time presenting them objectively as if from God's side, and at another expressing them in terms of personal experience.

Limits of the Theme

There is the subject of Decree. God's Decree is the eternally active will of God, embracing the entire universe, the eternal idea of reality unfolded, as far as this world is concerned, in time making the temporal the image of the eternal. This is regarded as source.

Election lies within the sphere of Predestination for which the N. T. term is 'προοριζω'. The Vulgate used for this term the word predestino, hence our A.V. translation, or transliteration, predestinate. ζω

The Confessional Symbols of the Scottish Church make a distinction between predestination and foreordination: a distinction which does not belong to the words themselves. They apply predestination exclusively to the elect, and foreordination to the reprobate in an attempt to make a distinction in the nature of the two realities involved. Predestination in the case of the elect is altogether of a different order from that of the reprobate. And so it is used as belonging to an experience of salvation, and not in any other context. They recognised that election and reprobation proceed on different grounds, the one on the grace of God, the other on the sin of man.

Our theme is Election, which finds so prominent a place in the Biblical setting of redemption. The Bible, being a soteriological manifesto, views all from that standpoint.

I. Election looked at objectively as a doctrine of theology

This will involve a rationalisation that may not seem to do justice either to God or man. The fundamental principle that sustains the doctrine is the sovereignty of God. By that we mean that God makes His own plans and carries them out in His own time and way. This would seem to be involved in our acceptance of a Personal Deity.

If God is supreme Personality He is in possession of Intelligence. He is Supreme Mind. He plans: there is a purpose resident in His mind. If God is Almighty, He carries out His plans. And He is Supreme Power. He does not need to harness existing energy. He is the font of energy for the entire universe in its breadth and depth.

If He is all-wise, He carries out His Plan in His own time and way. And God is Supreme Wisdom. If God did not carry out His Purpose or Plan in His own time and way it is because there is some limitation in His wisdom in planning, or in His power in executing.

Let us apply this elementary definition to the theological doctrine of Election, which is supposed to be undergirded by the sovereignty of God.

God Plans

The N. T. ' προθεσιζ' (purpose) presupposes intelligent and purposeful planning in the activity of God. There was a cosmic purpose behind the creation of the universe, and in bringing the world into existence.

I suppose we can say that personality is of necessity creative, and that its creative purpose is to share the vision and beauty that lay behind the creation. This is the case with an artist. He has resident in his mind the complete form that his work is to take before he puts a brush on canvas. He has an urge to produce it in order to share his vision with others who are capable of understanding and enjoying it.

The Bible speaks of this Divine Purpose as 'before the foundation of the world'. It was resident in the mind of God before His creative activity began. This counsel (Gk. βοολη) of God is given in the Bible in two settings, 1. In the creation of the Race. This is the terminus a quo, 2. In the eschatological consummation. This is the terminus ad quem.

1. In the Creation of the Race

'And God said: Let us make man (i.e. mankind) in our image and after our likeness and let them have dominion.'

2. In the Final Consummation

Paul refers to the mystery of God's will 'that in the dispensation of the fullness of the times he might gather together in one all things in Christ, both which are in heaven and which are on earth, even in him'. Or from Phillips translation: 'He purposed in his sovereign will that all human history will be consummated in Christ: that everything that exists in heaven or earth shall find its perfection and fulfilment in him.'

In the first statement we have a record, the only record there is, of the beginning of the race. And implicit in it is the purpose of God in what is presented as a new departure in the order of creation. God, the supreme Artist, gave expression to His purpose to create mankind in order that He might share with them the Fellowship that constitutes His own Being. The constitution of their nature as free moral beings, with quickened spiritual instincts, fitted them to respond to this fellowship, and to develop in spiritual life as they entered more deeply into that communion with their Maker. It is true that the purpose of the creation is quite often put as 'for His own glory'. This must be understood biblically. The glory of God is His moral excellence and spiritual perfection, and when God glorifies Himself He is communicating His blessedness to His moral creation. God thus manifesting His glory is as beneficial to His moral creatures as is the shining of the sun to the natural creation. And for the same reason, in that when the sun shines it communicates to natural life, by way of radiation, what stimulates the growth and strengthens the life of nature. For the chemical elements of the sun are also those of the earth and of every living organism. Thus it is with God and the creature He made in His own image: when God's light shines it supports and sustains the moral and spiritual life derived from Himself. Such are the affinities between God and the creatures that bear His moral and spiritual image. That was the Creator-creature relationship that constituted man's blessedness over the rest of creation.

When we follow on to read the simple, perhaps pictorial, record of man's history we learn that his development came under arrest by the entrance into his experience of moral evil. It was then that God revealed His further purpose to recreate the race of mankind under a Second Adam who would secure for them the certainty of attaining the goal set for them. The relationship now was stronger, closer, higher, than the creature-Creator relationship, it was that of a sinner-Saviour relationship. And far from this being introduced as an expedient to meet an unforeseen emergency, it is presented as belonging to the eternal purpose of God, as integral to the eternal counsel(Gk.βοωλη). It was not chance but choice.

In the purpose of this recreation, the emphasis is placed on the particularity of God's choice. It is the selective choice of a personal love. It is a Father regenerating, not so much a race, as a family, in vital union with an elder Brother, the First-Born of the family of God.

But in spite of this particularity of personal love, the individual cannot conceal the race. Men cannot be regarded as isolated units, they are members of an organism, the human race. And it is the race of mankind that is to reach the goal of God's destiny, and fulfil His purpose to bring man into His fellowship. But it is not a matter of chance, but of grace: the new race is to be known as the election of grace. But grace is not parsimonious: there shall be brought into God's fellowship a multitude which no man can number of all nations and kindreds and people, and tongues, a new race of mankind that in number is not unworthy of the Headship of its Divine Sponsor and Surety.Though many shall drop out in the process, and many be lost throughout the course of the race's advance to complete salvation, they shall be but as branches withered from the tree, but the stock will be saved, and in the end of the day it will be seen to be a racial salvation. It is mankind as an organic whole that shall be saved through Him of whom the N. T. speaks as the Saviour of the world. This is not chance, it is choice, the choice of grace and love, that ensures its complete and perfect realisation.

Now that, as simply as I can put it, is the Plan, in its design, activity, and execution, that introduces us supremely to the sovereignty of God in election. It does not hang as a dark pall over humanity and its destiny, but is a light that shineth more and more unto the perfect day.

II. Election as a fact in history

From what has been said, as well as from observation, it must be clear that God is controlling history teleologically. It is the unfolding of the divine plan of ingathering the family, the new race of mankind, into His Presence and Fellowship. For this reason we claim that election is a decisive factor in history.

The religious interpretation of history is for us given in the Bible as nowhere else. The Bible in its entirety is the record of God's pursuit of His purpose, working in history and in individual lives, a loving pursuit to recover fallen man to Himself. And we cannot fail to see, from the opening pages of Scripture to its close, the operation of a selective purpose of God. There is no chance, but there is choice everywhere. There election is given a pretemporal reference, and its global eschatology presupposes God in complete control of events from beginning to end, from the terminus a quo to the terminus ad quem.

In the O. T. throughout it is presented as a necessary consequence of the nature and character of Israel's God, seen as a Person worthy of trust, seen in particular in the history and development of the Kingdom of God in the world. The Kingdom is viewed throughout as the creation of God Himself, and not the product of man's effort. Man is made to fit into it by divine calling and obedience.

In the N. T. election is seen in a clearer, closer and warmer light in the teaching and activity of Jesus Christ. It is not too much to say that it is the controlling thought in the ministry of Christ, and that His teaching on the upbuilding of God's Kingdom in the world is an exposition of the meaning of the divine election. But it casts no cloud of pessimism on the ministry of Jesus. Even when conditions are difficult and results disappointing, His response to the situation is an immediate and joyful acceptance of His Father's plan: 'I thank Thee, O Father, Lord of Heaven and earth, because Thou hast hid these things from the wise and prudent, and hast revealed them unto babes. Even so Father, for so it seemed good in Thy sight.' But this presented no restrictive limitation to Him, no curb on His gracious ministry, for immediately afterwards, He cried: 'Come unto me all ye that labour and are heavy laden, and I will give you rest.' Thus He preserves in perfect balance the two complementary truths, even if they remain to us antinomies; seemingly contradictory in form, they are both aspects of the one reality.

There are subjects undoubtedly, on which the Gospel narratives present this spirit of double front, excluding the reader, as it seems from adopting a simple uncomplicated approach.

The theme of divine election is set by Christ in the context of divine sovereignty and human responsibility, and it is done very naturally yet very firmly. At one time the words of our Lord would suggest that it lies within the competence of man freely to make up his mind to come to Jesus, and receive from Him the gift of eternal life: 'Come unto me and I will give you....' and 'him that cometh unto me I will never cast out'.

And then we hear Him say: 'No man can come unto me unless the Father who has sent me draw him', and 'Everyone who has heard and learned from the Father cometh to me', and finally 'No one can come unto me unless it were given him of my Father'.

Thus two positions seem established. That it is within a man's responsibility to make up his mind freely to come to Jesus, and yet that his coming lies within the freedom of God who alone determines who shall come to Jesus. Christ's whole dialogue with His disciples at this time closes on this last personal note: 'Ye have not chosen me, but I have chosen you.' The divine and the human run so far on parallel lines, but by definition parallel lines do meet in infinity.

III. Election in personal experience

This is the subjective aspect of election, a department in which we may feel slightly more at home.

1. Look at it first in the context of the Gospel Call

In human experience there is no contradiction, far less conflict, between the election of God and the responsibility of men to accept the call of the Gospel.

The call of God is the divine contact with us, and we are called, not because we are elect, but because we need Christ, as sinners need a Saviour. And we trust in Christ not because we are elect, but because we were bidden to trust in Him and we found Him completely trustworthy. It is within the competence of man as a rational being freely to make up his mind to come to Christ, and the response of early N. T. Christianity was 'Come and see', as if no man has a right to make up his mind until he has investigated the claims of Christ.

And so man, in full possession of all that constitutes him a man, directs himself to God's call and makes a whole-hearted compliance with its demands. The terms used by Christ, to come, to hear, to learn, to take, all fall within the normal activity of a man's life. How true it is that the Incarnation has put the truth of Heaven into human categories.

The truth will soon become clear that God was all in it, while we too were all in it. It is not a co-ordinate relationship that exists – so much God's, so much man's – it is all God's and all man's. God's enabling does not mean a coercion, but a liberation. We have our freedom in the freedom of God, free as a bird is free in the air and a fish in the sea, each in its own native element.

Thus shall we feel when we enter the freewill of God and make it freely our will.

2. See it again in the context of our Redemption in Christ

Paul emphasised more than once the engrossing thought that we are 'elected in Christ'. This has occasioned an immense amount of discussion. Is our election a sovereign act of God the Father, representing the Majesty of the Trinity, who elected a people, and entrusted to His Son their restoration and redemption ? This would seem to make Christ the executor of election: 'thine they were and thou gavest them to me' would seem to imply this.

Or does it mean that God elected His Son to be the Second Adam under whose headship a new race would be formed and presented to God for a people?

I think there is a mix-up between the objective and subjective aspects of the doctrine, not helped by Barthian attempts to unravel it. Here and now I am to deal only with the subjective side. It is no abstract doctrine of election that we now consider, for that can be very deadening, and Barth has done us service by insistence on the concrete.

The fact is that we can see see our election only in Christ: it is there we meet it for the first time in our experience. No Christian can see his election apart from Christ: it is one of the secrets made known to the Christian heart and made known only in Christ.

John Calvin argues it in this way: 'But if we are elected in Him we cannot find the certainty of our election in ourselves, and not even in God the Father, if we look at Him apart from the Son.' And so he calls Christ the speculum or mirror of the election of God. We can see our election only from where Christ stands, for the electing act of God became revealed in time in His act in Christ. Only in Him it became revealed as a historical reality, even if it has its roots in the soil of eternity, 'before the foundation of the world' as Paul expresses it. In other words we are elected in Christ – into union with Christ – and it is in that redeeming relationship that we can view our election with wonder, love and awe. Or to borrow J. S. Stewart's phrase 'it bows a man to the ground in amazed adoring gratitude'.

We do not, therefore, seek our own election or that of others in the labyrinth of predestination, but in the redeeming love and the regenerating grace of the Lord Jesus Christ. Thus our election becomes to us, as the early Reformers claimed it was, a means of grace, a channel whereby the redeeming liberating grace of God took hold of us and we knew ourselves to be His. And it remains the channel by which we receive daily and hourly the grace of God for our continued living.

3. We must look at it also in the context of character and service.

Election is not presented in the N.T. as a matter of special favour, but of special reponsibility. It is perhaps noteworthy that the Hebrew 'Bachar' carries the thought, not so much of 'choosing from', as of 'choosing for'. It is an election to service as well as to salvation, and so it is a spur to ethical endeavour. It is not an end, but a beginning. It is an election to holiness, to character, and to fruitfulness. 'Ye have not chosen me, but I have chosen you and sent you that ye should bear fruit.'

So privilege and responsibility, as always go together. For that reason we cannot isolate election from sanctification and service and obedience. 'God has chosen us in Him', said Paul 'before the foundation of the world that we should be holy and without blame before him in love'. Though it is true that no human failure can deprive a man of the destiny set out for him, yet no man can so presume on his own election as to be indifferent to his character and conduct. You cannot – no man can – have any true sense of election if you are choosing to live in sin and wilful disobedience.

IV. Election as a Revelation and Experience of Divine Wisdom and Grace

1. The Divine Wisdom

In trying to define sovereignty I ventured to say that it meant God's intelligence plannng, and His wisdom carrying out His plan in His own time and way. Now wisdom may be defined as the using of the perfect means to attain the end desired. God uses means, and I think His wisdom may be seen in the fact that by these means He unfailingly attains the end He desires.

It was no chance that attained the end, but choice, the choice of the perfect means.

The entire Fellowship of the Godhead was involved in the plan to recreate a race of humanity that would respond to God's Fellowship. That meant dealing with the matter of moral evil in man. And God's way of dealing with sin is the supreme manifestation of His wisdom.

The problem was one worthy of the Divine Intelligence, how to condemn sin and save the sinner, to save him, not merely to make him salvable, to save him, and in saving him to save his entire personality. This was the purpose (Gk. $\pi\rho o\theta\epsilon\sigma\iota\zeta$) of salvation. It was executed objectively by Jesus Christ in His life, death, and resurrection, and subjectively by the Holy Spirit in regeneration and salvation. And the result was worthy of God.

There is no possibility of chance there – it is all choice from beginning to ending. God undertook to make Himself responsible for it, and no effort of His creatures had any place in it, no foreseen faith or anticipated obedience. This is not the foreknowledge that is spoken of in the Bible. The biblical foreknowledge (Gk.$\pi\rho o\gamma\nu\omega\sigma\iota\zeta$)

is much, very much, more than foresight. That is not the meaning of knowledge, let alone of foreknowledge, in the O. T. or the New. This principle that governs election (Gk.εκλογη), is not a merely passive foreknowledge, a mere condition of mind. It implies a definite relationship to the objects of the foreknowledge. It signifies predetermination. That alone would ensure that there would be no flaw in the operation of the divine purpose: God attains His end, and the end is recognised as worthy of his wisdom, as we hear the Heavenly Choir sing: 'Blessing and glory and thanksgiving and honour and power be unto our God for ever and ever'.

2. The Divine Grace

Grace places the hall-mark of supreme wisdom on the operation of the divine election. By making it operate in grace it ensures two things. First, that God bestows all and leaves nothing to man's merit or goodness. Grace meets man only at the point of his utter helplessness and self-despair.

And grace does not destroy human responsibility. The response to grace in God is faith in man. Grace is never the end of responsibility in man, but it is the beginning. Though God makes Himself responsible for our situation, this invests us with responsibility to work out our own salvation with fear and trembling. The Christian life thus becomes existence in a responsible relationship.

God in grace bridges the gap between freedom and determinism. It is the knowledge that He assumes responsibility for us that most truly awakens us to a sense of personal responsibility. In other words, Grace is not an outrage on human personality but a restoration of its dignity and honour as made in God's image and after His likeness.

CONCLUSION

It is good news that it is not chance but choice. And the divine thing about God's choice is that sooner or later it becomes our choice, and harmony is restored. We are reconciled to God and at peace with His will. He took away the heart of stone and gave a heart of flesh, restored the natural order, and by grace man becomes most truly man. There is no element of chance in the vast universe of God nor in the reality of human destiny. Every man goes, at the end of the day, to his own place, the place of his choice, the place for which character and conduct fit him. It is the final verdict of man's moral nature, that it could not be otherwise.

But the election of Divine Wisdom and Grace illumines the firmament from one end to the other as we gaze with bewilderment at the terminus ad quem — the purpose of God to sum up all things in the universe in Christ as the One who gives unity and cohesion and mercy to it all. In that light we may see that our salvation is but one element in the cosmical purpose of God for His universe. But all according to the good pleasure of His will in Christ Jesus as Lord.

Group 2

The Cross

THE SUFFERING SERVANT
(Isa. 52:13 – 53:12)

Our main interest in this remarkable page of prophetic writing is that we can see the waters of redemption that course through the whole of the Old Testament coming to the surface here.

It is like a moorland stream that runs underground for long stretches and then comes to the surface to form a spring of water, particularly cool, clear, and refreshing, and then submerges again, through peat and moss bogs, with only the low rumble of running water to be heard.

So the stream of human redemption that courses through the whole of the Old Testament, through symbol and sacrifice, through law and prophecy, comes so near the surface here that we can see the fountain of redeeming grace opened up for us, enabling us to draw with joy out of the wells of salvation.

The entire passage of fifteen verses can be divided into two main sections, representing two speakers, *God* and *man*. God and man both enter twice, *God*, beginning with an introduction to the Suffering Servant, and ending with a vindication of the Suffering Servant. In between these we have man's approach to the Suffering Servant, first in unbelief, (53:1 – 4) and then in faith (53:5 – 6).

To scan this passage as a whole it may be worth our while to follow this order: God's introduction to the Suffering Servant at the close of (52:13 – 15), then man's approach to the Suffering Servant, first in unbelief (53:1 – 4), and then in faith (53:5 – 6), while after that comes God's vindication of the Suffering Servant in vv7 – 12.

I. God's introduction to the Suffering Servant (Is. 52:13 – 15)

Here the Eternal Father presents the Suffering and Triumph of the Servant as He views it. These are the two notes struck, and they are struck twice – Suffering and Triumph. God sees the whole as the eye of man can never see it.

(a) In His Suffering v.13a. 'Behold My Servant shall deal prudently.' The Son is Servant as He comes forth on a mission of Redemption to carry out the will of His Father. 'Shall deal prudently' rather conceals the imagery and mutes the note of suffering. The figure is that of a farmer who casts his precious grain into the cold soil of Spring, harrows it and covers it out of sight, in the knowledge that it shall return to him in the increase of harvest. This is the prudence of the sower; he does the very thing that might be thought to bring loss and decay: he casts the precious seed into the cold inhospitable earth of Spring and buries it there. But he does it in the wise knowledge that only in this way can the increase of harvest come – abundant life out of apparent death and decay. In this case, however, the seed sown is precious life – life throbbing with the warm vitality of the Son of God. It cannot be forgotten that this was the symbolism He used Himself when the Greeks came with the plaintive request: 'We would see Jesus', 'Except a corn of wheat fall into the ground and die it abideth alone, but if it die it bringeth forth much fruit', and then he added: 'And I, if I be lifted up will draw all men to Me.' He thus pointed to His Suffering and Death as the cause of the Harvest that would bring Greeks as well as Jews, into His Kingdom. This is the Divine presentation of what happened at Calvary – the life of the Son of God falling into death that He might become the First Begotten from the dead, and the first fruits of all them that sleep.

(b) Triumph (v.13b). Then comes the Triumph that emerges from humiliation and suffering.: 'He shall be exalted and extolled, and shall be very high.' God the Father already sees the increase of harvest: exalted and extolled and very high – resurrection, ascension, and enthronement. These were the fruits of His humiliation unto death: the Son of God in His manhood raised, ascended, enthroned, so that Dr John Duncan long ago could put it daringly, 'The dust of the earth is on the Throne of the Majesty on High'. Christ in our nature, bearing the scars of His suffering, in the very nature in which He died – The Lamb as if it were slain, in the midst of the Throne.

We now come to the second pair of Suffering and Triumph

(a) Suffering 'As many as were astonied at Thee, (appalled at Thee); and then, as if it were an aside for us to hear, 'His visage was so marred more than any man, and His form more than the sons of men.' (unlike the sons of men). This is not a reference to His physical appearance. There is no reference in Scripture that He was different in appearance from the general run of His fellows. It is His spiritual position as the Sin bearer and the substitute of the spiritually deformed and guilt laden. In person he was the beloved Son of the Father. But Christ, for us men, and for our salvation, was assuming a position in relation to sin, so close and inseparable that He, who knew no sin, was made sin for us. God's reaction to sin is, and always must be, sore displeasure, not less when it was borne by One so dearly loved as His own Son. This is the key to many expressions of self abasement found in the Messianic Psalms, which are in very truth the autobiography of Christ in His humiliation. This consciousness belonged to Christ in His substitutionary relationship to His people: He was acutely sensitive to His position as Sin bearer.

(b) Triumph(15). 'So shall He sprinkle (or startle) many nations. Kings shall shut their mouths at Him, for that which had not been told them they shall see, and that which they had not heard shall they understand.' If the word 'sprinkle' be retained it points to His royal priesthood by which He shall reconcile men and nations to God. It denotes the utterly unexpected change in His circumstances, the reversal of His humiliation in a triumph that is spectacular and awakening.

II. Man's approach to the Suffering Servant (53:1 – 6)

Here we have man's approach in two relationships – that of unbelief and that of faith.

1. Man in unbelief (53:1 – 4)

Isaiah complains in the opening verse of the chapter of the reaction of those to whom he presented the Servant in His Suffering and Triumph.

They had no faith. 'Who has believed our report?' He brought them a report, a message in all its relevance to them. But it was met with utter unbelief.

They had no sight or feeling. 'To whom is the arm of the Lord revealed?' He told them that this was God's provision for their sin, but they could not see or feel the arm of the Lord in it: God's hand in it was hidden from them through unbelief. So the witness was rejected and the operation of God was not recognised. Why? Because of unbelief.

(a) The Servant's appearance was unattractive. It was the aspect of humiliation and suffering that made Him offensive and unattractive. We are now at the foot of the Cross listening to the mockery, the hatred, the utter rejection of the Jewish Rulers. It was always so, but it had reached its climax then. To the onlooker, without faith or feeling, He would grow up increasingly unattractive:-

(i) As a sapling, 'a tender plant'. It is a reference to the growth that you find in many plants where a sucker is produced that does not belong to the developed plant. So this Messiah was not of the real stock in their estimation: not a true Jew. He was lacking in the fierce animosities and prejudices of the real Jew of the period. Therefore He was rejected.

(ii) A root out of a dry ground, black, dead, unpromising as to its future growth. So the antecedents of Christ made Him unacceptable. True, when we read the genealogy of Christ we do find a strange assortment –

> Rahab   – the harlot
> Ruth   – the Moabitess
> Bathsheba – the adulteress
> Manasseh – the iconoclast

The Messiah was a root out of a dry ground indeed. He owed nothing to His genealogy. The Jews could only sneer: 'Is not this Joseph's son?' in derision. He derived nothing of His uniqueness, of His glory and grace, from His ancestry.

(iii)   No form or comeliness – *Form* refers to His physique e.g.'in good form'; *comeliness,* to His natural attractions. He was not a superman in appearance or appeal. 'When we shall see Him there is no beauty that we should desire Him.' By our standards there is nothing out of the ordinary about Him. It was moral and spiritual uniqueness that He possessed, and unbelief was totally incapable of appreciating this form of beauty.

Thus in His own day on earth, and to this day, unbelief sees nothing attractive about Christ. On the lower levels of this world He is mysterious and remote.

So much then for His appearance. Unbelief has no eye for the moral and spiritual beauty of a sinless character, and a Divine Person.

*(b) **His Person was rejected*** – v3 'despised and rejected of men – a man of sorrows and acquainted with grief'.

(i) despised – nothing to foster pride. He did not come up to the world's ideal.

(ii) rejected – Here was an act of will. His terms were not attractive. His conditions were hard, His veracity and faithfulness unbiassed and unflattering. So a decision was taken and He was rejected.

(iii)a man of sorrows. While there is no suggestion of gloom in the portrait of Christ given by the four Evangelists, we must remember that the dark side of His mission and message had at its heart much sorrow. His experience of sin-bearing added sorrow to His lot. From the cradle to the grave He bore the sins of many. His environment was often hostile and unfriendly as He exposed its hypocrisies. He was deeply sensitive: 'reproach hath broken my heart.'

(iv) Ignored. 'We hid, as it were, our faces from Him', literally 'there was a hiding of faces'. Men, in unbelief, turned their faces from Him to show their lack of interest in Himself and His message. This gives substance to much in the Old Testament psalms regarding the experience of the Messiah. 'A worm I am, and no man; a reproach of men, and despised of the people' (Ps 22). So, 'He was despised and we esteemed Him not.' We cared not for it. Unbelief cannot reverse the popular verdict.

Studdart Kennedy said that 'if Christ came now to Birmingham we would not crucify Him, we would just leave Him out in the rain' – polite rejection. But unbelief today, as yesterday, would join in the clamour 'Away with Him, away with Him, crucify Him'.

*(c) **His sufferings were misinterpreted*** v 4. 'Surely He hath borne our griefs.' This is not light breaking through yet. We see in Him all forms of human grief – all our bitter sorrows we see mirrored in Him – but we do not recognise this as having any reference to us. We could not see that our sorrows could be made over to Him. Rather did we think that God was punishing Him for sins of His own. We misinterpreted His sufferings completely. Unbelief reckoned that His unparalleled suffering meant that He was being punished by God. The cause of all His sorrows lay in Himself: He took the wrong course, He opposed the world order, He was a

misfit who refused to come to terms with His environment, and He dashed Himself violently against the hard facts of life.

So unbelief said then – so unbelief says still.

Thus it is that when Isaiah uplifts Christ in His sufferings, the people in unbelief turned away their faces – 'there was a turning away – hiding of faces' – unacceptable, unintelligible, utterly unlike their expectations of their Messiah. It was historically so when He came, suffered, was condemned and crucified. It is so still. If we speak of Him as a heroic soul, a noble spirit, a superman among men, they might listen to us. But speak of Him as a sin-bearing Saviour and they turn away: 'they leave Him out in the rain.'

2. *Man in the Vision of Faith* (53. v5 – 6)

Here we see the light breaking through like a flash from the spiritual realm, illuminating the whole scene, but illuminating above all the Person of the Sufferer.

(a) Faith's interpretation of His sufferings (v.5a)

But: The reversal of the findings of unbelief.

Faith now looks stedfastly at His sufferings, from the outer circumference to the very centre, and tells us what it sees.

(i) He was wounded. That was the external and visible aspect – His physical suffering. His body was wounded – by the crown of thorns, by the scourging, by the blow of violence, by the sword thrust into His side, by the nails into hands and feet, penetrating wound of thorns, contused wound of the blow, incised wound of the sword, lacerating wound by the scourge. That attracts our gaze first.

(ii) He was bruised. This was deeper and not so readily seen. Behind the violence inflicted on His body there was a crushing of His soul and spirit under a burden that only He could bear, when the Lord laid on Him the iniquity of us all. That burden, that bruising, only the eye of faith can see and understand.

(iii) He was chastised. This is something quite beyond the reach of the human eye. It was a rod of chastisement that struck Him at the very heart when He was forsaken, abandoned and alone.

But the vision of faith sees the reason why.

(i) Wounded for our transgressions. We are back to the circumference, the outer form of sin. It is transgression – that is to go across the border – line into territory that is not our own. It is an act of trespass. That is the outward aspect of sin, and anyone can see it.

(ii) Bruised for our iniquities. Faith has this further understanding of sin. It is iniquity – inequity – unjustness, crookedness, perversion. It tells us what is behind the transgression – it is a crooked disposition – a radical twist in our inner nature: it is guilt.

He was bruised for our iniquities; He bore this burden of guilt until it crushed Him into death.

(iii)Chastised for our peace. To secure our peace. Chastise is a domestic word. It suggests dispeace in the family circle.

Sin is rebellion in the heart of man. It is an act of revolt, bringing to light all the sinister motives of hatred and dislike and disharmony. And He was chastised for our peace – to restore our peace – to bring harmony into the disrupted family again – in short, to secure reconciliation.

And so faith has a very penetrating understanding of sin, and so of the meaning of sin – bearing. Only the Cross can reveal sin with this realism and intensity, and only sin can make the Cross intelligible.

(b) Faith's experience of His sufferings v 5.

'And with His stripes we are healed.' Because of transgression, iniquity, dispeace, our spiritual nature is sick, nigh unto death. 'With His stripes we are healed.' 'Stripes' mean 'sores' – stands for the net result of His sufferings: His sores withdrew the deadly poison, – and we are healed :

(c) Faith's Witness to His sufferings   v 6.

Faith now comes up with a Witness to sin and salvation through His sufferings.

(i) *General Confession (6a).* 'All we like sheep have gone astray' – all, without exception – like sheep, foolish, truant, wayward, witless.

(ii) *Personal Commitment* *(6 b).* 'We have turned every one to his own way.' Confession breaks down into penitence. We accept our personal responsibility; we rejected God's way and took our own: the very essence of sin.

Personal revolt
Personal guilt
Personal judgment

(iii) *Personal Deliverance.* 'And the Lord laid on Him the iniquity of us all' – of each of us. Here we have the good tidings – not of what we have done, but of what God has done. 'The Lord has laid on Him the iniquity of each of us.' The Lord is the One in charge of the transaction – who stood behind the outward scene, whose hand laid the burden on. 'The Lord made to meet on Him the iniquity of each of us.' There the flood-gates of penitence are opened – as we look on Him whom we have pierced, and mourn for Him. At the foot of the Cross penitence is the sinner's true moral response.

III. God's vindication of the Suffering Servant (53 v.7 – 12)

1. *He speaks of the manner of His sufferings* *(v 7).* His conduct under suffering made Him stand out in all the annals of human suffering as unique and alone.

His silence. Oppressed and afflicted yet He opened not His mouth. As a lamb to the slaughter, and as a sheep before her shearers is dumb – 'He opened not His mouth.' Only God could unfold the meaning of that silence. Was it patience? Truly it was that. Was it forbearance? Yes. Was it self-denial? Yes. But there was something deeper than all that which we could not see – the sin He bore was inexcusable. He stood before His God charged with sins that were not His own. And there is the voluntary aspect noted: 'He suffered Himself to be afflicted.' He was laying Himself voluntarily upon the altar.

2. *The extent of His sufferings (v.8).* 'He was taken from prison and from judgment, and His generation who shall declare?' This points to His apparent extinction: He was utterly liquidated – as it was thought. 'His generation who shall declare?' – His origins, His ancestry, nobody will discuss that. Hanged on a scaffold or a cross of shame, He will be disowned and left covered with shame – 'cut off out of the land of the living' – blotted out under the shame of His Cross. He went through death outright – and it was thought that this was the end of Him.

*3. **The Divine acceptance of the offering (v.8b)**.* 'For the transgression of My people was He stricken.' God unveils the mystery, unfolds the inner meaning; and the whole of the moral universe listens in. It was not a mere tragedy, not merely a miscarriage of justice, not a mere casting Him to the fury of His foes. It was meaningful, and measured and definite, and its inner meaning God alone makes clear: 'For the transgression of My people was He stricken.' Justice speaks: for transgression He suffered. Love speaks: For My people was He stricken: Covenant faithfulness speaks: 'He was stricken for My people': this was the eternal bond between Father and Son. 'In an eternal Covenant I gave Him My people that He might redeem them by His blood.' Christ never lost sight, amidst all the injustice and wrong, of that eternal engagement. 'You could do nothing' He said to Pilate, 'except it were given you from above.' God accepted the offering, and we now accept it in receptive faith and trust.

*4. **The Divine Intervention (v. 9)**.* 'He made His grave with the wicked –.' This must be changed to its true meaning. The construction is quite impersonal, 'It was so that His grave was made –', or more simply, 'They made His grave –.' The meaning is clear. The intention of those on the scene was that He should be buried with the other two crucified with Him, – probably at the foot of the Cross. But at that point God publicly intervened; He moved His secret servant, Joseph of Arimathea, to come forward and ask for the body of Jesus. And He was buried in Joseph's own rock-hewn tomb. And so we read it 'They made His grave with the wicked, but He was with a rich man in His death'. This was an act of God, the Judge and Controller of all. He was no longer to be numbered with the transgressors – the debt was paid and the victim was delivered, and the inscription on the rock-hewn tomb was 'He had done no violence, neither was any deceit in His mouth', – outward life without violence, inner life without deceit.

*5. **The Divine purpose revealed (v.10a)**.* Here God the Father and the final Judge speaks; 'It pleased the Lord to bruise Him.' God now reveals that He was behind and underneath it all. It was not left to the human actors however much it may have seemed so. 'It pleased the Lord' – not that it gave Him pleasure but that it was His purpose, – that it was integral to the purpose of redemption.

'To bruise Him', – to crush Him – 'He has put Him to grief.' The hidden hand of God was there in the innermost springs of grief and sorrow. Only the Father above could unveil those inner sufferings: they were no accident, but the purpose of God as the only way to put away sin.

6.   The Divine results assured (vv.10b–11). 'When Thou shalt make His soul an offering for sin' or 'When He shall make an offering – a trespass offering – for sin'. In either case the Divine purpose was that it should be a sin-offering: that when His soul, His entire being, was laid upon the altar it was as a trespass offering. And God ensured the results that would follow. There are three directions in which they can be seen.

(a) **Godwards**: 'He shall see His seed, He shall prolong His days, and the pleasure of the Lord shall prosper in His Hand'. God's plan and purpose entrusted to Him shall be fulfilled. His death shall accomplish all it was meant to do.

(b) **Christwards**: 'He shall see of the travail of His soul and shall be satisfied'; or, 'because of the travail of His soul He shall be satisfied.' The results are commensurate with His travail. His expectations shall be fulfilled.

(c) **Manwards**: 'By his knowledge shall My Righteous Servant justify many, for He shall bear their iniquities.' By knowing Him, the Righteous One, My Servant shall justify many, for He shall bear their iniquities. Manwards His sufferings are the ground of justification since He is for them the Sin-bearer. Knowing Him in His sin – bearing capacity is the way of justification. That is Paul's doctrine of justification; He, the Righteous One, who became the bearer of our iniquities; when He is known and accepted in the intimacy of faith, He shall become our righteousness and to share in His righteousness is to be justified.

7.   The Divine Vindication and Reward (v.12).

In this final verse we have a review of all that went before, and what issues from it.

(a) **His exaltation.** 'Therefore will I divide Him a portion with the Great.' God is in charge of this transaction from first to last.

(b) His widespread influence. 'He shall divide the spoil with the strong.'

He will distribute the fruits of His victory.

8. *The ground of His exaltation.*

Four acts of His are reviewed:

(i) 'He poured out His soul unto death.' 'He exposed His soul unto death.' It was the voluntary acceptance of a victim state. He put His soul in a position in which death could assault Him and pour its bitterness into His soul. He who did not need to die died death outright. Why? Because He became the Representative of those who were sentenced to die. That is *Representation.*

(ii) 'He was numbered among the transgressors.' He permitted Himself to be numbered among the transgressors. He yielded to an unjust judgment, and underwent condemnation for transgression that was not His own. Christ reminded His disciples before His capture that this was to be His position. A *substitute for the transgressors.*

(iii) 'He bore the sins of many.' He took the guilt of many upon Himself in order that He might wipe it out in death. That is *atonement.*

(iv) 'He made intercession for the transgressors.' We can hear Him from the Cross put in the plea – 'Father forgive them —', a plea based on the fact that He liquidated their debt so that they could be liberated and put right with eternal justice. 'Because He humbled Himself and became obedient unto death, even the death of the Cross, wherefore God has highly exalted Him, and given Him a name which is above every name.' That is *reconciliation.*

This summing up by the only One who can see it as a whole, and see the end from the beginning, now presents it as an accomplished fact. The Servant took on a representative position. He substituted Himself for those doomed to die. He made atonement for the guilt and wrong. He brought them into a state of reconciliation.

These are the pillars of His Throne of Grace, before which a great multitude which no man can number shall proclaim: 'Worthy is the Lamb that was slain to receive power and riches, wisdom and strength and honour and glory and blessing.'

And to that we all say: *Amen.*

THE MASTER SAITH
'WHERE IS THE GUEST – CHAMBER?'

A s it was a common practice in Jerusalem on Passover occasions that inhabitants should open their houses freely to strangers coming in to the feast, we are set awondering if the man 'bearing the pitcher of water' really knew what Stranger he was to have under his roof, or what memorable transaction was to be enacted in his home that night. From the minuteness of detail it is apparent that the Lord had His eye upon this special man as the one chosen to render hospitality on that memorable night, and from the response given to such an imperative demand we are left to conclude that such ready obedience and generous provision must surely betoken a soul that feared the Lord and a heart that loved the Saviour. If this indeed be a case of a hidden disciple of the Lord, unknown and unacknowledged among his immediate followers, we are led to realise the power and authority with which that Divine command came, 'The Master saith', when the doors of the home were so readily flung open to receive the Heavenly guest, and such ample provision made to meet His demand. When we, in like manner, shall feel the Divine command press heavily on heart and conscience, we shall realise that neither obscurity nor timidity shall warrant us to deny Him His claim. And when the 'guest-chamber' is yielded up to Him, it becomes a place where He fulfils a Heavenly purpose and imparts a Heavenly blessing.

We notice, here, that the guest-chamber yielded up became a place of intimate fellowship. When our Lord asked for a place where He might eat the Passover with His disciples, He gave expression, no doubt, to a deep desire for a short hour of communion and fellowship with those who shared His confidence and His affection; He sought a place where He could have a closer and more intimate heart-to-heart communion with His disciples, undisturbed by the world. And what an inner sanctuary of communion that guest-chamber became that night, when the Lord, with such infinite tenderness, sought to lead His disciples into the fellowship of His sufferings, and the mystery of His sacrifice, and the depths of His redeeming purpose! And He asks for their fellowship in a way that makes us think it was to be a strength and a comfort and a joy to Him as well as to them. They had ample opportunity for fellowship as they travelled together those three years or more – but they were crowded years, years of preaching and teaching and miracle – working. Now in the stillness of a parting hour, with the world and its distracting cares shut out, with none to intrude upon their privacy, He leads them into the most 'secret place' and brings them into closest fellowship with Himself, with His mind, with His heart, with His purpose. And so though there are abundant opportunities in daily effort and service of knowing that the Master is *with us*, yet He desires to create an inner sanctuary of communion and fellowship where we may be *with Him*. It is only when the guest-chamber is yielded up at the Lord's bidding that we can hope to enjoy such a time of communion as that.

The guest-chamber became, too, the place of glorious revelation. The Master had been a patient Teacher, but His followers were slow to learn the meaning of His mission and the nature of its fast – approaching end. Though He dropped hints all along of a coming ordeal of suffering and separation, these were sufficiently dark to enable the disciples to dismiss them as unreal, or, at any rate, as beyond their comprehension. But now it is different, for He brings them face to face with the coming doom, and He lovingly and patiently unfolds to them the nature and significance of His sufferings and death; He even places in their hands symbols of His body broken for them and His blood shed for them. Did they not at that hour, however dimly, realise, if never before, that there was some vital connection between His death and their life, His suffering and their salvation? They had been over three years in His company, but I venture to think they saw and understood more of the Master in that hour in the upper room than they did in all those years. He opened to them His mind as never before, He unveiled His heart, He unfolded His purpose, and in the light of His presence they saw something of their own mission, their own standing, their own safety and security. When the guest-chamber is yielded up to Christ it becomes a place of Heavenly illumination, where the Lord may give wonderful views of our sin and His salvation, of our weakness and His strength, of the love and mercy, of the grace and glory He has prepared for us.

We must also realise that the guest-room became the place of imparted strength. Let us not think that this provision of the Lord for His disciples was merely the promptings of affection and human sentiment. His was the love that was an utter stranger to any kind of weak sentimentality that desires its own pleasure. His was the love that serves, the love that burns to enlighten, to instruct and to bless. And were not those symbols received at the hands of the Master a very real blessing? It was not merely new light He imparted : it was also new strength He infused – a strength in which they were to go for many days of darkness and trial and tribulation. There was a real tangible blessing He had to bestow in the breaking of bread – it was Himself as the Bread and the Wine of life unto their souls. As they received the sacred symbols, did they not feed by faith upon Christ? As they partook of the common plate and the common cup did they not feel afresh their unity with Christ and with one another? Who knows what comfort and strength they afterwards found, as they stood before the Cross, in those mysterious words, 'My body which is broken for you'? At any rate we remember how quickly and eagerly they went back to the Supper in after days to receive that inflow of strength that came to them at the first. We, too, must lay to heart that when we neglect to prepare the guest – chamber for the Lord we are sapping our spiritual life and denying ourselves the strength and the comfort that the Lord is willing to impart to us. Let us yield to Him this obedience, and He will communicate Himself to us as the Bread and Wine of life in whose strength we may have to go many days – days perhaps of darkness and sorrow and trial.

Last of all, we notice that the guest–chamber became the place of holy song. Before they left the upper room we read that 'they sang an hymn'. Was there ever a hymn sang under such shadow as this? Facing the mockery and ribaldry of ungodly men, facing the agony of Gethsemane, and the suffering of Calvary, 'they sang an hymn'. It is not, it cannot be, a buoyant rapturous outburst of joy – it is more deep, more sacred than that; it is the melody of a heart that receives its cup of suffering and sorrow as from a Father's hand; it is the song of a heart in full harmony with the will of God. And the disciples – eleven of them – joined in that song – a song in face of the Cross, a song, indeed, under the shadow of Calvary.

Was there ever such a song as this – so full of sadness and sorrow, yet so full of resignation and peace? Yes; when the guest-chamber is yielded up to the Lord, He gives us, as He gave to a suffering servant of old, 'songs in the night'. But if it be sung at all, it must be sung *with Him*; apart from Him the soul can only sigh and groan before its burden of sorrow; but with Him the soul can take its cup of suffering and sing 'Of mercy and of judgment'.

Thus we see that when the Lord entered that upper room it was to fulfil a wonderful purpose of blessing for His immediate followers; but He saw unfolding from that upper room a larger purpose of blessing for His followers to the end of time; a purpose that here should be instituted that Feast of Remembrance and that Sacrament of loyalty that should link Him in all ages, openly and publicly, with His own, and that should revive strength and faith and be to the world the visible pledge of His coming. Purposes like unto these unfold themselves to us that day the Lord finds a guest–chamber in our hearts and radiates within the light and peace of His own Presence.

THE TRIUMPH OF THE CROSS
(Colossians 2:15)

His Epistles everywhere show that Paul was no stranger to the military strategy of his day. He frequently borrows a figure from the textbooks of the Roman army and presses it into the service of Jesus Christ. For to him the Christian life was an incessant conflict, the Christian ideal was ever at war with pagan values, and the Kingdom of Jesus Christ progressed and advanced through territory whose every acre was claimed and occupied by the forces of darkness. He had no illusions as to the fierceness of the conflict, but he had likewise no uncertainty as to the final issue. Both had become realities to him in the light which the Holy Spirit of Christ shed for him upon the Cross of Christ. Calvary it was that unveiled for Paul the real nature of the conflict that was being waged in the spiritual world; Calvary it was, too, that provided the certainty of final victory for truth and righteousness.

In his Epistle to the Colossians he notes this fact when he reminds the Christians at Colosse of what God had done when He blotted out 'the handwriting of ordinances' that was against them and 'took it out of the way, nailing it to the Cross'. But this Cross that secured for them this personal triumph had a wider and deeper significance than their personal salvation. Through it God, 'having spoiled principalities and powers, made a show of them openly triumphing over them in it.' This great declaration has been elsewhere rendered as follows: 'And the hostile princes and rulers He shook off from Himself, and boldly displayed them as His conquests, when by the Cross He triumphed over them.' As this translation is more graphic and does no violence to the figure employed by Paul, we shall make use of it side by side with the more familiar rendering. The passage, however translated, is an exposition of the triumph of the Cross of Christ, and as such it has a message that is especially applicable in days of conflict and upheaval.

1. Here we have indicated, first of all the Objects of Christ's Triumph. Paul speaks of them as 'principalities and powers' or 'hostile princes and rulers'. The early Church never lost sight of the real nature of its conflict because it understood so clearly the true nature of Christ's conflict on the Cross. It was a conflict with the

principalities of the world of darkness and with the rulers of this world; in other words with the combined forces of earth and hell, of the invisible kingdom of evil and its visible agents in the world. That this was the true nature of Christ's conflict no serious student of Scripture can doubt. Flinging their full strength against the One Who suffered on the Cross were more than human forces; there were the legions of Satan's empire unseen by the eyes of men, but not unfelt by the One Who challenged them to battle. The outward scene contained elements of fierce opposition: the priests, the Roman power, the hateful and hating mob. But these were but mere tools in the hands of powers more fierce and terrible than any that naked eyes could see. 'The Prince of this world cometh' was Christ's own description of the coming conflict, and it is easy to see why it should be so. Christ lived and died for the deepest things of life, for the hidden things of the spiritual realm; for the redemption of the human soul, for the liberation of the human spirit, for the cleansing of the human heart, for the reign of righteousness and love, for the establishment of a kingdom that is not meat and drink but peace and purity and joy in the Holy Ghost. In thus redeeming men, He came into conflict with the mysterious powers of darkness that held rule over the spirits of men. They challenged His authority to lay down the ransom price for man's redemption. They disputed His power to effect man's deliverance. He joined battle with these hidden forces that were in possession of the spiritual nature of man, and there was waged a conflict that was fierce and hot. They disputed every inch of territory and refused to yield any of their possessions. Therefore was the battle, in its intensest form, fought on spiritual soil. The real conflict was an inner one with forces more fierce, more powerful, more cunning than the human enemies that surrounded Him. And in triumphing He triumphed over the principalities of the spiritual kingdom as well as over the powers of this world. The conflict of the Cause of Christ is still with those hidden, but powerful forces; they are behind the outward turmoil and strife. There is a master-mind, cunning and unscrupulous, planning the campaign. The resources of the world of darkness are taxed to maintain the conflict. Human rulers are only pawns in the game, tools in the hands of more powerful agents than themselves. We understand this in the light of the Cross. For it was the Cross that brought these into the open and that compelled them to show their hand. The Cross was the devil's master-stroke, his bid for everlasting dominion. And he lost decisively and finally.

2.   The nature of Christ's triumph is also described here when it is said that He 'spoiled principalities and powers' and 'made a show of them openly'. The two thoughts here would seem to be that the triumph of the Cross was decisive and complete.

It was decisive inasmuch as Christ *spoiled* the powers against Him, that is to say He upset their plans, resisted their advance, seized their arms and shook off their mighty legions. Satan's plan and God's plan were pitted there the one against the other, for both came into full exercise in the culminating events of the Cross. As the Cross was the fullest manifestation of God's wisdom so it was also the masterpiece of the devil's cunning. As the legions of hell were marshalled in dreadful array to do battle with the solitary figure on Calvary's Tree, so the resources of Heaven were behind the Divine Sufferer as He wrestled with the powers of darkness. Whatever the issue it would be decisive; for all was staked there. With what avidity the forces of darkness, therefore, fastened on Christ as He entered into death and the grave! But in His resurrection 'He shook them off from Himself' for it was 'impossible that He should be holden' of death. In that triumph He vindicated the superior wisdom of God's plan and the exceeding greatness of God's power in a manner that could never be gainsaid. Let us hold fast to this assurance that Christ's victory on Calvary was a decisive event, that it decided eternal issues, and that the apparent mastery of evil in any age does not and cannot detract one iota from the virtue of that victory. That conviction will give us stability and balance when evil appears in the ascendancy, and righteousness seems overthrown. On Calvary where opposing forces were matched, the eternal dominion of righteousness, truth and peace was decisively secured.

And the Triumph was likewise complete, for not only did the Victor of Calvary spoil principalities and powers, but He 'made a show of them openly' or openly displayed them as His conquests. Not only did He make use of the powers of darkness to serve His own ends, but He publicly and openly took the captives into captivity, and having delivered the dupes of Satan He carried them with Him in the train of His triumph. Never was the Prince of this world more completely foiled with his own weapons than when his artillery was captured by grace and turned upon the citadel of darkness! We believe that the wrath of men can still be made to praise the Lord Christ, and that the forces of evil will serve His purpose and open doors in unexpected places for the Gospel of His Kingdom. Although the triumph of the Prince of Peace may not always be apparent its foundations are solid and real, and the forces of evil will be overthrown, and He will make a show of them openly.

3.   The means of Christ's glorious Triumph are clearly indicated here: it is His Cross. 'Triumphing over them in it' can have reference only to that Cross on which the hostile 'handwriting of ordinances' was nailed. It is useful to note how that Cross that seemed to seal the doom of His cause and spell defeat for His Kingdom became the means of His triumph and the talisman of victory for His Church.

It was in death that He laid down, finally and forever, the ransom price for man's redemption. The shedding of His righteous blood was the uttermost farthing exacted, and it was paid to the full. Not even hell can challenge the validity of that price or dispute its eternal competence. The value of earth's currencies may rise and fall till eventually our silver and gold shall have no standing in a realm where the only real values are spiritual, but the blood of the Son of God shall never lose its inherent merit or depreciate in the scale of spiritual values. That is the first and great reason why His triumph on our behalf is complete and eternal.

Through death also the Stronger One entered into possession of the strong one's goods, to use the language of Christ's own parable. In death Christ wrestled with the power of death, and attacked the very citadel of the enemy's kingdom. Through death He entered into the domain where death's power had remained unchallenged and supreme. The battle was carried into the enemy's territory and was finally won on the enemy's own soil. For when He appeared in His resurrection glory He appeared as still the Great Shepherd of the sheep, but brought back again from the dead by the blood that sealed the everlasting Covenant. This is, therefore, a further pledge of the completeness of His triumph that He has despoiled death and the grave because 'He humbled Himself and became obedient unto death'.

Through death, likewise, He has contradicted and overthrown all that the principalities and powers of this world hold their power by. These hold their subjects by force, Christ in dying proved that His Kingdom could be held by love. The kingdom of this world is ruled by self-interest, Christ's by self-sacrifice. The realm of darkness is kept in subjection through fear of punishment; Christ's empire is bound to His rule through gratitude because of forgiveness. Thus the wisdom of the world is overthrown by the Cross of Christ; its teaching is contradicted, and its sway for ever broken.

Truly this is Divine and wondrous in our eyes! The Cross that was the symbol of shame became the revelation of honour; the Cross that was the symbol of weakness became the weapon of power; the Cross that was the final stroke of defeat from the principalities of the world became the means of a Triumph that is decisive and complete, and the channel of power that shall operate in the hearts of men as long as a soul abides in immortality. This is what we mean by the Triumph of the Cross.

NO CROSS, NO CROWN

Our Bible suggests an indissoluble link between Cross and Crown, between suffering and triumph, between shame and glory, between the darkness of the Cross and the light it ministers gloriously to man, between the character it develops and the destiny we inherit. If this be a universal truth in the spiritual realm, then it is applicable to all who live in that realm, and come under its laws.

Our concern here is to trace this connection first in the Life of Christ, and then in the lives of those who follow Him. He and we come under the same eternal principle that regulates the life of the Kingdom in which He is Head and we are members.

1. Trace it in Christ's Life

A study of the life of Christ makes it clear that He Himself linked together His Cross and His Crown, His sufferings and His Throne. There was a necessity running through His life giving it cohesion and purpose and direction. It was the necessity of the Cross: and from that there could be no deviation.

(a) *Attempts to Break the Link*

(i)   In His temptation this was the offer made to him, to reach the Crown without His Cross. 'The devil taketh him up into a high mountain, and showeth him all the kingdoms of the world and the glory of them. And saith unto him: All these things will I give thee, if thou wilt fall down and worship me.' He was offered the easy way to His crown – a short cut to His destination and goal. Christ knew that the kingdoms of this world and the glory of them had been promised Him by His Father. But it was to be a hard road: there were to be wars of conflict and sacrifice, through death and shame. Here is an offer to escape the Cross, 'if thou wilt fall down and worship me.' One act of disloyalty in secret, behind the scenes, and it would all be His. Our Lord dismissed the thought at once: no treachery like that would find a foothold in His nature. The way to His Throne – to His dominion, was already prescribed for Him: it was by His Cross that He could lay hold of this power.

(ii)   The temptation returned later through a different channel. Christ had reached the place where He must disclose to His disciples that His path to the throne lay through suffering and death. 'From that time forth began Jesus to show unto His disciples how that He must go unto Jerusalem, and suffer many things of the elders and chief priests and scribes, and be killed, and be raised again the third day.' And Simon felt at that moment the offence of the Cross, the ignominy of all this, the absurdity of this lot falling to His Master. 'Far be it from thee Lord: this shall not be unto thee.' You must put the thought out of your mind – you must get another way, any way to escape the welter of suffering and shame. And the Lord recognised the old temptation returning through another channel. 'Get thee behind me, Satan, for thou savourest not the things that be of God but the things that be of man.' You are taking the human way out – and turning your back on the Divine way. God's way is predetermined: by the Cross to the Crown.

(iii)   At His last trial, the temptation returned. 'I adjure thee by the living God' said Caiaphas, 'that thou tell us whether thou be the Christ, the Son of God.' Let Him in but a word renounce His claims to the Crown, and He could escape the Cross. Solemnly He told them that one day their positions would be reversed, and they would appear before His judgment seat. 'Hereafter shall ye see the Son of Man sitting on the right hand of power, and coming in the clouds of Heaven.' His throne was secure. But there could be no evasion of His Cross: for He went by the Cross to His place of universal dominion and judgment.

Even on the Cross itself the temptation assailed Him as they shouted to Him 'If thou be the Christ of God come down from the Cross – and we will believe in thee'. Escape the Cross and we will crown thee.

(iv)   In the Garden of Gethsemane our Lord in His utter weakness may have asked if there was a way out. Otherwise, what is the meaning of His cry 'Father if it be possible, let this cup pass from me' ? If it be possible – if I can fulfil Thy will and reach my place of dominion without drinking this bitter draught – let this cup pass. But immediately He yielded a willing and a loyal obedience, 'Not my will, but Thine be done'. Thus He recognised with utmost solemnity that it was the will of His God that He should pass this way to His Throne.

On the Road to Emmaus the Risen Lord shed new light on this link between the Cross and the Crown. 'Ought not Christ to have suffered these things and to enter into his glory' – to enter through these sufferings – a Divine ought about it.

(b) *The Realisation of the Crown by the Way of the Cross*

Is it true that our Lord went to His Crown by the way of His Cross?

(i)   Look at His exaltation after death and resurrection. Paul tells us what the connecton is, 'He humbled himself and became obedient unto death, even the death of the Cross. Wherefore God hath highly exalted him and given him a name which is above every name, that at the name of Jesus every knee should bow' (Phil. 2:8-10). Paul is here speaking of the one who 'was found in fashion as a man', Jesus. He has been exalted to this place of centrality as the reward of His obedience unto death. It is an altogether new position conferred on the God-man Christ Jesus that He should be so exalted. The life that He had laid down in death He now lifts to the Eternal Throne, to be invested with a Name that is above every name.

Man below is still struggling against sin and sorrow and death. 'For we see not yet all things put under him; but we see Jesus, who was made a little lower than the angels – crowned with glory and honour.' The man of Nazareth has gone from His Cross to His Crown.

(ii)   We see it also in His investiture with dominion over all God's creation. He Himself, the Risen Lord, while still lingering on the borderland of two worlds here below, said to His disciples: 'All power is given unto me in Heaven and in earth: go ye therefore and teach all nations, baptising them in the name of the Father, and of the Son, and of the Holy Ghost.' And now He claims that dominion, He enters upon His reign. But it is the Lord that was pierced that holds the sceptre, the brow that was crowned with thorns that bears the Crown of Glory. Is there a connection between the crown of thorns and the Crown of Glory? What were the thorns but the emblems of earth's curse and sorrow and rebellion ? And when He bore, all unseen to mankind's eyes, the burden of earth's sin, it was proper that He should visibly and publicly bear the symbol of earth's curse – its thorns. But it was in virtue of that sin-bearing that He is now exalted to the Throne, and the crown of thorns is exchanged to a Crown of Glory.

And it is through His grace of redemption that He now wields the power of the Throne. He exercises His gracious redemptive dominion through the Cross and the victory over sin and guilt that He had won there. The One who died in human history is now Lord of History, and all history becomes the unfolding of the redemptive drama of which He is the pivot and centre. History continues to be written only because He who once died now lives to save, and when His salvation is complete the book of history will close, and its last chapter will have been written. 'In the midst of the Throne is the Lamb as if it were slain.'

(iii) What is true of His general dominion is also true of His rule in the hearts of men. He has been given a name that is above every name, a name to which every knee shall bow. And that name is Jesus – the name inscribed on His Cross, a name redolent with sacrifice. And He wields His crown rights over our hearts in virtue of His death for us. It is through His Cross, through His sacrifice, through His dying love, that He reigns in the heart of man. It is because He was lifted up that He still draws all men to Him.

(iv) Yes and His reign among the rebels who reject His overtures of mercy is exercised by right of His death. When they shall see Him – they shall see Him whom they pierced. When they experience His displeasure they shall feel the wrath of the Lamb. Thus we see in the Lord Jesus Christ the inseparableness of these two – the Cross and the Crown. Without a Cross He could not wear His Crown. Had He not sunk so low He could not ascend so high. His exaltation followed His Humiliation as its natural sequence and moral consequence. ('He drank of the brook in the way, Therefore shall He lift up the head')

2. Trace it in the Disciple's Life

How are the Cross and the Crown linked together in the experience of believing men? What is our Cross here? What shall be our Crown hereafter? Our Cross is what comes to us in witness-bearing, what is meted out to us because we name the name of Christ, and dare to follow in His steps. Our Cross is something that bears such a moral and spiritual resemblance to His Cross that He calls it 'Taking up His Cross'.

He has left us as much of His Cross as we are able to bear. He took away the guilt, the curse, the desertion, the death. But He left us something of His Cross – its mystery, its reproof, its offence. But also its power to slay, and make alive. Its power to condemn and deliver. Its power to crucify and quicken. It was His good pleasure to leave us this much of His Cross. Why? It has meaning for us here in our personal life and witness. It has meaning for us in the hereafter. It casts not its shadow, but its light into the eternal state. It stands for abiding values – our Crown.

And what is our Crown? It is the realisation and fulfilment of our highest desires and aspirations; it is to us the conscious mark of His approbation and 'well-done'. It is that which comes into our experience when we enter into the joy of our Lord as souls redeemed and servants honoured and blessed. And the N. T. does speak of that realisation and fulfilment as our 'Crown'. There are four crowns specially mentioned and they are all concerned with our fidelity to Christ in service and witness-bearing. Fidelity often brings the bitterness, and even the agony of the cross into our experience, but it also brings the crown.

3. Different Crowns

(a) Crown of Joy for Fidelity in Soul-Winning

Paul asks of the Thessalonians 'For what is our hope or joy, or crown of rejoicing. Are not ye in the presence of our Lord Jesus Christ at his coming' ? Souls won for the Saviour will be our crown of joy when He comes. 'They that turn many to righteousness shall shine as the stars for ever and ever.' And what trials, what pains, what suffering Paul underwent to reach these souls with the Gospel and win them for Christ. He travailed for them, he says. How sharply the cross bit into his sensitive nature as he met with reproach, endured hardship and suffered unspeakable wrongs. But they were won – and souls thus won were to be his crown of joy at the coming of the Master.

(b) Crown of Righteousness for Fidelity in Waiting and Expecting

Again Paul says, this time to Timothy, 'Henceforth there is laid up for me a crown of righteousness which the Lord the righteous judge shall give me at that day, and not to me only, but to all them that love His appearing.' A heart -throbbing expectancy for the Lord's appearance is to be met with the crown of righteousness. A crown which is righteousness realised, possessed and triumphant. But how much misunderstanding, ridicule, reproach there was to endure for one who loved the Lord's appearing: so unrealistic, so otherworldly, so futile. Paul refers here to the righteous judge: but at that time he was under the unrighteous judge awaiting his last trial under Nero. Yet for those who were loyal to the absent Lord and looked for His eventual triumph: a crown of righteousness would be theirs.

(c) Crown of Life for Fidelity in Endurance

James says: 'Blessed is the man that endureth temptation, for when he is tried he shall receive the crown of life which the Lord has promised to them that love him.' And John in Revelation says 'Be thou faithful unto death and I will give thee the crown of life'. The crown of life means life in all its meaning and fullness. It puts life in all its fullness at the disposal of the faithful servant. That is the grand consummation to which a life of faithful endurance is moving.

(d) Crown of Glory for Fidelity to the Church

Peter says 'Feed the flock of God which is among you – and when the chief Shepherd shall appear ye shall receive a crown of Glory that fadeth not away'. But fidelity to the flock often spells cross-bearing: open to abuse, to misunderstanding, to reproach. But it leads to the crown of glory – the crown that is glory in all its manifestations.

4. The Link between the Cross and the Crown.

What is the significance of the Cross in the believer's life?

(a) It tests the loyalty of his faith. Christ never ceased to demand that His followers should submit to His test before they accepted His call to serve Him. Many of His parables are concerned with depicting men and women who did not stand the test, who began well and ended in eclipse. For that reason He has left his cross for those who would pass

His test. 'If any man will come after me, let him deny himself and take up his cross and follow me.' And no man shall receive the crown until he has passed the test of his Master. Some, we are told, will be disappointed.

(b)   It deepens our nature. Only in this way can we stand the weight of His Cross. Shallow natures can never stand either prosperity or adversity. But the plough-share of sorrow comes to cut down and deepen its furrows within us. Psalm 90 says 'Make us glad according to the days wherein thou hast afflicted us, and the years wherein we have seen evil'. Joy sounds only as deep as sorrow has gone. Of Christ it has been said 'That it became him, in bringing many sons unto glory, to make the captain of their salvation perfect through suffering'

(c)   It sanctifies our character. There is a refining and a sanctifying influence in cross-bearing. 'Our light affliction which is but for a moment, worketh for us a far more exceeding and eternal weight of glory.' So the cross in affliction works: it does service. It spells victory over sin within. It slays sin in our inner nature: by it we are crucified with Christ. Through it we are with Christ daily. And however bitter and sore that cross may be, holiness shall not crown our lives without it. 'By which the world is crucified unto me, and I unto the world.'

5. Conclusion

What does it all sum up to? Just this: Is character worthwhile? Is there any eternal relevance in the struggles and triumphs of the Christian in his endeavour to do the will of God? Does it matter much what we are and do if we have found the promise of eternal life through Christ?

It is a fact that for the believer in Christ there is now no condemnation. He has passed from death unto life and will not come into condemnation. His person is completely delivered from sin's power and sin's guilt. Of that there can be no question. Is there any abiding value then in the Christian character he develops, in the way he walks in the will of God, in the obedience he yields to the bidding of his Master – if all believing men, in virtue of what Christ has done for them, are saved with an everlasting salvation? If that be so then much of the N. T. has been written in vain. The N. T. makes it everywhere clear that every thought, every desire, every word and action in the Christian's life is of eternal moment, that every Christian is building up his eternal estate, for we must all appear before the judgment seat of Christ that we may get back – returned to us – the things done in the body, whether good or bad.

And in the final reckoning it is clear that some will suffer loss – the wood, hay, stubble in our obedience and service will go up in flames. We will agree that it must be so – for these things cannot follow us into the Eternal State. But every Christian put in trust by his Lord must surely make some return.

That which stands the final test, that which is permanent in life and service – that will be our crown. But there is a law of the Christian life that only the Cross prepares us for the Crown. The Cross in some of its manifestations – its offence, its reproach, its denial, its suffering, its death to self – that is the Divine way to equip us for the Crown. Its acceptance here and now is the key, not only to many of life's problems here, but to many of life's possibilities in the hereafter. As a man, a Christian man, sows in the here and now, so shall he reap in the hereafter. Christian life, Christian conduct, Christian character matter – they matter eternally.

BETWEEN THE CROSS AND THE CROWN
(Psalm 23)

It is difficult to say why the Psalms were placed in the exact order in which we now find them in the Book of Psalms, but we think it was no mere coincidence that placed the Twenty-third Psalm where it is. Coming between the Twenty-second and the Twenty-fourth Psalms it is a gem in its natural setting. The Twenty-second Psalm deals with the sufferings of the Saviour and the Twenty-fourth Psalm gives a dramatic preview of the triumphant home-coming of the Church of God. What more natural, then, than that the Twenty-third Psalm, the Psalm of the Christian life, should lie between the Cross and the Crown! While the Twenty-second Psalm tells of the sufferings and the sorrows of the Shepherd who went to seek for the sheep that was lost, and the Twenty – fourth Psalm echoes the welcome home given to the Shepherd as He carries His sheep into the safety of the Heavenly Fold, so the Twenty-third tells of the wilderness experience of the sheep as she is being borne home on the shoulders of her Shepherd. Thus it is that the life of the Christian believer is lived day by day between the Cross of his redemption and the Crown of his eternal glory, the shadow of the Cross and the light of the coming Glory co-mingling as they play and inter-play upon his faith, giving him cause to mourn in deep soul affliction and to rejoice with a joy that is unspeakable and full of glory.

1.   We do well to note first, that *the Christian's possessions are entered upon and claimed between the Cross and the Crown.* The song opens with two great claims: the soul's claim to the Shepherd Himself, and then to all His resources. These two claims are so related that the first becomes the foundation of the second; it is because faith can say, 'The Lord is my Shepherd' that it can add, 'I shall not want.' But these great claims can have no validity except in the shadow of the Cross and the light of the Crown. Only in full view of the Cross can faith stake its claim, *'My* Shepherd.' Christ in all His relationships is personal, but in a supreme and paramount way, He is a personal *Saviour* who has made Himself over to the soul. His sacrifice is thus seen to be personal, the identification of the Sin-bearer with the sinner is fundamentally personal, and under the shadow of Calvary faith has confidence in claiming 'He loved me and gave Himself for me'. Then again as the eye of faith penetrates within the veil and views the ineffable glory of the enthroned Lord, and

is assured that all He is, He is for His own, the Christian heart can face the wilderness journey with the song 'I shall not want'. Only between the Cross and the Crown can such a song be given and maintained, receiving its deeper notes from the sore experiences recorded in the Twenty-second Psalm and its higher notes from the echoes of triumph that sound from the Twenty-fourth.

But these are not *all* the possessions that the Christian heart can lay claim to between the Cross and the Crown, though they are the source and the pledge of all the others. There is, for example, the possession of peace or rest: 'He maketh me to lie down in green pastures', and there is in that peace a progressiveness, a developing apprehension, that finds pictorial expression in the words 'He leadeth me by the still waters'. But where can such an experience of 'the peace of God that passeth all understanding' be received except it be between the Cross and the Crown? For what is it that turns the wilderness into 'green pastures' save the reconciliation made by the Shepherd? And what is it that turns the raging torrents of the way into 'waters of quietness' save the vision of the enthroned Christ and the touch of His right hand as He lays it upon the fluttering heart saying, 'Fear not, I am the First and the Last, I am He that liveth and was dead, and behold I am alive for evermore and have the keys.' Was that the meaning of the two-fold peace that the Lord spoke of to His disciples: 'Peace I leave with you; my peace give I unto you' – the legacy bequeathed from His death, the gift bestowed from the throne?

2.   We note next, that *the Christian's walk is between the Cross and the Crown*. His is not a stagnant life, even though it may be one of unbroken peace and quietness. His path is determined for him, it is the King's Highway over which all His pilgrims are led. For this Royal Road he needs Royal sustenance and grace: 'He restoreth my soul.' Only the Lord Himself has this access to the soul, and He alone can supply the restoratives that revive faith, quicken hope and stimulate love. Yet this very grace of restoration is itself the premonition of a trial to be faced and a difficulty to be overcome. And it is even so here: 'He leadeth me in the paths of righteousness even for His own name's sake.' The 'paths of righteousness' were never found to be easy, and many discovered them to be a severe test of faith and courage, leaving the traveller at the end of the day footsore and

weary. But since He 'leads' in that direction there can be no withdrawal and no pining for the easy path. Were we to ask our Guide why it was necessary for us to take this uphill road, His only reply would surely be, 'Even for His own name's sake.' Must all this be experienced between the Cross and the Crown? Where else can we find the restoratives that revive our spiritual life save at the foot of the Cross where the Lord of Life died that we might have 'life more abundant', where 'by His stripes we are healed'? And how can we persevere in 'the paths of righteousness' if it be not in the power of His resurrection as well as in the fellowship of His sufferings, if it be not that the enthroned Lord gives the promise 'I will guide thee with mine eye'? Dare we, then, shrink from taking this hard road 'for His name's sake', when we look back into the Twenty-second Psalm and see there the road that He took for our name's sake!

But 'the paths of righteousness' lead through strange country, often inhospitable and alien country. For one thing, 'the valley of the shadow of death' is on the King's Highway, and it is doubtlessly a place of gloom, and oft of trial and distress. But the traveller here sings of two things that comfort him: 'thy rod and thy staff, they comfort me.' Surely it is under the shadow of Christ's Cross that the believer discovers the 'rod' and the 'staff' that the Lord Himself used when He passed this way. For Him the valley was not merely one of 'shadows', but, in very truth, one of stern and grave realities, yet with His rod and His staff in His hand He passed through. But there is more – infinitely more – than the rod and the staff in the valley of dark shadows; there is the intimacy of a living Presence: 'for Thou art with me.' Here is struck the first note of intimacy – the first 'Thou' in the Psalm – it took the valley of the shadow of death to do that! And where can the assurance of the Living Presence be given save from the Throne and from the lips of the Crowned Lord? Thus the shadow of the Cross and the light of the Crown flit across the traveller's face as he sings, 'Yea, though I walk through the valley of the shadow of death I will fear no evil, for Thou art with me, thy rod and thy staff, they comfort me.'

3.   We note, lastly, that *the believer enjoys his choicest spiritual privileges between the Cross and the Crown*. There are festive occasions in the believer's experience when he enjoys to the full the privileges of communion and sweet fellowship that turn the wilderness into a banqueting house: 'Thou preparest a table before me in the

presence of mine enemies.' Such a table can be set and furnished only in the shadow of the Cross, under the canopy of reconciliation, a reconciliation that sin cannot mar nor the enemies of the soul destroy. And yet, there is more than the Cross here in the enjoyment of the believing soul: there is the Living Lord Himself anointing the head, and filling the cup. These are the 'extras' that a loving heart never fails to provide, the 'extras' that Jesus missed that day that He was guest with Simon the Pharisee! How can we receive these tokens of special love from His hand without recalling – unable to hide the blush of shame as we recall – that when He was guest with us we put upon His head a crown of thorns, and in the day of His deep thirst, we gave Him vinegar to drink? For hatred He gives love, and for cruelty infinite tenderness and patience!

And now as the song draws to its close, there is one more glance behind at the Cross whence all our blessings flow, and lo! there is the realisation that the fountain cannot run dry: 'surely goodness and mercy shall follow me all the days of my life.' Then there is a look ahead and the lights of Home are already streaming down, and through the break in the clouds we can see the doors of the Eternal Abode flung open in obedience to that command of the Twenty-fourth Psalm: 'Lift up your heads, ye gates, even lift them up ye everlasting doors.' Nay, more, we see a place reserved for us within, a place that none other can claim, and we, who have met the mercies of God in the way, who have tasted so deeply of the Heavenly wine while still on this side of Jordan, know with an assured confidence that grace is the prelude to glory and that we 'shall dwell in the house of the Lord for ever'.

THE THREE MEN OF CALVARY

It is not too much to claim that all our studies in the life and character and teaching of Christ must inevitably lead to the subject of Calvary and to the death of our Lord outside the City Gate. That was the place to which He was travelling right through His life as the grand climax of all He was, all He said, and all He did. All roads led to Calvary, and in the Christian's thought and experience it must always be so. This is in line with Christ's own mind and with His will for us. And yet when we reach Calvary it must prove a bitter and heart-searching experience. Our Lord is there put to open shame, and He is there in the company of two common thieves. This is Luke's simple and graphic record: 'And when they were come to the place which is called Calvary, there they crucified him and the malefactors, one on the right, the other on the left.' The scene, as thus depicted, cannot fail to strike one, prepared by many references of the Master Himself for a great dramatic culminating act of majesty and grace, as singularly inappropriate and disappointing. That He at the last should be found there, and in such company! That a life which began amidst the worship and adoration of wise men and holy angels should end in the company of common thieves! That one whose cradle was surrounded by gold and frankincense and myrrh should spend His dying hours amidst the oaths and curses of tortured, broken and outcast men! That there should be on Calvary not one man and one Cross in solitary splendour, but three men and three crosses! This may prove a bitter disappointment to the earnest seeker who is on a spiritual pilgrimage to Calvary. We recognise in it, indeed, the malicious design of the Jewish rulers to add insult to injury by designating the Prophet of Galilee a common criminal and giving Him in death a place between two malefactors. But we recognise in it, too, the finger of God who had from eternity not only pinpointed the place where His Son should render satisfaction for the world's sin, but also pre-ordained all the circumstances surrounding that sacrifice. For that reason we are warranted to find in it something of abiding spiritual significance. It is, indeed, a clue to the inner meaning of Calvary, and an interpretation of what was happening that there should be at the place of crucifixion not one man but three. The three men and the three crosses belong spiritually to that setting as truly as they once did historically. That shall be our approach to Calvary on this occasion.

1.   The first man of Calvary is a malefactor on his cross, criminal in life and now defiant in death, greeting the Divine Sufferer on the centre cross with a sneer of unbelief: 'If thou be the Christ, save thyself and us', his spirit obviously untamed, his heart unchanged, his will unyielding, a rebel to the last! What an exposure of the man, even now when his nature is breaking in death!

And that is, indeed, the meaning of Calvary in relation to the human heart. It is a great and a ghastly exposure of unregenerate human nature such as could be made only in the revealing presence of the Son of God. For there on Calvary man and God came together, man in the ascendancy and the Son of God in chains. That was man's hour, given to him by Him to whom Time as well as Eternity belongs, an hour that witnessed man's most complete exposure and condemnation. There for his brief hour, man, under the control of 'the power of darkness', threw aside all restraint and eagerly snatched at the opportunity to strike at the heart of the only Righteous and Holy One. There man's age-long malice against God has its completest exposure and his sin in all its venom and daring is seen portrayed against the background of Divine Holiness and Grace. Man is there seen to be what sin has made him, a deicide, at heart a murderer of God! This is seen to be as true of religious man as of pagan man, of Jewish rabbi as of Roman judge; for religion at its purest, as represented by the spiritual leaders of Israel, and justice at its highest, as represented by Pilate the Roman judge, combined to thrust the Son of God outside the camp and there put Him to open shame. What an unveiling of the bankruptcy of the world's wisdom and goodness, of the hollowness and sordidness of the world's law and equity, of the utter criminality of human nature!

Thus the first man of Calvary is a representative man, representative of natural man, fallen, depraved, impenitent, lost. That malefactor, arrested, exposed, condemned, sentenced, yet unsoftened, impenitent, rebellious to the last breath, represents all that man is in the presence of God. The Cross is thus our condemnation, testifying to the utter hopelessness of improving a nature so antagonistic to God, so daring in its malice, so steeled against mercy, so utterly fallen and lost.

2.   The Second Man of Calvary is on the middle cross. He is truly and uniquely the Son of God, but He is nonetheless a man, for He is indeed

the only one who is truly and completely Man. When Pilate pointed to Him, the victim of injustice and cruelty, and exclaimed 'Behold the Man!' how little he understood of his own exclamation! For this was not any man, but the Representative Man, the new Head of the Race, the Second Adam. If the race is to fulfil its Divine destiny it must have a new start under a new head, it must be built again upon new foundations. Thus it was that the Second Man, the Lord from Heaven, took the field where the first man had failed. The contest between God and man is raised again and brought to a direct issue as the Representative of a criminal and ruined race took His place before God to make restitution and yield obedience. For Him this was no merely formal and academic position to assume, but a position that was truly terrible in its implications. There on Calvary, outside the camp, Christ stood alone over against the God of the Universe to meet the due consequences of man's rebellion and disobedience. He became a sin-bearer, and God thus ordered that He should be numbered with the transgressors. As sin-bearer He became an outcast, abandoned of men and forsaken of God, absolutely and completely alone in the transaction He took in hand. Though He were a Son, when He knocked at the door of the Heavenly Home, it was shut against Him, He called and there was no answer. He was enveloped in the darkness of impenetrable night, at mid-day, darkness that was the emblem, not indeed of sorrow, but of judgment and condemnation.

When out of that darkness there came forth eventually the cry 'It is finished', we believe that with His perfect manhood upon the altar He yielded the last sacrifice, He officiated as the last priest, He provided the last altar, and complete restitution was made. He 'restored that which He took not away', He made an end of sin and brought in an everlasting righteousness.

That was the Second Man, the Lord from Heaven, the Man who stood for fallen man,who made restitution for man's rebellion and wrong, who restored the righteousness and honour which man's sin took away, who laid the foundations on which a new manhood could be built to the honour and glory of God.That is the Cross of Redemption.

3.   The third man is also upon his cross, and his life is forfeit. He, too, had been a rebel and had lived in open defiance of God and man. He, too, had apparently joined in the railing against the guiltless Sufferer by his side. But something happened: we can never fully know what or

how, except as we interpret it in the light of our own spiritual experience. Was it something he felt when he sensed the majestic calm that enveloped the Sufferer by his side? Was it something he heard when the strange cry sounded forth amidst the shrieks of the revengeful mob, 'Father, forgive them, for they know not what they do'? Was it something he saw when he looked up at the board Pilate had smeared with the first verse of the New Testament to be written, 'This is Jesus of Nazareth, the King of the Jews'? Again we cannot tell, but he looked out on One who suffered yet had done nothing amiss, and the vision of vicarious suffering, of the sin-bearer for the sinner, broke upon his soul and he prayed. It is the first time, surely, that a man on a cross prayed to a man on a cross, a dying man to a dying man! And what a prayer – all the humble brokenness of a soul on the brink of despair, with the simple trustfulness of a little child, with the vision of a prophet who sees the Crucified One returning crowned!

And what an answer it received, giving hope, certainty, eternal life! He who seemed an outcast Himself took an outcast by the hand and took him safely home! And He did it as of perfect right, asking permission of none to bring this guest home to His Father's Table, the fruit of His passion!

And that is the Regenerate Man, redeemed by the agony of the Cross, and reborn as he is linked by faith to an atoning Saviour. And that is the further meaning of Calvary, it contains a cross on which man dies to self and comes alive to God. There man, a rebel, is reconciled, man, depraved, is recreated, man, an outcast, is restored to God.

In that darkness that enveloped Calvary we believe that the foundations of a new creation were being laid. Our minds go back to the first act of creation when darkness enveloped the earth and God sent forth His creative word: 'Let there be light.' Once more from a darkness as dense we hear another creative word, 'Verily, verily, I say unto thee, today shalt thou be with Me in Paradise.' And at His word there is a new creation! There the Cross means regeneration, as before it meant condemnation, and redemption.

Truly, Calvary is strangely peopled! Three Men and three Crosses – one man dying in sin, one dying for sin, and one dying to sin. It must always be so, for this is the Divine purpose concerning it. And when Paul beheld this he cried, 'God forbid that I should glory, save in the

Cross of our Lord Jesus Christ, by whom the world is crucified unto me, and I unto the world.' Still, three Men and three Crosses! Condemnation, Redemption, Regeneration!

WHAT I HAVE WRITTEN I HAVE WRITTEN

As we become conscious of the passage of the years with ever accelerating pace, we know instinctively, as we know for certain by the witness of God's word, that their record abides. We know that nothing through which we have lived is permanently lost so that it cannot re-enter our experience and we live it again in all its joy or sorrow. We know that the tenses of time have no relevance to the eternal state to which we most truly belong and in which all is an abiding, ever-living present. Into that timeless state we bear our record with us, as real a part of ourselves as thought, or feeling, or memory. For it is interwoven into the strands of moral character and spiritual consciousness. At such a time we feel a strange, haunting, inescapable relevance in the cry of Pilate, the Roman Judge. 'What I have written, I have written .' Pilate lived among events that turned the tide of history, he had a hand in a transaction from which have flowed hope and feeling to millions of mankind, yet Pilate himself retired from the scene, set his back upon its life and its light, and left nothing behind him – but an inscription! And not only is Pilate known in history by that inscription he smeared so hastily on the Cross, but the Cross itself is known to the ages by that inscription: 'Jesus of Nazareth, the King of the Jews.' That inscription, penned perhaps to wound Jewish pride, still overhangs the Cross, flashing its light like the beams of a lighthouse at the entrance to port, guiding stormbound mariners into the haven. Pilate, indeed, must have had some strange intuition that its relevance was not merely local, or temporary, for he had it written in Greek, and Latin, and Hebrew, as representing the world's culture, the world's government, and the world's religion at their highest. Had he, indeed, a premonition that the Cross it marked and interpreted had a message for the culture of the world, for its government and its religion? Be that as it may, Pilate displayed a firmness that does not seem native to so pliable and shifty a character when he replied to his instigators, as they turned round to reproach him: 'What I have written, I have written.' There it was allowed to stand, and there it still stands, the accompaniment and the interpreter of the Cross wherever it is uplifted and proclaimed: 'Jesus of Nazareth, the King of the Jews.'

Today our minds fasten on Pilate's resolute words that sound depths which he could not fathom and proclaim a truth which he could not comprehend: 'What I have written, I have written.'

1.   In their implications for Pilate himself, we see here *the finality of a spiritual decision.* There is some evidence that a conflict was waged within Pilate's breast – a conflict between the right he knew and the grievous wrong he was to commit. His inscription registered a decision that may well have been the true finding of his mind and heart. He had been probably several hours in all in the presence of his Prisoner whose demeanour in private as in public perplexed the Roman Judge and perhaps struck awe into his pagan heart. As a high official of Caesar, Pilate had been in the presence of kingly personages, and he sensed, we think, that he was in a royal presence now. Majesty radiated from every word and movement of Him who stood at his bar, and Pilate decided to record that one impression of his: 'This is the King of the Jews.' Ere he turned his back for ever upon the Cross and its manifestation of true Majesty, he was asked to change the inscription: he resolutely refused, he would not, for he could not. It was the record of a transaction that took place within his own soul, a verdict that was to leave its mark indelibly upon his heart for ever. He had gazed into the face of Divine Majesty, and turned away for ever! What he had written could not be unwritten: it stood there, as it stood on the records of his inner being, a permanent and abiding verdict.

It is wise for us to remember that there are some things in man's life that are irrevocable. Among these are the moral impressions of truth, and the sense of spiritual realities. Our book is to be closed, sealed, and laid aside. What we have written, we have written, and not till the Books are opened for the final reckoning shall we fully realise how the spiritual impressions of the past have been engraven in our destiny with abiding finality.

2.   We think we discover, also, in Pilate's resolute outburst the strange *sense of a great fulfilment.* History had testified, though Pilate had not known it, that One was to come who should reign in righteousness. And Divine history had shown clearly that the Regal One should come of the Seed of Abraham. The sacrifices of ancient Israel told of One who should be broken upon the altar as He met with God for men. The Song of Israel told of One who should be

pierced in hands and feet, and yet be fairer than the children of men, whose sceptre was a royal sceptre, and His Kingdom an ever-lasting kingdom. The Prophets of Israel told of One who should be a Man of Sorrows and acquainted with grief, who should be wounded for our transgressions and bruised for our iniquities, and yet have the government upon His shoulders, and be called the Mighty God, the Everlasting Father, and the Prince of Peace. And here in Pilate's description is the glimpse of recognition – 'Jesus of Nazareth, the King of the Jews!' Bring these ancient witnesses to the foot of the Cross – shall they fail to recognise in the outcast and suffering One, the King of Prophecy, the Lord of Grace, and the Prince of Peace? Is not the Cross itself the Throne of justice and mercy from which the empire of the redeemed is for ever ruled? Is not the crown of thorns He wore, thorns that were the fruit of earth's curse and the emblems of sin's sharp sorrow, the visible pledge of the curse He bore upon His soul, and the visible token of His sovereignty over hearts He has redeemed and cleansed? And the reed in His Hand, in all its expression of weakness and brokenness, is it not the sceptre of His grace and love that He holds over rebel hearts to bring them into subjection to His sway? Pilate saw and knew it not, and yet he had marked off the Victim of his injustice as the Promised of God who should gather the dispersed of Israel into homage to His crown rights. And in Him 'all Israel shall be saved'.

3.   May we not see in Pilate's decision to abide by his inscription *the operation of a gracious purpose of God* towards a soul in sin. There was the dying malefactor on his cross by the side of Christ, and as yet he knew nothing, or could know nothing of his fellow-sufferer in the midst. Perhaps in his youth, at a mother's knee, he had heard the Jewish Scriptures read, and listened to the promises of the Hope of Israel, the King of Zion, who was yet to come. If so, all that must have been forgotten in a life of violence and crime. He had left the Home and the Book and the Religion of Israel far behind. In a dying hour there was none to open the Book or speak of the Hope of Israel to a dying malefactor. Yet there was another Divine Book being written – the New Testament, and the first line of it to be formed is inscribed upon the centre Cross – 'Jesus of Nazareth, the King of the Jews.' The thief of Calvary, with the mist of death gathering upon his eye, looked out and read there God's message

to his soul, and saw the fullness of all that the Law and Prophets had promised. Light dawned, prayer dawned. He saw the One who was going crucified coming crowned. He saw the sun that was setting in darkness and blood rise again on a day of coronation and royal appearing. He cherished the hope that on that day there might be a place for the malefactor of Calvary, a misfit and a criminal in the world-order below, in the Kingdom that was to be in Grace. Strange, indeed it is, that Pilate should have written with a rough hand words that became God's Gospel to a soul in darkness and death! What he had written, he had written irrevocably and unchangeably, for a Heavenly hand was directing him and a Heavenly purpose had him in its grasp. The inflexible decree of God was laden, as it so often is, with mercy and grace for the outcasts and malefactors of earth.

Truly we do well, as we survey our lives, to go to Pilate, learn the solemn message, and experience the healing balm, of his inscription, that he sealed with that utterance, 'What I have written, I have written.'

THE SACRAMENTS

1. Definition

The word *Sacrament* is not found in the Bible. It is derived from the Latin sacramentum which is supposed to have some connection with the oath which a Roman soldier gave in loyalty and obedience to his supreme commander. It is not at all probable that the military association of the word had anything at all to do with its adoption for a religious rite. We owe the word rather to a translation into Latin of the Greek word μυστηριον (mystery), by the translators of the Greek Scriptures into the Latin Vulgate. Perhaps the N. T. sacraments were supposed to have had some resemblance to the mysteries of the Greek religions, and so the name μυστηριον (mystery) came to be used. It is true, however, that the word is used both in the N. T. and especially in the early Church for many kinds of customs and ordinances which were supposed to be 'signs' and 'seals' of the new Faith.

Its specialised name in the N. T., however, is not open to doubt. It was used to designate baptism and the Lord's Supper, and quite a comprehensive definition is that given in the Shorter Catechism as 'an ordinance instituted by Christ, wherein by sensible signs Christ and the benefits of the New Covenant are represented, sealed, and applied to believers'. It came to be used, in addition to this, as an opportunity that believers have of renewing their vows to God and making a public witness of their faith, and expressing their oneness in Christ. This will suffice by way of definition.

2. The Distinctive Elements in the Sacraments

It is clear from our definition that it has outward and inward elements, material and spiritual elements, and that these are connected. It is a Parable not in words, but in action.

(i) The outward elements are material, water in baptism, bread and wine in the Supper.

There cannot be a Sacrament in a true sense without these outward material elements.

(ii) But there is the inner element of Grace signified by these elements. In the case of Baptism, baptism in water signifies washing or cleansing. In the case of the Supper, bread and wine signify nourishment, food for strength and growth.

(iii) There is also the union between the material sign and the spiritual Grace. This is apparent on the very surface: the material sign openly and expressively signifies the nature of the inner grace. The water of baptism signifies the cleansing by the blood of Christ, and the bread and wine the nourishing of the spiritual life by the living Christ who died for us.

So the material sign puts an outward seal or mark upon the inward grace, and so it exhibits to ourselves what grace has inwardly wrought. To our faith this is very expressive and must be very helpful. It is doing in another way what the word of God in the Bible does – assures us of our cleansing and our life in Christ. It is more expressive than the mere word because it appeals to our sight, our feeling, and our taste. For this reason it has access to our nature in more ways than by the mere hearing of the Word: it conveys a spiritual message to our eyes, our touch, and our taste.

The Word of God, however, establishes a union between the outward sign and inward grace which faith can perceive and appropriate. This is spoken of as a sacramental union – the union between the outer sign and the inward significance. It is the promise of God in His word that makes this union, and it is faith in us that recognises and receives it.

It is not a physical union, so that the material elements contain some spiritual power inside them, and by receiving them, or swallowing them in the case of the Supper, we swallow Divine Grace with them. A mechanical action of this kind is alien to the spirit of our religion. You don't get divine grace in virtue of washing or eating. But in this washing and this eating, we have a better understanding of the grace of forgiveness and the grace of life that is new – and our faith enjoys it and is supported and strengthened. Moreover the signs promise Christ and seal to us the Presence of Christ. It is a communion. The Spirit takes of the things of Christ and makes them real to us in a special way. How it happens is one of the mysteries of our faith, but it is a reality that on such an occasion we are brought into contact with the means of our salvation.

So the two things necessary to make this union are understanding and faith. Understanding is necessary, for a blind performance will not profit us much. The Sacraments do not fully explain themselves. They are dumb symbols in themselves. So they can have no meaning for those who do not understand what they represent. This is what Paul calls 'not discerning the Lord's body'. For that reason we are indebted to the Scriptures – to the Word – to shed light on the sacrament and tell us what it means and what it is to do. The Word must therefore go before the Sacrament to shed light on its meaning.

And faith is necessary since without it there is nothing to respond to this outward sign. It presupposes that we are spiritually alive, since there is no use at all washing or feeding the dead. No food will benefit a lifeless body. So we hold that where the Sacrament is approached with an enlightened understanding and received by faith the grace of God does accompany it. In other words, it is a means of grace, a very rich and expressive means, a parable in action.

3. The Necessity of the Sacraments

We do not hold that the Sacraments are necessary for salvation: that a person cannot be a Christian without them. If the reality is there the lack of observance of the outward sign cannot invalidate it. Many have been saved without observing the Sacraments, and today neither the Salvation Army nor the Quakers have sacraments. Yet, to dispense with material signs is not a proof of spirituality. It rather obstructs and stultifies spirituality. All bodily manifestations – speaking, laughing, handshaking – are material signs and we would be much the poorer spiritually without them.

The Sacraments are special signs – they give expression to relationships which gain depth and meaning by being expressed. They personalise our relationship to God, and we think their absence impoverishes the spiritual life. If Christ commanded us to observe them for our spiritual growth we are stunting that growth by disobedience. Though faith alone is necessary for salvation, there can be weak faith and strong faith, and since the sacraments strengthen faith they are designed to build up the Christian life. Where for any reason it is not possible to observe the Sacrament,

God can strengthen grace in some other way, but wilful neglect is disobedience – it is neglect of the grace of God.

4. What is Involved in Receiving the Sacrament

In receiving the sacrament a person makes public profession of several things, and he has to ask himself if these things are true of him or not.

(i)   He professes that he has had cleansing from sin: that he has received the divine forgiveness, and that he has tested and proved that the blood of Christ cleanses from all sin.

If that experience took place it is very strengthening to have this outward expression given to it. The spiritual reality becomes, as it were, visible.

If that experience has not taken place, it is an empty show, and a solemn mockery to go through this symbolism, and it cannot but cheapen spiritual things in our minds.

(ii) He professes that he has his life now in Christ. The bread and wine are symbols of the body and blood of Christ, of Christ in His death. When we eat the bread and the wine, we profess that we have one life in Christ, that He is our daily food, our meat and drink.

Bread and wine were part of the daily food of the people of Palestine in Christ's day: the poor man's portion, the labourer's daily meal. Christ was teaching how accessible He was to anyone who wanted to live by Him. And so if we live our daily life in Christ – if we approach Christ through His death for us, and live daily on the life He bestows, then it is no empty show, but a great reality, to take these symbols of His body and blood. And if Christ has no influence on our daily life, if we do not rely on Him for daily strength, it is a vain show to eat and drink.

(iii) The person who takes the Sacrament professes that he is one of a family – the family of God. The Lord's Supper is a family meal. One table, one loaf, one cup, signifies a family oneness of the closest kind. The person who sits at that table professes that he belongs to that family and that he is living in their fellowship in his daily life. That alone makes his profession real.

If his society is not with his fellow Christians but with the non-Christian world, it is an empty force – a foolish pretence to sit with them at this table. The Sacraments give admission not to a congregation or a denomination, but to the Church of God universally – to the fellowship of all believers. You are admitted on the condition that you named Christ as your Saviour, and no other conditions should be imposed.

Thus the Sacraments have their value in inter-communion. Among human beings – as distinct from animals – a meal is an occasion for fellowship, a token of solidarity. In the Bible the breaking of bread – whether sacramental or not – has profound spiritual significance. This is not because we are animals needing food, but because we are more than animals.

(iv) The Person who sits at the Lord's Table is making an act of public witness in two directions – that the Lord has come, and that He will come again. This is the meaning of Paul's words: 'As often as ye eat this bread and drink this cup, ye do show the Lord's death till He come.' The Sacraments link us to the death of Christ on Calvary – the fact of His death, the manner of His death, – from violence, the significance of His death as a means of life to us. The Sacrament also stands as a pledge that He is returning: and so it links us to the coming again of Christ.

Each time we observe this supper, we add a stone to the cairn of remembrance that He came and died, and we add a link to the chain that pledges to us His return. It is not the Last Post over His grave. It is the Reveille that is sounded in anticipation and hope.

The Sacrament is thus a link with the Living Lord, and a channel whereby He can return to us in the presence of His Spirit. It is a line of communication kept open between His people and their absent Lord – a means by which His presence may be ministered to them.

5.The Mutual Relations between the Two Sacraments

The Sacraments of the N. T. are related to the corresponding rites of the O. T. Circumcision and Passover are used of the N. T. rites as when Paul says: 'Christ our Passover is slain for us' in the context of the Lord's Supper. He also says that Christians in Colosse were 'circumcised by the circumcision of Christ made without hands, (when ye were) buried with Him in Baptism' (Col 2:11-12). Similarly

Baptism and the Lord's Supper are applied to the O. T. Church in 1 Cor. 10: 'all were baptised in the cloud and in the sea' and 'all did eat the same spiritual meat and drank the same spiritual drink'. That is they are related too in Christian experience.

Baptism, like circumcision, is a N. T. initiation. It is an enrolment into the membership of the Church: as such it is a break with the past, and an entrance into a new mode of life – a cleansed life. As such it is not repeated. The Lord's Supper is in the nature of sustaining life, and so it is repeated.

But logically the one should go before the other in time, as enrolment should go before enjoyment of privileges of membership. Should unbaptised be forbidden to take the Lord's Supper ? No, if the circumstances are such that he cannot be baptised. We have to remember that validity in the spiritual realm depends on the spiritual condition of the recipient and not on conforming to precise rules and regulations.

As in the case of baptism no one should receive baptism who does not profess to have received forgiveness and cleansing – and in the case of Infant Baptism baptism is not given to the child – it is given to believing parents on a renewed profession of their faith – so in the Lord's Supper no one can benefit from it if they are not sincerely attempting to live daily in Christ.

Anyone living in sin – unconfessed and unforsaken – cannot receive this benefit. In Paul's words, they are only drinking judgment to themselves.

6. What relationship has the Officiating Minister to the Sacrament?

Just this : that he is the minister in ministering this to us

(a) Does he have any effect on the Sacrament? Just as much as he has on other things he does in the service of God – no more, no less. In preaching, for example, he could do it expressively and instructively. So he can administer the sacrament instructively or in a cold, unedifying way. But does he not bless the elements of water, of bread, and wine? He 'gives thanks'. He blesses in the sense that he asks God to make them a blessing to us. He does the same in preaching. He exercises no magic whatsoever in either case.

(b) In the case of the Supper, is he not making an offering? Of course he is not, for there is nothing to offer, except our gratitude and obedience. Christ by one offering has completed that and no one can presume to do it over again. Why then have an ordained minister as essential in most of our Churches? He is acting purely in a representative capacity. In the case of baptism, it is only the body of believers that can admit into their fellowship. They ask the appointed office-bearers to attend to it and see that it is done worthily. And the office-bearers entrust the minister to us, in order that there may not arise mistakes due to too many people acting in the matter. It is the same in the Lord's Supper – the congregation gathers their fellow-believers into this fellowship, and the minister acts for them. All this is to safeguard proper order and discipline in the Church.

7. In the Lord's Supper what are we 'remembering'?

(a) Christ. 'Do this in remembrance of me.' He was to be absent. Remembering in Biblical thought is a much deeper conception than with us: it is a link of fellowship: for example 'Lord, remember me'.

Christ meant this act of remembering thus to be a link of fellowship bringing His Presence near. The Presence of Christ is what makes the Supper a blessing in the highest sense.

(b) It is a remembering of Christ in His death. It is Christ in His broken body and shed blood we remember. It is symbols of the broken body and shed blood that make our banquet: it is a profession that we have life in His death.

(c) It is a remembering of Christ in the fellowship of His people. They are all sharers – partakers of the one bread and the one cup. That is why the one cup is much more expressive of fellowship than individual cups. Is it hygienic? It is certainly not more unhygienic than some other acts of ours – eating bread handled by others, shaking hands, kissing.

(d) It is a remembering of the other Supper – the marriage Supper of the Lamb. It was so of Christ 'I shall not drink of the fruit of the vine till I drink it anew in the Kingdom of God'. Did He mean to imply that wine would be drunk in the House of God? No – it simply meant 'till I reach home – till it is all fulfilled – till the symbol gives place to reality'.

'As often as ye eat this bread and drink this cup ye do show the Lord's death till He come.' Faith is strengthened. Love is exercised. Hope is quickened.

Group 3

The Resurrection

THE RESURRECTION OF CHRIST

It is highly significant that foes as well as friends of the Christian faith make the resurrection of Christ from the dead the foundation and touchstone of the faith.

Festus the Roman governor of Judaea put the case for Christianity in simple terms when he told Herod it was a matter of 'one Jesus who was dead, whom Paul affirmed to be alive'. That was the issue as it appeared to him – it still is as it appears to all the enemies of Christianity.

And when Paul, the Apostle of the new Faith, argued 'And if Christ be not risen, your faith is in vain', he grasped the same issue: it meant that if the resurrection were disproved the entire edifice of Christianity would collapse. For if Christ were not risen, the supernatural could be eliminated from the Christian message, and Christianity that eliminated the supernatural could not deal with the vital issues of human sin and salvation. But the very fact that the chief exponent and missionary of the early Church could state the issue thus, indicates his confidence that the resurrection of Christ could not be disproved.

The Christian approaches the resurrection from three angles: as a fact, as a message, and as an experience, and these three cohere and stand or fall together. If the resurrection is not an historical fact, it cannot contain a spiritual message, and it cannot become a living experience. There is a tendency today, even among theologians, to remove the resurrection from history and place it merely in experience and faith. They place doubt on the resurrection as an historical fact at any rate. They claim that it is irrelevant to ask whether or not it was a verifiable historical fact, since only its certitude to faith is all that matters.

But to us a faith of this kind is useless unless it is based on factual truth. If the substance of belief is not true as a matter of fact, it cannot long remain true as a matter of faith. What is false in the realm of fact cannot be true in the realm of faith. Otherwise faith is not far removed from mere credulity.

Now it is the interrelation between these three I am to discuss with you – fact, faith and experience.

1. The Fact of History

I think that if we read the Biblical references to the resurrection only as historical documents we must be impressed by the fact that they bear on their face the mask of authenticity. They read as sincere, honest, unbiassed evidence of eye witnesses, and they bear the cold critical scrutiny of history. What is the fact to which they bear witness?

(i)   That the tomb was empty on the first Easter morning. The body that had been laid in Joseph of Arimathaea's rock -hewn tomb was not there when the investigators went to look for it. And this fact is testified to by all the witnesses, friends and foes, Jews and Romans. No one at the time attempted to disprove it, though they were ready to offer several explanations of it.

(ii) The tomb had been broken open from within. At least once before this day the grave had been invaded from without, the reign of death had been interrupted, and its prey delivered at the command of 'one stronger than he'. But never before since death had claimed its first victim had the tomb been broken from within and its tenant able to emerge in triumph. But it was obvious that this is what had happened on this occasion. It was not an act of violence by which the grave had been rifled from without. There was no body-snatching here – the orderliness of the tomb, the placing and wrapping of the grave clothes showed clearly that it was neither an act of force from without nor the stealthy escape from within of one who may have recovered from a swoon or a collapse.

(iii) The Fact of the Resurrection meant that the Lord had been seen alive. This was attested by a vast number and a great variety of witnesses, who knew Him in the years before His death and could testify to His identity. Some of them were very slow to accept. They were not psychologically constituted for its occurrence, and they refused to accept the evidence of eye-witnesses, till they had seen and recognised the very Christ for themselves. Most striking of all is perhaps that of James the Lord's brother who apparently had remained outside the faith until the Risen Lord had appeared to him. There could be no illusion in his case, for since he shared the same home with Jesus, and remained impervious to the witness of His life and character there, it is indeed significant that this event had shattered his unbelief and swept him into the company of Christ's followers.

(iv) The Fact of the Resurrection meant that the Lord was now in possession of a life superior to death or decay in a resurrection Life. This was no mere resuscitation as happened in the case of Lazarus, not a mere re-uniting of body and soul. It was a life that was in so many respects the same, yet so very different. It was the same Jesus, His identity was beyond doubt, but He was different. He was in possession of a life in which human nature had been lifted immeasurably above that of the ordinary human level. It had qualities that no human being living under natural law has.

Though the forms of the Risen Lord's manifestations varied, at one time predominantly spiritual, at another time unquestionably material, yet it was evident that He conformed to the law of our present life only as an accommodation to others. He obviously had a life transcending physical limitations. He appeared for forty days to be standing between two worlds, visible and invisible, His closest affinities being with the realm of spirits and with things invisible and eternal. Yet the narrative dealing as it does with something that is utterly above our own comprehension, shows a remarkable self-consistency. There was so much about it that the narrators could not fathom or explain, but they did not attempt to embellish it or to add the element of the miraculous or the merely spectacular.

The first occasion on which a comment of this kind is made – and it is a factual comment – is when John writes 'Then the same day at evening, being the first day of the week, when the doors were shut, where the disciples were assembled for fear of the Jews, came Jesus and stood in the midst'. It is quite clear that John means us to understand that the door was still shut, bolted from within, when Jesus had appeared. He means us to gather that no one had opened the doors, as they would be very unlikely to do to an unknown stranger or an unidentified visitor.

That is the account and no explanation is offered. We are left to draw our own conclusion, which is the only possible one that Jesus came in through the shut doors. There is no attempt then or afterwards to give significance to this phenomenon: it is only stated in its proper place as a fact. But to us it is the break in the narrative, the point of departure from the material to the supernatural. And in its light we can re-read some other statements, made or not made.

That the linen wrappings had been left undisturbed in the grave. That there is no suggestion that the stone had been removed from the tomb to get the Lord out. That He could appear to the women, to Simon, on the first resurrection day, then to two on the road to Emmaus some seven miles away, then to the gathered company at Jerusalem – all without what we would regard as the necessary passage of time for the ordinary movements of a human being. They all come together to give the impression that we are dealing with the supernatural, at least with a body that is not in its movements restricted by physical laws.

2. The Resurrection – a Message

For the entire body of believers – and for all who would listen to them – the Resurrection was a message. If the early Christians hailed each other daily with the greeting 'The Lord is risen' it was because it had a relevance for their daily life, it bore to them a message which could be interpreted and translated into personal living. The Risen Lord had Himself formulated the precise message He wished His resurrection to convey. To Mary He entrusted that message that was evermore to live in His Church. 'Go, tell my brethren, and say unto them: I ascend unto my Father and your Father, and to my God and your God'.

(a) *It is a message of unbroken relationships.*

'I ascend unto my Father and your Father, my God and your God.' It was a message that the vital spiritual ties that bound them to Him were not severed. 'Tell my brethren' – unbroken kinship. Death and the grave behind Him, they were still His brethren, closer in spiritual kinship than before. 'My Father and your Father' – an eternal relationship that death was powerless to disrupt.

It proclaims to us, perishing men in a decaying world, part and parcel of a natural order whose disintegration seems to be a fixed law, that there are ties which death cannot break, nor the grave dissolve. Our real possession is undisturbed by the upheaval of death or the dissolution of the grave.

(b) *It is a message of eternity entering time.*

'I ascend', linking Heaven and earth in one. When Christ sent the tidings 'I ascend' He lifted for ever their hearts and aspirations to the heavenly Throne, bestowing upon them a heavenly citizenship, making them even in this world while they suffer reproach and shame, conscious of their affinities with the Eternal. 'I ascend' fixes our gaze as it fixed theirs, upwards, drawing aside the veil that severs earth from Heaven, time from eternity, the material from the spiritual. A message of spiritual affinities.

3. The Resurrection – an Experience

Soon, very soon, the Resurrection became an experience. It was an experience of the Presence of the Risen and Living Lord. They met Him and this meeting in terms of personal experience meant three things: peace, purpose and power.

(a) Peace. As Christ's presence was realised, suddenly and unexpectedly, in the Upper Room a hush fell on all gathered, fear and joy, hope and uncertainty battling with each other. And then Christ spoke 'Peace be with you: and He showed them His hands and His side'. That is the sight that gave peace – a peace that was closely related to those wounds – to His suffering unto death. It was the peace He died to secure, and now lives to bestow: peace with God, the peace of God, the peace of reconciliation by which the moral nature of man enters into possession of fullest rest and peace. And men and women throughout the world since that day have linked their experiences of peace with those wounds, with that sacrifice unto death, and with the pardon that He bestows on the ground of what He has done.

(b) Purpose. Along with the sight that gave peace to their hearts, there was the command that put purpose into their lives. The Risen Lord shared 'As the Father has sent me, so send I you'. What a vision of their high calling for those who had been a few hours ago dispirited and broken men. They were being sent as Christ had been sent. They were sent to witness as Christ witnessed, by obedience, by suffering, by death itself. What a wonderful realisation they had of life's lofty purpose, as they go forth into a world for which Christ died. It is the morning of a new day with them and heaven's lights gild with glory the common task.

(c) Power. As well as the sight that gave peace and the command that gave purpose there was the breath that gave power. 'He breathed on them and said, Receive ye the Holy Ghost.' Thus were they to rise above their weakness and failure, to face their new task and fulfil their

mission. New energy was introduced – the breath of Christ brought to them the energising power of the Holy Ghost.

Now that is what the resurrection experience does in human life still. It is good to have mental satisfaction that the Resurrection is a historical fact worthy of credibility – that the foundations of faith are stable. But it is not enough.

It is good to receive the Resurrection message assuring us that eternity and time are linked together by Him who was dead and now lives for evermore.

But it is essential to have a resurrection experience: only thus can the spirit of man enter into possession: and it is a possession that fully satisfies: it is peace to the conscience, purpose to the spirit and power to the life.

THE RESURRECTION – AN EMPOWERING

It is perhaps true that the most spectacular result of the Resurrection of Christ was the change in the character and demeanour of the disciples of Christ. Changed from timid, frightened, hesitant men to bold, fearless, courageous proclaimers of the faith. And so Christianity moved from behind closed doors into the arena of public life, into the market place, into the synagogue, into the meeting places of the masses of men. All this was the outworking of the power of Christ's resurrection. They felt a new infusion of power that equipped them for a fearless witness to their Lord and His cause. How did this come about?

1. The Recognition of Christ: 'It is the Lord'

Christ is often in the Christian's experience when He is not recognised. It is a valid experience, a rich and enriching experience, heart supplying, heart filling and heart burning.

So it was with the disciples on the lake: (Jn 21). Let us be careful not to misjudge them for going for a night's fishing. There was nothing unworthy of Christ and the resurrection in that. It was not a return to the world. That lake – the Sea of Galilee – had sacred associations and many sacred memories for them. And above all the Master Himself gave His presence and His countenance. He came there to meet with themselves and I do believe He was there all the night through – though He was not recognised till the break of day.

As far as the fishing was concerned it was a blank night. They got no fish, – a night of empty nets, of fruitless toil, of frustrated effort. But is Christ not in an experience like that? May He not have had something to do with the empty nets and the fruitless toil. He was what Bishop Handley called 'the Lord of the fishing grounds', and He had the movement of the fish under His control. And for a reason best known to Himself, and becoming clear to us now, He saw to it that the nets were empty – that there was no catch that night.

The experience of fruitless toil,of empty nets,may be a Christian experience for us. It may be that it is only in our hour of disappointment and failure that He will be recognised.

As the light of day broke and they were heading for home they saw a shadowy figure standing on the shore. He called to them:'Lads, have you had a catch?' And the answer was that of tired and disappointed men: 'No.' Then He directed them as to the right side of the ship on which to cast their nets with the promise of success.

And strangely enough, they obeyed. Skilled fishermen are not ready to take direction from land men, and in this case if the fish did not enter the nets during the night, it was not at all likely they would in the light of day. But at His bidding, they cast their nets as He directed. And the unexpected happened – 'they were not able to draw it for the multitude of the fishes.'

It was at this point that John put a whisper in Peter's ear: 'It is the Lord.' How did John reach this recognition? 'When John therefore saw the draught of fishes he said 'It is the Lord'. Therefore the big draught of fishes had something to do with the leap of faith into recognition.

That miracle took John back to his first acquaintance with the power of Jesus. It was on this very lake – when He and James were partners with Simon – that the event occurred. Then too it was a blank night – they caught nothing, but at His bidding they let down the nets and caught a great haul of fishes. It was then that Christ said to his disciples "Fear not, from henceforth thou shalt catch men".

And when they had brought their ships to land, they forsook all and followed Him. That was John's call to discipleship – into the travelling fellowship of Jesus. Never forgotten, never set aside. And here it is repeated with the same display of power. And faith leapt over the years and brought the two together. The similarity between the two was too striking to be lost on him. That first experience illumined this one – because of it he was able to trace the Master's hand and feel His presence and recognise Him in this miracle. Faith does not act in a void.

A first experience of Christ in His power and grace is an abiding possession of the soul. It sets the pattern for all that is to follow. It leaves a sensitiveness in the soul to His presence, a responsiveness to His touch, a power of recognition. This will abide.

Heaven is illumined by the expression of God's grace in all our journeys here.

2. Recognition Leads to Communion

It is clear here that recognition was given only as a prelude to communion on the shore, and only those who desire this communion can have this moment of recognition. It was so here.

The fellowship on the shore was His provision. The fire and the meal had been prepared by Him, for when they went ashore, they found a fire and fish laid thereon. And yet He asked for their contribution to the fellowship: 'Bring now of the fish which ye have caught.' Not because there was any lack in what He had provided – but because He decreed it to be mutual fellowship – His and theirs.

Communion fellowship is His desire for His own. And He makes provision for it. It was He who instituted the Lord's Supper. Amidst the distractions and distress of that hour He had planned it: 'With desire, I have desired to eat this passover with you.' It was to be a mutual fellowship.

This fellowship with Christ proved to be a very heart-searching experience – so Simon found. The thrice repeated question recalled to him his thrice repeated denial. He was eating the bitter herbs of the Passover. So do we experience the bitter sweet of penitence when we enter our Lord's communion. Do not be surprised or dismayed at this: it deepens the communion. There is no real joy in the heart that has not known sorrow. To remember the bitterness of sin is to enjoy the sweetness of forgiveness, to recall our unfaithfulness is to taste of the faithfulness of His love.

3. Fellowship with Christ is an Empowering for Service

Not even fellowship is an end in itself: it is to equip for service. Thus the commission is given, and the commission is restored, if lost: a commission based on Simon's personal love for Jesus, a superlative love greater than redemptive love for men. So we believe that the faith of Christ's people should move to the place of recognition, and that recognition brings us to the place of fellowship, and fellowship sends us to the sphere of service, commissioned and recommissioned.

And it shall be so in the larger pattern of events still to be ours. Today we have His word over the dark waters guiding us in our night of failure, telling us the right side of the ship on which to cast our nets. And one day that same voice shall bid us to the fellowship prepared by Him on the further shore .Blessed are they who shall not be so ill at ease when the bidding comes they would fain decline. Blessed are they whose faith is moving towards that recognition and whose experience can interpret that provision as the Marriage Supper of the Lamb.

So three things are linked together in the equipment of disciples for His service.

(1)The sight that gave faith.
(2)The communion that gave purpose.
(3)The breath that gave power.

THE RESURRECTION MESSAGE

We frequently speak of the Resurrection Message, and there is a sense in which all the heart-stirring messages of that eventful day crystallise into one, and that one the most transforming the world has ever heard: 'Christ is risen indeed.' In that respect it may be held that all the messages of the Resurrection Day go to confirm the one great fact that Christ was truly and indubitably risen. Yet all three messages of the Resurrection Day, considered in their natural order, have a sequence about them that suggests the breaking of a new day and the gradual rising of the sun from morning's dawn to noon- day light.

Let us consider each in turn.

1. The Resurrection morning brought, first of all, the message of the Broken Tomb.

And it was the first message of hope to a world that dwelt under the shadow of death: *the tomb was broken from within!* Never before in the history of mortal man had that happened! Death had reigned supreme; the tomb was its fortress that no man was yet able to take by storm. Humanity had awaited the approach of death with fearful heart and the grave cast its sombre shadow everywhere. Mary's heart knew it all that early dawn as she wended her way to the grave, saying to her companions, 'Who shall roll us away the stone?' Humanity had been asking that question through the ages, and no hand was found strong enough to roll away the stone! But the Resurrection Morning brought new tidings into the experience of men: the stone was rolled away, the tomb was broken, and it was broken from within! That much was quite clear immediately to Peter and John. Mary merely brought the tidings of an empty tomb: but they looked in and saw from the condition of the grave clothes that the dead had escaped from its folds and its wrappings so quietly and triumphantly that nothing had been disturbed or displaced. It was wonderful tidings to a world that had been living under the shadow of death's power and dominion: the tomb was broken from within! It had received an unwonted visitor who broke its seal and snapped its fetters! That is still wonderful tidings to the darkened hearts and sorrowing spirits of men. The burden of our hearts is still that of Mary's: 'Who shall roll us away the stone' ? Is not the grave impenetrable and its seal for ever? Has it not been locked and its key for ever lost? And so the sadness of death, its irrevocableness and its finality, grips us and devastates our hearts. But the first message of the Resurrection morning comes to lift the burden and dispel the shadows: the tomb is broken from within; a power has entered the grave stronger than death, and he has snapped its fetters and broken its sceptre! 'Come', said the angels 'see the place where the Lord lay!' See, it is empty, yet not empty, for it holds the assurance that the Lord of life has proved His lordship over death and the grave, and has left in the empty tomb the pledges of His triumph and might.

2. The second message of the Resurrection morning was the message of the Living Christ Himself.

It was Mary who was chosen to bring this still greater message to those who dwelt under the shadow of death, the message, not merely of the empty grave and the broken tomb, but of the Christ who rose from the dead and stood on the other side of the grave, and sent to His own these words of consolation: 'Go, tell my brethren, behold I ascend to My Father and your Father, to my God and your God.' It was, as we can see, a message of *unbroken kinship*; they were still His 'brethren'. Death and the grave, instead of unloosening that tie, only served to make it closer and warmer, inasmuch as this is the first time He chose to call them brethren. He came back from the tomb as their Elder Brother and, though He now stood on the other side of the grave, with death and the tomb for ever behind Him, He was not ashamed to call them 'My brethren'. It was moreover a message of Heavenly Hope: it contained the majestic declaration, 'I ascend.' We thank God for that message, for it has lifted our eyes upwards more than any other message that ever reached us. 'I ascend' has snapped the cords that bind us to the dust; it has given us a Heavenly citizenship and a Heavenly hope. It has ensured that the Christian's eye should gaze evermore not backwards but upwards! It was essentially a message of spiritual relationships: 'My Father and your Father, my God and your God' was His definition of the new Christian affinities. He has thus given us a new spiritual lineage, and a new spiritual relationship such as was never within our reach before. He has given us His Father to be our Father, and His God to be our God. True, He marks a distinction between His relationship and ours, for God is His Father and His God in a sense in which He can never be ours. But He is our Father and our God, notwithstanding, because He is His, and we are His brethren. How much this message of spiritual relationships, of unbroken ties, of Heavenly affinities, must mean to those who, in the presence of death and the grave, are so conscious of their kinship with the dust and their brotherhood with death!

3. The message of the Resurrection Day was, lastly, a message of Personal Experience.

It is enshrined in the soul – stirring cry: 'We have seen the Lord.' The experience of those who have seen the Lord and who know Him in the power of His resurrection is thus, an integral part of the resurrection Message. For the first disciples that experience of the resurrection day meant the communicating of the Divine peace, the unveiling of the Divine purpose, and the bestowal of the Divine power for daily living and daily witness-bearing. We know not which to single out as the most transforming experience of that wonderful day – *the Sight that gave peace, the Commission that gave purpose to their lives, or the Breath that gave power.* All three make up the experience of the Resurrection Day. When the risen Lord proclaimed peace, 'He showed unto them His hands and His side', thus unveiling before their wondering eyes the foundations of their peace in His sacrifice even unto death. 'As My Father hath sent me, even so send I you' was an unfolding of the Lord's purpose for them that was infinitely higher than anything they could themselves contemplate, for it linked their life mission in an intimate way with His own. But for the carrying out of this exalted purpose they needed singular equipment, and so 'He breathed on them and saith unto them, Receive ye the Holy Ghost'. In this symbolic manner, He signified the new energy they were to receive for carrying out His commission in the world. And so in this Resurrection experience of His disciples we have the threefold blessedness of seeing, of understanding, and of receiving.

What message has the Resurrection for us – a broken tomb, a Living Christ, a sacred experience? It has brought us Hope, Life, and Liberty that produce in us a resurrection life and make us evermore 'new creatures in Christ Jesus'.

CHRIST'S RESURRECTION AND OURS

Much has been written in interpretation and elucidation of the resurrection hope of the Christian believer. Much of it lays claim to fidelity to Scripture, and yet is but an attempt to explain away the resurrection as merely spiritual, and altogether unrelated to the body that had been reverently laid aside in the tomb. What strikes one most forcibly in reading these dissertations is that so few of them make any reference to the Resurrection of Christ. It is true that the resurrection of the dead presents many difficulties to minds that grapple with it in the light of human reason and on the lower plain of human analogies. But seen in the light of our Saviour's glorious Resurrection, it becomes to our faith one of the most luminous realities of the Christian life, shedding its radiant light upon some of life's deepest problems, and upon the gloom of death and the grave. It is good for us, therefore, to trace the line of connection which Scripture draws between Christ's Resurrection and ours.

1. In Scripture Christ is said to be *the First fruits of them that slept* (1 Cor. 15:20). In this respect He is the PLEDGE of our resurrection. Resurrection is undoubtedly typified in Nature: the advent of Spring clearly speaks of a general resurrection, while the germination of the seed-grain speaks of an individual resurrection. Moreover, resurrection has been embraced in the Covenant blessings of God, 'Who promised us eternal life before the world began' (Tit. 1:2), and Who made Himself known in time as 'the God of Abraham, of Isaac, and of Jacob', thus linking Himself eternally with those who had long since passed out of the sight of men. But it is in the Risen Christ that we have the visible and final Pledge of our resurrection. It is in this respect that Christ has become 'the firstfruits of them that slept'. The allusion is richly suggestive. When we sow the grain, be it wheat or oats, or any other grain, we commit it to the cold, damp earth in good hope, because we believe each grain contains the living germ that the dampness and coldness of earth cannot destroy. And we see this faith justified when we reap the first sheaf of harvest! Now, Christ is the first sheaf of a great resurrection harvest. His resurrection from the dead proved that there resided in Him a life indestructible and imperishable, which death and the grave could not destroy. This life He imparts in germ

to all that are His. 'I give unto them eternal life', He says, and therefore 'they shall never perish'. That life, so quick and powerful, takes hold, in its warm embrace, of body and soul. Christ's quickened ones may go down into death, and their mortal bodies may disintegrate into dust, but they possess a life over which death has no power, a life that has already gone through death unscathed and unhurt. Rather, as we should say, that life possesses them, for they are bound, body and soul, to their Living Lord by cords which death cannot break, or the grave dissolve. Christ is the first sheaf of harvest. And as sure as the first sheaf has been gathered in, so shall every grain yield its own harvest, and be gathered in. So then, Christ, risen, living, real, is the pledge of our risen and living humanity beyond death and the grave.

2. Christ is also called *the First-begotten of the dead* (Rev 1 v5). In this respect He is the PATTERN of our resurrection. Why should Christ be called the First-begotten of the dead? Were there not others who had come back from the dead before He rose? In the three instances of restoration from the dead mentioned in the Gospel story, one at least seems a resurrection comparable to Christ's own. By His Divine power He manifested that He would interrupt the process of death at any of its stages. The daughter of Jairus, just newly dead, He snatched from the jaws of death ere it had begun its work of corruption. The widow's son at Nain was being carried to his burial when He stopped the procession, and robbed the grave of its prey. But Lazarus had already been four days dead, and was restored from corruption. How, then, is Christ spoken of as Himself the First-begotten of the dead? Because these others were miracles of resuscitation, rather than of resurrection. They came back to live under the same physical conditions as before, and in due time they succumbed to death again. They had only a temporary respite from death; but He was delivered from death to die no more. They, to put it so, rose on this side of death and the grave, while He rose on the other side, beyond the reach and power of death for ever. He was, therefore, in very fact the First-begotten of the dead, the possessor of a humanity that death could not hold captive. But because He is the *first* begotten, all who are begotten from the dead by His quickening power must, in some measure, resemble Him. In other words, He, in His risen life, is the Pattern of our resurrection. We are not forgetful that a gulf must ever separate His Person from

ours, inasmuch as He was Divine, and His Humanity both before and after the Resurrection, was inseparably bound to His Divine nature in one glorious Person. But inasmuch as He was the Firstborn of the dead, all the children of the resurrection must in their measure conform to His resurrection. Believing this, we reverently enquire into the facts revealed to us about His risen humanity, and we learn that He came back in the identical body in which He had lived, died, and been buried. It was the body in which He had lived, for He was recognisable by those who had known Him; yet it was the body in which He had died, for in His risen body there could be seen the mark of the nails; it was the body in which He had been buried, for the grave was seen to be empty. But though it was the same, yet it was vastly different. It was a spiritual body, for it could – as we have reason to believe it did – leave the grave without requiring the stone to be removed, just as it could enter the Upper Room 'the doors being shut'. It could leave the grave without as much as disturbing the grave-clothes from the folds in which they had been wrapped about the body. For this is the only satisfactory interpretation of John's testimony that the linen clothes that covered the body were in one place, and the napkin that was about the head was lying apart where the head had been. It was, moreover, a body that was no longer subject to the laws of time and space, for He could be in several places a distance apart without requiring the passage of time to intervene, as we, under our physical conditions, now require. It was a body that did not need shelter or warmth, and though He took food after He had risen it was not because He needed it, but rather to demonstrate the reality of His physical resurrection. It was thus a spiritual body, or a humanity spiritualised, that He had brought back from the grave. It was, likewise, a body that could be glorified, for it could visibly ascend to Heaven, and share in the ineffable glory of the Heavenly Throne. And though we must be careful to recognise that He sustained a relation to Deity that the mere sons of men can never attain to, yet we are assured that in the respects we have indicated, He the Risen One, is the Pattern of our resurrection. The body of our resurrection shall be recognisable as the body that descended into the grave, nevertheless it shall be a spiritual body possessed of new capacities and higher powers, and capable of sharing the Heavenly glory of our redeemed spirits. The pattern to which our bodies shall ultimately be conformed is none other than His glorified body, for He 'shall change the body of our humiliation that it may be fashioned like unto the body of His glory'. This is the fullness of the blessed Hope of a Resurrection Day.

3.   Christ is further spoken of as *the first-born from the dead* (Col. 1:18). This, we take it, signifies His HEADSHIP of the resurrection life. As the Firstborn from the dead, Christ is Head of a new family, the children of the resurrection. The first family of humanity had been, as we know, wrecked by sin. What man could have become if sin had not entered we are not called upon to conjecture. What we do know is that God became the author of a second creation, a new humanity, over which sin and death can have no power. And the Risen Man, Christ Jesus, became the head of that new humanity. As the Firstborn and the Elder Brother, He unifies the family, exercises control over them, and brings them into, and maintains them in, a state of perfect holiness. This new humanity is, therefore, of necessity, of a higher order than the first, since holiness is a higher state than innocence. But this is ours only in union with the Firstborn from the dead. It is possible for us here below, encompassed though we be by many infirmities, to 'know Him and the power of His Resurrection', and by that power He will yet recall us from the grave, and cause that our 'mortality shall be swallowed up of life'. By that self-same power He, as the Firstborn from the dead, shall maintain His brethren for ever in the perfect holiness that is the crown of our new humanity. Thus it is that as the Firstborn from the dead He has been given 'as Head over all things to the church, which is His body, the fullness of Him that filleth all in all'.

These blessed truths, however dimly we perceive them, must have a powerful practical bearing upon our daily lives. They inculcate respect for the human body, both in life and in death. If our bodies share the union of our spirits to Christ, and are yet to share in His resurrection life and glory, how precious to Him must be the dust of His saints! For this reason, the Christian consciousness recoils from the modern practice of 'disposing' of the body by cremation. The glory of His Resurrection casts its light into the darkness of the tomb, and, knowing as we do, that He, the Living One, links Himself to us in our deepest humiliation, we believe that 'our bodies being still united to Christ do rest in their graves till the resurrection'.

THE ROAD TO EMMAUS

The experience upon the way to Emmaus was the experience of comfort and peace from the hands of a fellow-traveller, unrecognised and unknown. It is this chance wayside experience of two humble unknown disciples of Christ that contains for us the hope that the same master is often travelling with us along life's sad road while our eyes are 'holden that we should not know Him'. But the companionship of the Lord, even when He is still unrecognised, makes the journey, and invests that mile of the rough road with a sacredness that will never allow us to call it common ground. Thus, as we look back upon the path we trod, we find springing from it a definite experience that lends reality and weight to our personal testimony as we essay to tell 'what things were done in the way'. Can we analyse such an experience as this – the experience of a soul who has the Lord's company by the way and yet knows not that He is the Lord?

For the two disciples it was, first of all, a heart-emptying experience. If the road seemed unusually long and the way unusually rough, it was because their hearts were sad and their souls overwhelmed with a burden of grief. And of all kinds of sorrow, theirs was the most galling, for it was the sorrow of spiritual disappointment and disillusionment and despair. Their hopes had been linked with this Jesus of Nazareth, and His untimely death had shattered all. They had felt the peace and power of His message, but they thought they had also understood His prospects and His plan. Now that they are deceived in the one, may it not be that they were deceived in the other too! Thus are they thrown back upon the beginnings of things, the origin of spiritual impressions, the reality of sacred experiences; and the foundations of their faith seem to tremble. Truly, converse as they might, the heart's real anguish was unexpressed and inexpressible – until the Stranger joins them. And then the strange thing happens – in answer to a friendly query the pent-up heart is unlocked, the floodgates are opened, and the whole plaint of unsatisfied desire, and disappointed hope, and all but shattered devotion is poured at the Stranger's feet: the tangled mass of hope and despair, of faith and unbelief, of knowledge and ignorance is cast before One who is but a fellow-traveller for part of the road. Truly the key to the pent-up heart was at that hour in the hands of the Divine Craftsman, or such an outpouring of its inner sorrow was impossible. But it is ever the unmistakeable sign of the Lord's nearness when the soul can unbosom its grief and the heart can unlock its sorrow as in the Lord's presence. In those days the Throne of Grace is very near, the errands of the soul there are many and frequent, and the heart is being continually poured out in confession and contrition and earnest petition. We are not conscious then, maybe, that the Lord is so near, far less do we realise that we are in His company, but there is a continuous self-emptying, a continuous outpouring of heart, a continuous unburdening of the spirit as the soul finds access at the mercy seat. Christ is the Great Emptier, and He must empty ere He fills. Thus, it is not without significance that our Risen Lord's first appearances were all given to the sorrowing; first to Mary in her bereavement and loss, next to Peter under conviction and contrition, and now to two unknown disciples in perplexity and dismay: in each case did He appear as the great Emptier of the grief-flooded heart and the great Unburdener of the sin-laden soul. This is His office still, and this is the sure evidence of His presence with the contrite soul.

But this was clearly a heart-enlightening experience. At the Master's touch the festering wound of unbelief is laid bare, and the fountain of all their bitterness is revealed: but that sore is probed only to make it respond all the readier to His balm, that fountain is emptied to make it receive a fresh supply. And so once the heart is emptied the Divine infilling begins. And what waters these were – how freshly they gushed from the smitten Rock, how fragrant with sacrifice and victory! And all came from – Moses and the Prophets! It is nothing new – and yet it is all new, for He takes the old Book, and in His hands it shines with a new light. The familiar page, where they never saw their Messiah, where they could not discover His Cross, is now aglow with His sufferings and sacrifice, and with throbbing hearts they follow the blood-stained footprints where before was a pathless desert. In symbol and ceremony, in type and sacrifice, in history and prophecy, it is all their Messiah and His Sacrifice: the Cross that was the great stumbling-block to them before now becomes illumined with light and glory as the pledge of their salvation; once the source of disappointment and despair, now it is the spring of a new and a Heavenly hope.

Such is the joy of a new-found faith – a joy that flows from the living streams of God's written Word. It is not revelations of new and mysterious truths that the darkened soul needs in the hour of its emptiness and despair – it is a new understanding of the old and familiar truths that were known but were never fully understood or experienced before. And that new light upon the old truths comes only when the Lord is in the company and when 'He expounds in all the Scriptures the things concerning Himself'. It is only when the Risen and Living One bends over the open Book that we see His countenance mirrored on every page. The eyes may be 'holden' that we may not see Him in our company, but the understanding is enlightened to see Him in His Word, and under that illumination He can be seen as the Alpha and Omega of the Truth and the One that gives unity and coherence to the Sacred Volume. Chapters that may have seemed an arid wilderness now become green pastures to our souls: 'in the wilderness shall waters break out and streams in the desert'.

This was also a heart-burning experience. This is a further manifestation of the wonder-working power of the truth in the hands of the Great Interpreter. It not only serves to enlighten the darkened mind, but it percolates through to the cold and desolate heart. And as it worked mightily in the understanding, so now it works effectually in the heart; the cold ice-bound heart, under the impact of this truth, begins to thaw, then to warm, soon to glow, and eventually to burn. And that burning flame is a consuming and devastating fire, burning up the 'wood, hay and stubble' of prejudice and unbelief; it is a hungry fire ever seeking more fuel and making the soul cry, 'Abide with us'; it is a fire whose dynamic is felt within not only as 'the expulsive power of a new affection' but as the motive power of a new endeavour. Under its urgency the two lowly disciples hasten back to witness to the truth of their Lord's resurrection.

And it is under the motive power of burning hearts that the Church of Christ has done all its work throughout the ages. Inward light and spiritual illumination will not suffice to make the Church 'fair as the moon, clear as the sun, terrible as an army with banners'. That knowledge must be kindled by a heavenly spark, that new perception of the truth must become 'fire within the bones', ere there be active and consecrated effort for Jesus Christ. But when the 'light of the knowledge of the glory of God' is seen in the face of Jesus Christ in the Word, it is a burning and consuming light that sets the heart ablaze with an elevated and a holy passion, purifying, cleansing, constraining. At such an hour the Lord is near though we recognise Him not, and our hearts, under the influence of His instruction, cry, 'Abide with us, for it is towards evening and the day is far spent'.

The experience of having Christ in the company unrecognised for so much of the way was destined to be followed by a greater thing – Christ 'made known in the breaking of bread', the one was Grace, the other Glory. But just because the Christian life here below is lived between grace and glory, there are happy moments in the soul's experience when grace overtakes glory, and grace is transfigured into glory; yet, even then, glory is but the recognition of the Stranger who journeyed with us by the way and made our hearts burn within us as He opened up to us the Scriptures. And our testimony in the midst of our brethren is as much 'concerning the things done in the way' as concerning the appearance of Him who 'made Himself known to us in the breaking of bread'.

NOT TO ALL: THE MYSTERY OF CHRIST'S SELF-REVELATION

In Peter's account of the Resurrection of Christ, as narrated by him in the house of Cornelius, there occurs this significant passage: 'Him God raised up the third day, and showed Him openly; not to all the people, but unto witnesses chosen before of God, even to us, who did eat and drink with him after he rose from the dead. And he commanded us to preach unto all the people and to testify that it is He which was ordained of God to be the judge of quick and dead'. This raises one of the most perplexing problems of the Christian life, namely, why only a few, apparently a very few, should profess a saving knowledge of the Lord Jesus Christ, while so many – the majority it would seem – remain ignorant, unseeing and unbelieving. We can, at any rate, say that it is not a new problem. The disciples of the Lord Jesus felt it themselves, for that was the purport of Judas' question to the Saviour, 'Lord, how is it that thou wilt manifest thyself unto us, and not unto the world?'. They were perplexed and bewildered at the ways of Christ: why should He not give a great spectacular display of His glory, till all men would see what *they* saw. The same problem is before us in Peter's reference to the resurrection appearances of the Lord. The Lord of Glory was publicly put to death, uplifted on a Cross outside the Gate, but when He rose from the dead, proving beyond all doubt that He was the Son of God and the Saviour of men, He manifested Himself in His risen glory 'not to all the people, but to witnesses chosen before of God'. Here we are confronted with the mystery of Christ's revelation of Himself to men, that contains so much to baffle our weak understanding and oftentimes to stagger our feeble faith. For, in very truth, few things are more painfully real to the Christian worker than the mystery contained in the words, 'Not to all the people'.

We may, perhaps, discover here, first of all, the **Principle** of Christ's self-revelation. That there was a principle that governed Christ's revelation of Himself to men is apparent from the whole course of His earthly life, as well as from His spiritual manifestations since. In the days of His flesh, multitudes met Him on the road, and in the street, and in the synagogue, but to the majority it was but as man passes man on the dusty road, as ship passes ship in the night. Even in the intimacy of

His mother's home, His own brethren did not see the hidden glory! But here and there, in Bethany, in Capernaum even, in Jerusalem, there were homes where He was light and life. Here and there in the crowd there were souls to whom He was peace and salvation, men and women in whose lives He was all and in all. It was only to faith, and spiritual desire, and urgent need that Christ revealed Himself in the days of His earthly life and ministry; it was on the same principle that He acted in His resurrection appearances, and it is on that spiritual principle that He acts still. Not to superstition but to faith, not to curiosity but to spiritual desire, not to fancy but to real need, does the Lord Jesus reveal His hidden glory. He does not cast His pearls before those who have no spiritual faculty with which to appreciate their value. He does not thrust His grace upon those who have no conscious need of it. It is significant indeed that His resurrection appearances were specifically designed to meet some pressing need, to banish some special sorrow, to heal some painful wound; to Mary, for example, in the throes of disconsolate grief; to Simon convulsed by the pangs of bitter penitence; to the two travelling to Emmaus under the cloud of a lost faith and a shattered hope. And thus He acts still. While He passes by the multitudes who have no conscious need, He oft reveals Himself to those who sit by the wayside, maimed, bruised and broken. And they behold the hidden glory and find healing from His touch. 'Not to all the people', indeed, but to those who in need cry to Him, in desire go out after Him, in faith lay hold upon Him; to them He is the great and only Reality.

We may discover here too, the **Purpose** of Christ's Self-revelation. We believe that there can be nothing arbitrary in the ways of the Master, and at times we are able to trace out the hidden purpose underlying His operations. There is a clear purpose underlying Christ's principle of self-revelation as Peter is careful to note: 'not to all the people,' he says, 'but unto witnesses, chosen before of God, even to us, who did eat and drink with Him after He rose from the dead'. Peter here emphasises the fact that not only did all the people not see the Risen One, but those that did see Him entered into very close intercourse with Him and obtained this amazing intimacy with Him that they 'ate and drank with Him after He rose from the dead'. It was not a fleeting sight, a glimpse in the passing, they had, leaving them dazed, perplexed, stunned! He permitted them to enjoy the most intimate fellowship with Him, and He accommodated Himself to their fellowship by eating and drinking with them, so that the reality of His Presence was beyond all doubt. Why, it may well be asked, give so much of His company to a few, and none at all to the rest? Peter says it was in order that they might be *witnesses*. That was the great purpose underlying His self-revelation: they were to tell the world what they saw and knew, and they were to tell it in no uncertain way. If they were to be witnesses to an unseeing and unbelieving world, they must have unshaken conviction and certainty regarding the reality of Him of whom they witnessed. How marvellously was the Divine purpose fulfilled through this small handful of disciples. The certainty and conviction with which they witnessed to their Lord! This is still the great and grand purpose behind Christ's principle of self-revelation. It is more valuable for His cause and Kingdom that one man should know Him intimately than that a score should have a casual acquaintance with Him! It has been said that the greatest thing a man can do is to see one thing clearly and then tell the world what he has seen. The greatest thing of all is to see Christ clearly, come to an intimate knowledge of Him, hold deep and clear convictions regarding Him, and then tell of Him to the world that knows Him not. The present trouble is that the world, the Church, and even the pulpit have half-hearted convictions. And if they are not sure of themselves, how can they inspire any confidence in their hearers! They are thus of little service to the Lord or to their fellows. Had Christ left His cause to men of half-hearted convictions, to men who had uncertain knowledge of Him, where would we have been? It is little wonder that the note struck by the New Testament Church was certainty, for it was sounded by men who knew their Lord in the intimacy of personal communion.

We can also see here the **Power** of Christ's Self-revelation. Peter could speak as one commissioned by his Lord, for that was inherent in the intercourse with his Risen Master. 'And He commanded us to preach – and to testify', he explained to Cornelius and his friends. This intimate fellowship with the Lord invested the disciples with authority: they came out energised and endued with power that the world could not resist. Their very enemies witnessed to their boldness in declaring the certainties of their faith, and to their power in dealing with the consciences and lives of their fellows. They went out into the world to teach, preach, live and die for the certainty of the things they believed, and their blood became the seed of the Church! It is in this way that Christ would still invest His messengers with irresistible power: by bringing them into the inner sanctuary of His fellowship, by unfolding to them there His glory as of 'the only begotten of the Father', by burning deep into their inmost consciousness the truth of what they are to declare, and then sending them out into the world as His messengers and ambassadors. It has been said that it is possible to recognise in the street those men who do duty in the great Halls and Cathedrals and Palaces of our land: there is a dignity and nobility in their very bearing that suggests the grandeur of those places where they serve. It is even so with the disciple of Jesus Christ. If he does duty with his Lord and master in the secret place, he shall do duty with his fellowmen as one that speaks for God and from God.

In ways such as these we are led to recognise that what constitutes a wonderful mystery in the dealings of God with the world may be made to reflect the grace and wisdom and love of Him who is 'The King eternal, immortal, invisible, the only wise God'.

Group 4
Paul

PAUL, THE MOST COMPANIONABLE OF MEN

Paul was the most companionable of men. He had a rare faculty for friendship of the closest and most enduring kind. And in return he ardently longed for friendship himself : e.g. in 2 Cor. 2:13 he tells us that when he arrived at Troas 'I had no rest in my spirit because I found not Titus my brother' and he departed from Troas and went into Macedonia. When he arrived there he tells us in 2 Cor. 7:5-6 that 'without were fightings, within were fears. Nevertheless God that comforteth those that are cast down comforted us by the coming of Titus'.

Again writing of Onesiphorus he writes in 2 Tim.1:16-17 'The Lord give mercy unto the house of Onesiphorus, for he oft refreshed me and was not ashamed of my chain. But when he was in Rome, he sought me out very diligently, and found me'.

Then again in 2 Tim. 4 he writes in v 11 to Timothy 'Take Mark with you for he is profitable to me for the ministry'. And in v 20 and 21 'Trophimus have I left at Miletum sick' and 'Do thy diligence to come before winter'.

But perhaps the last Chapter of Romans gives us the most wonderful glimpse of Paul's gift for friendship. In this chapter twenty-six names are mentioned, but it is not a mere roll-call, a dry list of encumbrances. The names are instant with life; the life of Christ. They are all friends of Paul; we see them through his eyes.

They were all brothers and sisters in Christ, who kept the witness alive in Rome. How they came to Rome we cannot tell. Paul met them in his journeyings elsewhere, but he himself had not at this stage ever visited Rome. As to why they were now in Rome we cannot tell. Some think they may have been conscripted from the provinces into Nero's household, many as slaves. Nor do we know what they suffered. But their sufferings were not what Paul was referring to. It was their Christian character, and that still remains.

As Paul enumerates the names, he attaches some grace to each, some feature of character or life or service. That was what he saw in them, what he coveted in them. And yet they had one thing in common, they all loved the Lord Jesus Christ. But this love showed itself differently in each.

Consider a few examples: First

THE LOVE THAT SUCCOURS.

In verse 1 the list starts with the love of Phoebe. Hers was a love that succours. She was a Greek. a converted pagan. Paul describes her as a servant of the Church at Cenchrea. But we should not read too much into the word servant. She was a business woman – like Lydia, and she was going to Rome; she was not already there. Possibly she may have been taking the Epistle with her. And Paul tells the brethren in Rome to receive her and stand by her in any business in which she had need of them, for 'she had been a succourer of many and of me also'.

Now a succourer is one who runs to help another, or stands by him to champion his cause when he is abused, misrepresented, slandered or down trodden. Just picture this Christian business woman in Cenchrea, which was one of the two ports of Corinth. She had there found disciples who were abused, maltreated, victims of prejudice and injustice, and she did not hesitate to stand up for them, to plead their cause, to rescue them from injustice and wrong. Even Paul himself she had assisted and succoured. What a picture of loyalty, that natural instinct of woman, but here gripped, reinforced and elevated by love of Christ. And Paul here recalls this staunch loyalty, and the fidelity of her courage in his recommendation to the Church at Rome. It was a loyalty that dared for Christ, found in many Christian men, but in more Christian women.

Secondly, in verses 3-5,

THE LOVE THAT SACRIFICES.

Here we have turning up in Rome the pious devoted couple Priscilla and Aquila, as they did before in Corinth (Acts 18:2), and earlier still at Ephesus (Acts 18:19). The order is Priscilla and Aquila, i.e. the woman's name comes first. At each place her home was the centre of fellowship. The Church was in her home.

So now they are in Rome, and Paul remembers them for a very particular act of self-forgetfulness and self-denial, 'Who have for my life laid down their necks', or even more strongly 'Who have for my life's sake submitted their throats to the knife'. There had been some great crisis in Paul's life – a violent blast of persecution so that his life had been in dire peril. And that gracious couple, quiet home-makers and home-lovers, had stepped out into the storm and placed themselves between the Apostle and death, knowing full well that they staked their own lives. That act of self-forgetting sacrifice has shed its aroma about their names, and it is fragrant still. Paul breathes it in Corinth, although they are now in Rome, and we breathe it still.

Thirdly, in verse 5, consider

THE LOVE THAT STANDS ALONE.

Epenetus had been willing to give out a lone witness. This man who had been the first fruits of Achaia unto Christ. Let us think of the implications of that. The Gospel had been taken by Paul to Achaia, the Roman province in Greece of which Corinth was the capital. But there had been no wave of revival. As at Philippi (Acts:16:11 ff) where Paul and Silas had been beaten and had been asked to leave the city, so that their triple fruit of Lydia, the slave-girl with the spirit of divination and the Roman jailor was hard-earned, so in Achaia the fruit was hand-picked in the person of Epenetus. He was the first to yield to the claims of Christ, to come out from a heathen environment and then raise a lone witness for Christ in the pagan darkness.

To Paul, Epenetus was 'well-beloved', as all first converts are. Being first in Achaia meant that he had to raise and maintain a lone witness for the crucified One. In the case of Epenetus this meant he had to demonstrate strength of character, resolution and conviction. It is easier to go in on a mounting wave than to go in alone. But there was, as in all such cases, the joy of finding another and yet another as a Church was established there.

Fourthly, in v 7 consider

THE LOVE THAT CARRIES ON.

'Andronicus and Junias, men who are of note among the Apostles, who also were in Christ before me'. In using the phrase 'in Christ before me' Paul seems to mention the distinction almost enviously. They were his own kinsmen. Did he know them when they were Christians and he was a persecutor? Did they ever attempt to arrest his pursuits and put in a word for the Lord? Paul looks back with tearful eyes to those days, of which he wrote elsewhere, earlier to the Corinthians (1 Cor. 15:9) and later to the Ephesians (Eph. 3:8), of himself being 'least of the apostles', and 'less than the least of all the saints' respectively. But they, his kinsmen, were still carrying on, and were now prominent, – they were of note – among the Apostles. Their Christian character had opened, they had received the grace to carry on without their love going cold or their spirits becoming faint. In this they had achieved a distinction which is to be coveted; they grew old in Christ and retained the keen edge of their first love, which 'is a good thing to be said of a man when he is laid in his grave'.

Fifthly, in v 10,

THE LOVE THAT ENDURES THE TEST.

'Salute APELLES approved in Christ'. He was the one who was tested in Christ. We do not know the nature of the test, but to Paul he had come through, and that was enough. And Paul knew what testing was. He himself had to face a fiery testing since he came to Christ. And he must have known something of the testing of Apelles, whether it was by torture, or scourge, or being disowned by loved ones. Only ONE knew fully what happened and that was Christ Himself. From this testing Apelles graduated with a good degree 'Approved in Christ'. Those who are thus listed have a distinctive something about them. They are not arrogant or aggressive. Just the opposite, meek and perhaps even diffident, 'but approved in Christ'.

Sixthly, in v 12,

THE LOVE THAT TOILS.

The names TRYPHENA, TRYPHOSA, and PERSIS are those of women. If it is accepted that there were as many, or more, slaves in Rome as freemen, then they may have been slaves in service, conscripted from the provinces. Tryphena and Tryphosa, we read, 'toiled in the Lord'. If they were slaves, this gives dignity to their bondage. By the way in which they carried out their work, they magnified their station.

Also Persis, another woman, 'the beloved Persis', as she is called, must have been the object of special affection in the Christian community. She 'toiled much in the Lord', we are told. The quality of her service would have been unchanged whatever its environment, because that environment was in the Lord. Likewise the inspiration for her work she found in the Lord.

Seventhly, in v 13,

THE LOVE THAT TENDS.

In verse 13 we are introduced to RUFUS and his mother. A partnership between a mother and her son is a partnership to which the Church of Christ owes much. Who was Rufus? We are told in Mark 15:21 that there was a Rufus who was the son of Simon the Cyrenian, who was compelled to carry the cross of Christ. If this was the same Rufus then he and his mother were now in Rome. In any case these two provided a home for the saints in Rome, thus making up for the loss of friends who had been lost for Christ's sake.

> 'Hearts I have won of sister or of brother
>
> Quick on the earth or hidden in the sod
> Lo! every heart awaiteth me, another
> Friend in the blameless family of God.'

This is not a far-off world, nor so strange to us. Though in Rome, they were in Christ. What matter it, though we do not know Rome. Their true environment was Christ – in character, in faith, in aspiration – just as for Christians today.

SAUL'S HEAVENLY VISION
(Acts 26:19)

P aul is a magnificent figure in the presence of Festus and
Agrippa. Paul would be a striking figure in any company,
but in the presence of the world's authority – in the person
of Festus the Roman governor, and the world's empty pomp in the
person of the puppet King, Herod Agrippa – Paul shows himself to
belong to Heaven's nobility as Agrippa was not, and to be invested
with the dignity of Heaven's ambassador as Festus was not.

He was on trial for his life, but this is not the speech of one
pleading for his life; it is that of a missionary and soul-winner,
pleading for the souls of his hearers. His own immediate destiny is
not important to him. What is important is to commend Christ and
put His claims across to his judges.

And Paul does not hesitate to disclose where he got his
commission from, what the source of his authority and the inspiration
of his boldness and confidence. It was a meeting with his Kingly
Master – and a transaction that left its impression deeply and indelibly
on his life.

1. The Heavenly Vision

Fourteen years of missionary activity had passed – well nigh
thirty years since the experience on the Jerusalem-Damascus road.
And they were years of trial and testing and suffering – but to Paul
that experience was still the Kingly Vision. He could no more doubt
its heavenliness than doubt the sun in the sky. The vision was stamped
with:-

(a) Heaven's Authority
(b) Heaven's Purpose

(a) *The Vision of Heaven's Authority*

Authority – power – majesty is the landmark of Heaven's
visitation. Saul, a Pharisee, and probably a member of the Jewish
Council, was very conscious of the weight of authority, very sensitive
and susceptible to investment with official authority. On this occasion
he himself tells us that he travelled with the authority of the High
Priests and the Council, and that invested him with confidence and
the sense of power. Was he not commissioned by his superiors to
hunt out and destroy the devotees of a new faith?

The name that the Glorious One chose to reveal Himself by is significant – Jesus. That was the name Saul despised and hated – because it stood for weakness, for grace, for the crucified one. Now it sounds in awful majesty out of heaven. Saul was going to Damascus to escape the Cross of Calvary, and now the cross meets him on the way, bars his progress and challenges him to obey. Jesus in blood-stained garments stands astride the Damascus road: there is no by-passing Him now.

That is the test of your vision: does it leave you with a person – does it confront you with Christ ? The height, the power, the voice are not enough – unless they usher in the presence of Jesus in His grace. When grace visits you, you have to reckon with what happened at Calvary.

(b) *The Vision of Heaven's Purpose*

That was unfolded to the humbled soul – the programme of Heaven's purpose for his life. He was to be the chosen messenger, to convey the light of heaven to men. The programme was clear: verse 16 'I have appeared unto thee for this purpose to make thee a minister and a witness'. The light he had received he was to bring to the Gentiles to turn them from darkness unto God.

This was Heaven's purpose, clear, dependable, authoritative – and there could be no going back on it. Heaven's programme could not be altered. God had His plan, He also had His man. and from that hour Paul felt himself in the grip of that Heavenly purpose, and he pressed forward that he might apprehend that for which he was apprehended of Christ Jesus.

Friend, don't you agree that this was a Heavenly vision ? So it will be to you, when this Jesus meets with you in the way – arrests your soul in its mad progress in sin, reveals Himself to you as the One against whom you sin, the One whose compassion yearns over you, and then He takes hold of you in His Divine purpose to be His messenger and witness-bearer. That is to you a Heavenly Vision, which does not fade with the passing years.

2. What Obedience to the Heavenly Vision Meant to Paul

Paul could say in all honesty and sincerity before Agrippa and Festus: 'I was not disobedient to the Heavenly Vision'. And as he said it and looked into Agrippa's eyes, I am sure the King winced

— Paul was speaking of Someone greater than any earthly majesty. And what did the Heavenly Vision demand from him? It meant primarily a surrendered will.

His will was the citadel of Saul's resistance: the proud, stubborn, unyielding will of the self-righteous Pharisee. Christ laid His hand on that and asked for its immediate surrender. And Paul capitulated: 'Lord, what wilt Thou have me to do?' At that hour, he handed his will over to a new Master, and from that day Saul became the willing captive of his Lord. And he was willing to be led by the hand, as a little child, into Damascus.

3. What would Disobedience to the Heavenly Vision Mean?

Paul was not disobedient. Can you say as much? Many a man can say ruefully and sadly 'I am sad because I disobeyed the vision that came to me'.

Think seriously of this, while I try to indicate to you what disobedience to the Heavenly Vision may mean:-

(a) *An Extinguished Light*

Can a man's light go out? Remember the five foolish virgins — they set out with lamps alit — and then the midnight cry arose — the most tragic cry in all the earth: 'Our lamps are gone out'. Oh the tragedy, the thick darkness, of extinguished light — you can no longer see.

(b) *A Seared Conscience*

The phrase is not mine. It is the Bible's. What does a seared conscience mean? It is a conscience that can no longer feel. You know that if a wound in the body is allowed to heal without care, it develops a hard, thick skin, and perhaps the spot loses its feeling – nerves are no longer near the surface and a numbness sets in.

Many a man's conscience can be like that. Once it was wounded, sensitive, sore. But it was carelessly treated. You did not apply the Balm of Gilead. It is now no longer an open wound, but it has lost its feeling.

(c) *A Blighted Hope*

A blighted hope is often the first result of disobedience to the Heavenly Vision: a life that is left barren and bare. You can no longer do what once you did: the capacity is gone. And like a tree withered at the roots decay and death set in.

SAUL AND HIS FELLOW-TRAVELLERS
A Study in Borderland Experiences

A certain school of liberal criticism of the Bible has made much of the apparent discrepancies and divergent readings in the Gospel narratives as indicating composite authorship and contradicting the traditional view that any of the Gospels was the work of the man whose name it now bears. This form of criticism has likewise been applied to the Book of Acts, and divergencies in different accounts of the same incident have been taken as indicating different authorship. But the divergencies were often more imaginary than real. For example, in the two accounts of Saul's conversion, the one from the pen of Luke in Chap. 9, the other in Chap. 22 from the address of Paul himself before Claudius Lysias and the Jews, there seem two divergent accounts of Saul's actual experience on the Jerusalem – Damascus road. In Luke's account the narrative reads: 'And the men who journeyed with him stood speechless, hearing a voice but seeing no man', while Paul himself records the experience thus: 'And they that were with me saw indeed the light, and were afraid; but they heard not the voice that spoke to me'. One might be justified in saying at once that in recording an experience of an earthquake, two men could truthfully give different reports of what happened, and indeed the same man might not give his personal experience in the same way twice. Saul's experience was as convulsive as an earthquake, and he might be pardoned for not narrating it in the same way on the two occasions. But, far from there being any inconsistency, the two accounts are complementary and lay bare certain aspects of the Christian's conversion, in its relation to those who have not passed through a like experience, that convey many vital lessons to us.

1.   The first account suggests that **there is a Hearing, which does not Enlighten.** 'And the men who journeyed with me stood speechless, hearing a voice but seeing no man'. In the experience of Saul's companions there was a sound like distant thunder, but there was no Face. That sound did not unveil a Face such as Saul beheld, the Face that transformed his whole being from a persecutor to a saint and that haunted him evermore by day and by night, luring him on to face privation, and destitution and death itself. With his fellow-travellers it was wholly different: the sound they heard carried no

enlightenment and led to no personal recognition. For that reason the course of life for them was to go on as before and the experience on the road to Damascus faded out.

Thus it is in the spiritual life. To hear and not to see is to remain unimpressed. For example, *we may hear of sin, but if we do not see ourselves as sinners we are not enlightened.* There may be such a thing as the faithful exposure of sin in its guilt and corruption and power, but if it remains a mere theological abstraction, a doctrine which we are ready to accept as Scriptural, without any conviction regarding our personal sin, then it is merely hearing which does not enlighten. To hear of sin and yet not see ourselves as sinners brings no experience of penitence into heart or conscience.

We may, likewise, hear of salvation, but if we do not see a Saviour there is no enlightenment. To hear the way of salvation unfolded, to have its terms expounded, and its appeal presented may leave us unenlightened and unsaved. It is a voice we hear; the Face we do not see. It is only when the way directs us to the Person, and the terms bring us into the Presence of the Saviour, that we exclaim: 'My Lord and my God'. No exposition of the plan, no presentation of the terms, can in themselves produce the enlightenment that testifies: 'Come, see a Man who told me all things that ever I did. Is not this the Christ?'

We may hear of Heaven, but if we do not see its glory we are not enlightened. It is not much we know, or can know, of the habitation of the saints at rest, the House of many mansions, but what Scripture unveils in language and imagery accommodated to our feeble senses we can understand and appreciate, yet if the glory of Heaven has not shone into our hearts and the radiance of the Throne shed its illumination on our path, we are not enlightened. To hear of Heaven's bliss and not see its spiritual glory is to remain in the shadows, children of earth, and not pilgrims to the City that hath foundations.

Thus it is that in many ways we cannot enumerate there may be an experience that leaves no abiding impression because it lacks the illumination of a personal unveiling. It is an experience such as Saul's fellow-travellers had, an experience in which we may indeed hear a voice but see no man.

2. On the other hand we must realise that **there is *a Vision that does not instruct.***

When Paul related the incidents of his own conversion to the Jews of Jerusalem (Acts 22:9), he spoke of his fellow-travellers in somewhat different terms: 'And they that were with me saw indeed the light, and were afraid; but they heard not the voice that spake to me'. There he presents the situation from a different angle – they saw, but did not hear – and yet the result was precisely the same – they remained unmoved and unchanged. The experience they passed through left no abiding impression because it conveyed not to them the voice that spoke so powerfully to Saul's heart and conscience. A light indeed shone on their path, but it was unintelligible and unavailing for their spiritual good because it lacked the voice of majesty and authority that shook the proud Pharisee out of his self-righteousness and self-pleasing. So there are experiences in life that do lighten the path and shed a temporary illumination on the road we tread, but they carry no conviction and leave no abiding impression because they do not convey the voice of God to soul and conscience. We see the vision, but it conveys no saving knowledge.

For example, *we may see the Hand of Providence in our daily life, but if we do not hear God's summons, it has no message for us.* There are situations in the lives of most men in which they can discern the Hand of an almighty and overruling Providence. It may be in the experience of a bitter sorrow, or of a signal deliverance; it may be in the bestowing of unexpected and unmerited good, or in the withholding of some coveted blessing. Whatever it be, the Hand of God is clearly recognised and the light of a great Divine intervention is shed upon the path. But that experience never seems to convey to them the summons of God beckoning them to leave the path of rebellion and unbelief and yield obedience to the claims of the Most High. And because the experience does not contain for them the voice of God, they do not recognise in it a message for their souls, and they remain ignorant and unimpressed. It is only when the providences of God speak with Divine authority to heart and conscience that foolish men are instructed and become wise unto salvation.

There are occasions also in which *we may see the Way of Salvation, but if we do not hear the personal call of God we are unwon.* How often has it happened to men and women under the preaching of the Gospel that the way of mercy became strangely illumined, that 'they were once enlightened', and 'the light that never was on sea or land' had shone about them, yet they heard not the voice of God calling them from sin to pardon, from guilt to grace, from death to life. And because there was no Divine call, there was no arresting hand laid in mercy upon them, and the light faded, and the darkness of unconcern once again brooded over their lives. The experience of an enlightened mind that does not lead to an awakened conscience and a surrendered heart leaves no abiding impression; rather is the slumber deeper, the shadows darker, and the soul deader than before.

We could cite, too, the experience of *one whose conscience testifies to the truth, and because the soul does not receive it as the Word of God, there are no permanent convictions.* There are doubtlessly occasions in life when, not only the mind is enlightened to see, but the conscience has given its witness to the truth and so has 'tasted the good Word of God and the powers of the world to come'. And because the truth is not embraced and obeyed as the Word of God that liveth and abideth for ever, the conscience does not come under the authority of Divine truth and the deep – rooted convictions that give stability and security to the life are not formed. The light indeed was seen, recognised by the conscience as the truth, but the voice was not heard and no clear, intelligible impressions were formed. Thus in many ways is it true in the lives of men that experiences that lead to enlightenment and shed their illumination upon the path for many days convey not 'the still small voice' to the soul and are of no abiding consequence to the life.

3. The sum of the whole matter would seem to be that the Divine work in the soul cannot find adequate expression in human language, and when language must be used to testify to what has happened between God and the soul its limitations give rise to apparent contradictions and inconsistencies. Yet these very contradictions themselves testify to the reality of the spiritual experience and distinguish often between those we read of as having been 'enlightened', having 'tasted', and having been made 'partakers', who had reached the very borders of the good land, and those who, by the grace of God, had been brought into full and everlasting possession. On that borderland there would seem to be 'a field of magnetic influence', to use a scientific phrase, where strange powers and influences are let loose and experiences are felt that seem to bear the stamp of permanence and reality. And yet there is that 'falling away' that stamps them as evanescent and unreal. Regarding such experiences as these, the Scriptures sound out many warnings, and in many forms reiterate the promise that 'He that endureth to the end, the same shall be saved'.

PAUL THE PRISONER OF JESUS CHRIST

Paul is in his own person the classic example of the Christian transfiguration of misfortune and trouble. Although the transmutation of base into precious metals is not possible, the transmutation of suffering into joy and weakness into strength is a secret within the possession of every Christian, in the measure in which he accepts the will of God and cultivates the fellowship of Jesus Christ. Paul is the outstanding example in the New Testament of this grace by which the Christian is (Rom. 8:37) '*more* than conqueror'. He bore his sufferings not merely with courage and heroism unparalleled, but with a triumphant faith that made them means of grace and channels of blessing to himself and to his fellows. Perhaps there is no grander figure in history, apart from the Lord Jesus Christ, than Paul in bonds. How utterly disappointed and embittered he might be! How human to feel crushed in spirit and soured in heart! Is this all that comes of a faithful witness and a heroic faith and endurance! Those chains, did they not spell the disappointing of his fondest hopes, and the frustration of his life's efforts! Not at all! How could they, when they were recognised as forged by the gracious hand of his Divine Lord! A prisoner he truly was, but Paul in prison was 'Paul, the prisoner of Jesus Christ'. Always Christ's, he was not a whit the less now that he was in bonds! When we ourselves, and those we love, are passing through sorrow and often in bonds, it becomes us to learn something of the secret of this Christian transfiguration of misfortune and calamity.

1. Paul in prison tells us that here is *Affliction that increases his Joy.* Imprisonment is, and must always be, a great affliction, since it is a serious interference with the common way of living and a serious infringement on the liberties of men. It was so to Paul not less than to common men. His enemies had wrecked their vengeance upon him to the furthest extent possible to them. Since they were not allowed to deprive him of life, they would fill his cup of suffering to the brim. And yet how foolish they must have seemed even to themselves! True, he is now a prisoner, but 'the prisoner of Jesus Christ' he declares himself! As if he said 'I am imprisoned with my Lord, and 'tis no prison at all! The cell is irradiated with His presence till it has become an ante-chamber of Heaven!' And the communications that issued from that prison cell breathed no sadness at all. 'Rejoice in the Lord alway, and again, I say rejoice' was the throbbing exhortation he sent out to his fellow-believers. There was no sense of deprivation, for he wrote to his converts at Philippi: 'I have all and abound'. Some of the sweetest and most joyful doxologies he issued from prison, indicated that no sadness had touched his heart and no gloom had settled upon his spirit. 'We are exceeding joyful in all our tribulations' was not a formal and empty profession, but the genuine expression of his soul's gladness and mirth. How impotent, then, must his enemies have felt! His imprisonment was an utter failure, since it could not sadden or crush his spirit! There are times in life when the Christian realises that the touch of Jesus Christ can turn affliction into joy, can transmute the base metal of sorrow into the purest gold of spiritual rejoicing. At such times he can trace his afflictions to their real source, and he can see their spring and fountain-head in the good will and pleasure of God. And when that happens, he is led to ask and expect the presence of the Lord as the joy that more than compensates for all the sorrow, nay that changes the base alloy of sorrow into the refined gold of Christian joy! And so the yoke is easy, and the burden is light, because they are recognised as His Yoke and His Burden, because they are accepted as the expression of His good will, and because their acceptance is the condition on which He bestows His presence and makes known His hidden purposes. To be in prison thus, is to be 'the prisoner of Jesus Christ'.

2. Paul the prisoner of Jesus Christ suggests to us that here is *intimidation that strengthens his courage*. The rigour of prison was calculated to break Paul's spirit, to curb his boldness, and crush his brave heart. For it was designed to engender fear, and fear is a paralysing and disabling thing. But do Paul's letters from prison ever breathe fear, or betray any fretful apprehensiveness as to the future? Far from it! Here is a prisoner indeed, but not a captive spirit beating helplessly against the bars of his cage or a cramped soul clamouring for larger space and purer atmosphere! Here is the prisoner of Jesus Christ, and what can there be to fear in that! These chains are the chains of Jesus Christ, those fetters were tied and knotted by the hand of His Divine Master! And he was there waiting his Lord's pleasure and would be free whenever the Lord gave the word! It was no captivity, when his spirit was not bound, and when his lot was under his Lord's control. Once he had been the Lord's disciple, His Apostle, His ambassador, now he is His prisoner, and he has no reason to be dismayed. It only adds another title to his worthy calling, gives him another good degree! For Christ is the common factor in his changing fortunes, and there is, therefore, no real change at all. So must we learn that it is only the touch of Jesus Christ that can lift our spirits above the fettering circumstances of our lot. We may be cramped and caged in our outward circumstances, but our spirits may be free, and our courage undaunted. For our souls recognise in Jesus Christ the controller of our circumstances and the only disposer of our lot. We may be in prison, but we can be the prisoners of Jesus Christ, unfettered and free in spirit.

3.   Paul suggests to us that there is an *isolation that leads to a wider fellowship.* No doubt his enemies had felt that the sorest thing that could happen to Paul would be to cut him adrift from his brethren. He revelled in the fellowship of his brethren so much that to be severed from them would be a crushing and bitter isolation! A maker of friends, Paul was himself a warm and true friend. In truth he could say:-

> 'Hearts I have won of sister or of brother
> Quick on the earth or hidden in the sod
> Lo! every heart awaiteth me, another
> Friend in the blameless family of God.'

And now prison walls were to come between Paul and the wide fellowship of his friends. But 'the prisoner of Jesus Christ' acknowledges no isolation whatsoever. By the way of the Throne he is in touch with all his brethren as he is in touch with their common Lord. He dwells with his converts, 'joying', as he says, 'and beholding their order in Christ Jesus'. From the vantage ground of his prison cell he can look on them all as a father at the close of each day looks upon his scattered family in personal remembrance and fond devotion. So a prison life could not isolate Paul's affectionate heart and devoted spirit from his brethren. He was the Lord's prisoner, and the prison that shut him out from the noisy and clamorous world shut him in with the Lord and with the wide circle of his brethren. So it is with every true Christian. Our horizon must not be bounded and limited by the circumstances of our own lives. We do not need to live always in our own narrow world. In thought, in sympathy, and in prayer, we can travel through the broad expanses of earth and take wing to Heaven. By meditation and prayer our isolation may lead us into a wider fellowship from which our earthly lot cannot exclude us.

4.   Paul could also tell us that here was *inactivity that multiplied his labours*. His enemies, of course, thought that by imprisoning him they could arrest and stop Paul's labours. It was something when this man who had turned the world upside down was now caged! His tongue was tied; his busy feet were in fetters. But now we know how utterly they failed! This was the prisoner of Jesus Christ engaged in his Master's service in prison. It was a change of sphere, not a change of employment, far less a cessation of labour.

His lips were not silenced. How could they be when he had such a message to deliver! His imprisonment was probably in some part of the royal palace, and Paul eagerly grasped the opportunity of making his message felt there. 'But I would ye should understand, brethren,' he writes to the Philippians, 'that the things which happened unto me have fallen out rather unto the furtherance of the Gospel, so that my bonds in Christ are manifest in all the palace.' So *all the palace* came to feel the influence of this prisoner of Jesus Christ! With what result, we partly know. 'All the saints salute you,' he wrote again to the Philippians, 'chiefly they that are of Caesar's household'. Even Nero's household staff came within the influence of Paul's message! How foolish his enemies seem to us now! In cutting him off from the common people among whom he delighted to labour, they thrust him into the palace and gave him the opportunity to lay under Nero's cruel throne the dynamite that was to convulse the Roman Empire and bring the Caesars into submission to the faith.

Not only so, but Paul 'the prisoner of Jesus Christ' made the Church and the world his debtors by those wonderful Epistles that he wrote from prison. For 'the prison epistles of Paul' rank among the great literature of the human race, and are in truth the charter of their spiritual liberty to the people of God. Himself in bonds, he became the emancipator of those in chains! For the Lord's prisoner did the Lord's work in prison, and all the generations of men will go on reaping the fruits of those prison labours. Thus it is that there may come into our lives a circumstance that may set a restraining hand upon our customary activities and yet result, not in inactivity, but in widening our influence and multiplying our labours. Let us, therefore, beware of setting bounds to the possibilities of service for God, even when our outward circumstances may appear most unpropitious. We can do the will of God and yield Him service in any sphere in which His providence may place us, and the most crippling circumstances in our lives may equip us for the highest service.

Many good people are discouraged and their efforts apparently thwarted by an altogether new set of circumstances that never came into their reckoning and for which they made no provision. Let them accept these as a challenge to greater zeal and an opportunity for wider and greater service. Some readers may have loved ones in a captivity as close and as real as was Paul's. Let them not think of God's purposes as arrested by prison gates. Rather let them recognise in these circumstances a further unfolding of God's gracious purposes towards those who are called to be His servants. To become 'the prisoner of Jesus Christ' is not merely to attain to a good degree, but to enter into a sphere in which we may do the Lord most notable service. Above all, let us constantly bear in mind that amongst the changing fortunes of earth, there is one constant and unchanging factor, namely, Christ's saving relationship to us and our obligation to yield Him obedience.

PAUL'S PREACHING OF THE CROSS
(1 Cor. 1:18)

There is something refreshingly up to date about Paul's feelings and experiences at Corinth. They are somewhat similar to the experiences of ten thousand preachers of the Gospel at this very day.

Paul preached the Cross of Christ – Christ crucified, Christ in the significance of His death, and he now reflects upon the varied responses to his message. It must have been startling to Paul and it no doubt was puzzling.

To one set of his hearers, the message he brought to the wicked licentious city of Corinth, brought about such a mighty change that he had to conclude that it was the power of God that was at work. Men and women steeped and soaked in sin were now new creatures.

To another set, his preaching of the Cross of Christ, his exposition of the death of Christ was just so much nonsense. The wise men of Corinth smiled indulgently at his simplicity, listened cynically to his offer, and went on their way unmoved – to them it was all foolishness.

What made the difference was not their taste, or education or culture. It was much more radical than that. It was a matter of their spiritual position and their spiritual character. One set was being saved, the other was perishing. The state they were in made the difference.

These are still the reactions to the Cross wherever it is being presented. These have been the reactions always – and will be the reaction no doubt in days to come. But why was it foolishness to some? Why was the preaching of the Cross – the exposition, the interpretation, the application of the inner meaning of the Cross foolishness, emptiness, meaningless, absurd? It did not make sense, it did not belong to their world of thinking. Why? Were there seeming contradictions about it that puzzled them? Yes, there were. Let us consider some of these.

1. Paul's Gospel of the Cross Professed to Bring Light out of Darkness

To the wise men of Corinth the Cross and all it stood for was just black midnight darkness. We should not be surprised at this considering their spiritual condition. The Cross was just that – darkness – to many even at the time it happened. It was so to many of those who surrounded the Cross. 'He saved others, Himself He cannot save' shouted the people. 'If He be the Christ, let Him come down from the Cross and we will believe in Him' cried others.

Even his disciples were stricken down. 'We thought it was he who should have redeemed Israel' they mournfully confessed. And the darkness in men's minds was matched by the darkness that shrouded the Cross when the sun in the heavens was darkness from the sixth to the ninth hour. And there was darkness over the whole earth for these three or four hours.

And yet Paul tells his hearers that he and a multitude of others saw light – such light as made them blind to all else – light on God and man, on sin and salvation, on justice and mercy, and he told them that there alone they would see true light, that neither life nor death could extinguish.

2. Paul's Gospel of the Cross Claimed to Bring Power out of Weakness

This power was a power to transform the lives of men. The world already knew about other types of power – the power of brute strength, the power of the mailed fist, the power of the royal sceptre, but power out of weakness was just foolishness to the Corinthians. And yet that is what the Cross of Christ meant and still means.

That puzzled His enemies from the very first, as well as His followers, that Christ did not meet power with power, that He did not exercise power on His own behalf but submitted to all the humiliation and indignity of the Cross. Everything there pointed to His weakness, to His apparent helplessness. So feeble was He that He fell down under the burden of the physical Cross He was asked to carry, and a stranger had to be requisitioned to carry it for Him. He offered no resistance when He was arrested. He said not a word in self-defence when He was accused and condemned.

The Roman soldiers saw the irony of calling Him a king. With all the buffoonery of soldiers they carried out the heartless farce of a mock coronation – with robes, crown, rod and mock homage. And at the end He bent His head in death, apparently friendless and alone. After all this 'He saved others, Himself He cannot save' was perhaps the most rational comment.

But Paul would claim that the coronation was not the empty farce it may have seemed. The robe of human weakness, the crown of thorns and the sceptre of a reed befitted Him. For at that moment He was on His throne indeed. Crucified in weakness He was mighty to save. That is still the throne of His power – and power to save still flows from that Cross of a living Saviour, as it did long ago. With those pierced hands He lifted empires off their hinges . He stemmed the tide of history and turned it into new channels with them – He still governs the ages. What was weakness to unbelievers was glory to Paul.

3. Paul's Gospel Proclaimed that Pardon and Forgiveness Could Flow from Condemnation

Condemnation was indeed written over that death scene. Both Jews and Romans had combined to produce the condemnation. The Jews represented religion, and its pronouncers would only say 'We have a law and by our law he ought to die'. The Romans representing justice at its highest could only lead him away to be crucified. No one stepped forward to his defence – except for Pilate's wife.

The lonely sufferer uttered not a word in self-defence. Even the heavens above were silent. When He cried 'My God, why hast Thou forsaken me', He accepted its verdict of silence, and entered into a consciousness of being not only forsaken of men, but also forsaken of God. He was, as He Himself told beforehand, (Luke 22:37), 'numbered among the transgressors'.

Yet Paul presented the full and free forgiveness that that Cross brings into the experience of sinful men. It is a forgiveness through His condemnation. He stood there for sinners, He suffered for sinners and He died for sinners. There on the Cross He spoke no word of self-defence, but in prayer asked as of right 'Father forgive them for they know not what they do'. John Newton found this himself as he sang:

Thus while His death my sin displays
In all its blackest hue,
Such is the mystery of grace
It seals my pardon too

4. Paul's Gospel Proclaimed that Life flows from His Death

It seemed foolish to proclaim that life flows from His death. But this Paul did at Corinth. His death was real. He died outright: life was extinct. He entered into the realm of the dead. None questioned the reality of His death as the stone was rolled to the grave to seal it.

But was Paul's coming to Corinth to preach that life flows from that death foolishness? How can it be? Because He took the wages of sin, which is death, He secured the gift of eternal life to be channelled through his death. John Newton in his dilemna – the dilemna of an awakened soul – adds

Alas I knew not what I did
But now my tears are vain.
Where shall my trembling soul be hid ?
For I the Lord have slain.

Another look He gave which said
'I fully all forgive.
This blood is for thy ransom paid
I die, that thou mayest live'

5. Paul's Gospel Proclaimed there was Power in the Preaching of the Cross

'It is' says Paul – an experience belonging to many at Corinth – 'it is the power of God unto salvation'. It is an experience of the greatest spiritual power known to God's creation. How is this so?

First it fulfils the Redeeming Purpose of God. The will of God is the power that animates the universe; it is the mainspring of all power. And this will of God is expressed in His Purpose.

The Cross was not an accident. It was not merely an outrage committed by the malice of Satan and the enemy of man. It was the full expression of the purpose of God to redeem man. It was the operation of that purpose. It was released and it moved into known history to save, mightier than any power of nature that operates on earth. Christ always recognised Himself as fulfilling the divine purpose. He looked forward to the hour when the redeeming purpose of God would be let loose to all men – to save. And so the omnipotence of God is at work in the preaching of the Cross – His purpose grips us and His will locks us fast.

Secondly, preaching the Cross conveys the emancipating love of Christ. The love of God is the strongest emotion in the moral universe. And we make saving contact with this love of God in Christ Jesus our Lord.

And it is through Christ in His death that the love of God is channelled to us as we look upon Him whom we have pierced, and mourn for Him. Our slavish fear is then banished and our spirits become unfettered as the love of God is shed abroad in our hearts.

Thirdly, preaching the Cross of Christ brings into our experience the regenerating energy of the Holy Spirit. The Spirit of God is the executive of Deity, He is compared to wind, water, fire, all the strongest natural powers. It is the death of Christ that secures that power for us. On the foundation of what Christ has done for us, the Holy Spirit can work in us, and we are created anew.

Conclusion

Is the preaching of the cross still foolishness? If so is it not a sign that we are still in the state that Paul calls 'perishing'? The natural man receiveth not the things of the Spirit of God for they are foolishness unto him. Or is it in your experience the mighty power of God? If so you can say with John Newton once more

With pleasing grief and mournful joy
My spirit now is filled;
That I should such a life destroy,
Yet live, by Him I killed

PAUL'S VIEW OF THE RESURRECTION
(1 Cor. 15:17-18)

Paul was clear on one thing – that Christianity stood or fell on the fact of the literal, physical resurrection of Christ. He was open and frank about it – he faced it boldly and courageously – 'If Christ be not risen'. That is putting it at its plainest.

Paul was mentally honest – he did not seek refuge in any sort of subterfuge. Paul was morally honest – he could not hold on to anything that had no foundation in fact. Paul was spiritually honest – he would not go on believing when his faith had nothing to rest on.

And so he expresses the case for Christianity, and the case against Christianity in these challenging words.

1. A Vain Faith

The Christian faith is empty if Christ has not risen from the dead. It means that there was something supernatural about Christ.

The world will say that He was but an ordinary man, that He lived on ordinary levels and died an ordinary death. That in His birth, in His Life, in His death He was not different from other men of His day. But the Christian faith decreed that He was vastly different. In His birth, born of a virgin, nature stepped aside to let Him pass. In His life He spoke as never man spoke. In His works He controlled nature and death itself. In His character – and that was the strongest miracle of all – He was holy, undefiled, separate from sinners. In His death He gave Himself willingly – death was not His fate – it was His deed. And the transforming faith of Christianity is that He broke the grave open from the inside and rose in resurrection life – in a life over which death no longer has power. That put the copestone on the supernatural in Christ's life and death. That is the keystone in the arch of supernatural Christianity, and if that goes all goes – the Christian faith is vain.

And if so, if Christ be not risen, there is nothing divine about all the promises given in the Bible. The Scriptures contain wonderful promises of One who was to come who would conquer death and the grave. Promises that the stone rejected by the builders would become Head of the Corner. Promises that He would ascend on high and lead captivity captive. Promises that God would not leave

Him in the grave to see corruption. Promises that made Him cry 'O death, I will be thy plagues; O grave I will be thy destruction (Hos. 13:14). And the whole of the Bible is knit together by these promises, giving it cohesion and unity of purpose.

If Christ be not risen all these great and glorious promises are in vain – and the edifice of Scripture falls to pieces. But they have been gloriously and triumphantly fulfilled in part already and much is to follow. These promises are divine, given of God and fulfilled of God. And they place the divine seal on the resurrection of Christ who was declared to be the Son of God with power by the resurrection from the dead.

In short, if Christ be not risen we cannot regard the words of Christ Himself as trustworthy. He said again and again that not only would He be crucified but that He would rise on the third day. He based His Kingdom on this one fact and pledged His trust-worthiness that it would be so. 'If it were not so I would have told you'. If this central fact did not really take place, can we trust anything else Christ said or did? Our faith in Christ is vain. This we cannot for a moment accept. It is this or nothing. And the evidence for the resurrection is so strong, so compelling, so complete that we have confidence in basing our all on that – our Redeemer lives. Faith in Christ is faith in the Resurrection.

2. A Vain Experience

'Ye are yet in your sins'.

All that constitutes our Christian experience is built on the fabric of a rationalisation. In this case we have not yet been redeemed.

(a) Christ has not borne our sins in His own body on the tree if He was only human. He could only bear His sin and not ours. And we are still bearing our own sins.

(b) Christ did not give satisfaction for us to God. For if Christ did not rise or leave evidence that God accepted His offering for us, we have no receipt that the debt was paid for us – we have no evidence that He has made an end of our sins. We are yet in the guilt of our sins.

(c) And if Christ did not rise from the dead He has not broken the power of sin for us. We are still in its chains, it exercises its old dominion over us – the power of His Resurrection is not a power in us – we are yet in the bondage of our sin.

But we know that we have been redeemed, we have experienced forgiveness and the peace it brings. We have had emancipation and deliverance from our besetting sin.

3. A Vain Hope

'They also which are fallen asleep in Christ are perished'.

That is our dearest Hope – that those who lived in Christ, died in Christ. That death, no matter in what form it comes, is only a sleep. Compare Stephen who was stoned to death and yet the New Testament said he fell asleep. He saw Christ enthroned on the right hand of God, and Christ closed his eyes in sleep.

But if Christ be not risen we shall not awake on the other side.

(a) Our Hope of seeing Him will not be fulfilled. And that is our dearest hope – to see Him face to face. It was His face that lighted us in our pilgrimage. And His servants still serve Him and they shall see His face.

(b) Our Hope of being like Him will not be realised. We shall be like Him then and shall see Him as He is. That is the goal of our journey – the pinnacle of our Hope.

(c) Our Hope of eternal fellowship will be dashed. There is no fellowship beyond the grave. The Christian hope of a resurrection is an empty dream: men have been following a will o' the wisp that leads nowhere. No wonder Paul concludes 'If in this life only we have hope in Christ we are of all men most miserable'. But that is not the case for the Christian. 'But now is Christ risen from the dead and become the first-fruits of them that slept'. The Risen Christ is the First Sheaf of a great harvest, the pledge of all that is to come, the pattern of what we shall be when we are risen with Him.

And as such the early Church accepted it – the early Christians greeted one another with the words 'Christ is Risen'. It put joy, confidence and victory into their lives. Do we behave as if we had a living Saviour?

PAUL'S CHARGE TO THE EPHESIAN ELDERS

After the riot at Ephesus Paul decided to visit Greece again and made his way towards Macedonia. How long he spent in Macedonia on this occasion Luke does not say, but the three months he spent altogether in Greece were the winter months of AD 56-57. Most of this time was spent in Corinth from which he wrote his Epistle to the Romans. Among the things he did in Greece was the arrangements for conveying the collected gifts from the Greek Churches to Jerusalem. A number of Gentile Christians joined with him, probably representatives of the churches which contributed to the collection for the relief of the poverty-stricken Jerusalem Christians. They made the sea voyage from Neapolis, the port of Philippi, to Troas, and the description of the journey from there to Jerusalem is given by Luke in detail.

He was obviously one of the number himself and probably kept a log-book of the voyage. While his companions embarked at Troas, Paul himself did not join the ship till Assos. From there they arrived at Miletus on the south shore of the Latorian Gulf where the ship was to be in harbour for three or four days. It was here that Paul sent a message to Ephesus, some thirty miles away, inviting the elders of the Church there to come and see him. His purpose was obviously to discuss with them the affairs of the Church at Ephesus, and give them such further instruction and exhortation as they needed in view of opposition they were experiencing at Ephesus. And Luke recorded the gist of the speech. It is the only speech of Paul to a Christian gathering recorded by Luke.

1. Paul's Ministry in Retrospect (Acts 20:18-21)

Here Paul finds it necessary, in self-defence against his opponents and traducers, to remind the Elders of the kind of life he led during the three years he had been among them at Ephesus.

(a) *His ministry among them had three features (v 19)*

He served the Lord with lowliness of mind.

He served also with tears.

He survived all the trials due to Jewish plots against his life.

That was the spirit in which he served of humility, of sorrow and of suffering.

(b) *The substance of his ministry (vv 20-21)*

In spite of trials and persecution he shrank not from declaring to them anything that was profitable for their Christian life. His method was both public and private. It was public first in the Synagogue and then in the School or Lecture hall of Tyrannus. It was also a ministry in private homes to which he had access.

That ministry was exercised both to Jews and to Greeks. And the message of it was 'repentance towards God and faith towards our Lord Jesus Christ' (v 21). These were the two demands of his message – repentance and faith. Repentance is directed God-wards; faith is directed Christ-wards. In repentance we turn to God; in faith we are directed to Christ.

2. Paul's Ministry in Prospect (vv 22-27)

He tells them that he is bound for Jerusalem under a sense of spiritual constraint. He was doubtful as to the reception he would receive there from two sources:

(a)   From the unbelieving Jews who would be hostile in view of his ministry among the Gentiles.

(b)   From the Jewish Christians, whether the gifts from the Gentile Church might be acceptable to them.

Even now as he visits port after port, and church after church, the Holy Ghost, probably through the lips of prophets in each congregation, warns him of a hostile reception in Jerusalem.

But his speech is one of calm obedience. He is willing to surrender his liberty and his life if only he can reach the end of his appointed cause and fulfil the ministry entrusted to him. Life and death were not the real issues in Paul's sight; what really mattered was that he might fulfil his ministry and that Christ should be glorified in him. He had received that ministry from Christ and his only wish was to fulfil it.

And he could bring these brethren as witnesses to this fact that he proclaimed the message given to him without fear or favour. Many were to see him no more – but he asks them to witness to the fact that he was faithful to their spiritual interests and to the commission given to him.

For that reason he was 'free from the blood of all men', blood standing for the destiny of lost souls. He cannot be charged with the destiny of souls that are lost through not believing the message.

In Ezekiel God says of the wicked who will not warn his fellows: 'his blood will I require at thy hand'. Paul's confidence arises from the assurance of his faithfulness to his message in v 27 'For I have not shunned to declare unto you the whole counsel of God'.

What is the whole counsel of God? It is the way of salvation in all its parts. It includes what God offers to man and what God requires of man. It must exclude excessive emphasis on, for example, the second coming, infant baptism, election and predestination or dispensational teaching. It must always emphasise man's responsibility.

3. Paul's Charge to the Ephesian Elders (v 28)

As he has discharged his own responsibility so he beseeches them to discharge theirs. On them rests a heavy responsibility. The Holy Spirit had entrusted them with the charge of God's flock at Ephesus. The twofold commission of the Gospel minister is

(1) a call from God to preach the Gospel.

(2) a call from God's people to take charge of their souls.

Both go together – one gives authority – the authority of God. The other gives power – power to act in a representative capacity.

The word used for overseers can be translated as bishops. And the word used for these elders at the beginning can be translated as presbyters. So the same body of men are called presbyters and bishops – indicating that these words bear the same meaning. Thus they are elder men – presbyters as to their standing in the congregation. They are bishops as to their functions to oversee the congregations collectively and individually. They are also shepherds to feed the Church of God – to pasture, to nurture, to instruct, to edify and develop. And as a strong incentive to duty he indicates the relationship of the Church to God 'which he has purchased by his own blood'. Purchased here means 'got for his own possession', or 'made peculiarly his own'.

This consideration should surely lead the pastors to do their task with reverence, with awe, with diligence, with love: it made their responsibility the greater when it is said 'God has purchased the Church with his own blood'. Some would read it 'with the blood of his own', i.e. Son. The blood of God, though an unusual expression, may stand as indicating the Divine value of the sacrifice given – the Person who gave it was Divine, and so everything about

Him was Divine, a Divine birth, a Divine message, a Divine authority and a Divine sacrifice.

4. Their Responsibility in View of the Future of the Ephesian Church (vv 29-31)

As Paul looks to the future the prospects for the Ephesian Church are not bright. This means greater vigilance. Dangers will come from two directions:-

(1) Intruders from without – wolves they are called, ravaging the flock.

(2) From within – brethren will lapse into all sorts of heresies to draw their followers away from the truth of the Gospel.

'Therefore watch'. And they have Paul's own example to encourage them : 'remember', his own example for three years was one of constant watchfulness, 'warn everyone, night and day, with tears', – all elements of extreme care and vigilance.

5. But the Grace of God is Enough for them as it was for him (v 32)

'And now brethren I commend you to God and to the word of His grace which is able to build you up and give you an inheritance among all them that are sanctified' – the grace of God was able:-

(1) to develop them in their ministry.
(2) to sanctify them for the inheritance to come.

So the word that conveyed the grace of God was their equipment for the upbuilding of the Church.

6. Once again he reverts to his own example (v 33)

He lived for the flock, not of the flock. He did not even derive his living as was legitimate. He laboured as tent-maker to provide a livelihood for many of his fellowworkers. By this example they ought to labour to support the weak among them, rather than have them be a burden to them - weak in faith as well as poor in circumstances.

This they were to do in the spirit of our Lord's words 'It is more blessed to give rather than to receive'.

There is no recording of this in the Gospel sayings of Christ.

But it was the spirit of His whole life and mission and message.

PAUL'S SPIRITUAL RELATIONSHIP IN CHRIST

L uther is reported as saying that the heart of religion was in the personal pronouns. The same might with equal truth be said of the prepositions. They are the link-words of a language, placed before nouns and pronouns to express their relationship to the verbs that are the operative words of the sentence, thus giving unity and coherence to the whole. The prepositions of the spiritual life are similarly the connecting ties that are the channels of life, and grace, and security to the soul. Paul's exclamation in his Epistle to the Galatians is a striking example of this: (Gal. 2:20) 'I am crucified with Christ, nevertheless I live; yet not I, but Christ liveth in me; and the life that I now live in the flesh is by the faith of the Son of God, who loved me and gave himself for me'. Here the four prepositions *with, in, by* and *for* lay bare the vital spiritual ties that exist between the soul and God, the ties that are the channels of life, and strength, of obedience and sanctity, between the inner man and the source of all Grace. While Paul, in that grand outburst of spiritual passion, produced them in the order of experience, from the circumference to the centre as it were, it may be more profitable for us, with our less vivid experience, to reverse the order, and consider them in the order of the gracious operations of the quickening Spirit of God, that is from the centre to the circumference.

1. In this order we have laid bare first that basic tie that is the *Foundation of the Christian life*.

It is represented by the word FOR. This is a strange mystic tie; some would tell us that it is too flimsy to hang one's soul on, and that something more concrete, more palpable and real, must be sought as a foundation on which to build the edifice of the Christian life. But flimsy as it may appear to the mere investigator into spiritual origins, it is *Divine*, and each strand of it contains the hall-mark of its Divine origin. To Paul this was the vital, throbbing centre of his life, that it was God in the Person of His Son who loved him and gave Himself FOR him. This lifeline was cast over from the Divine side when man was wholly and hopelessly adrift from God. It was not man that dared to find kinship with God, but God that claimed kinship with man when by an act of humiliation and self-abasement the Word was made flesh and tabernacled amongst men. We may never fully understand how it happened – for Nature seemed to step aside to let God pass – but we base the foundations of our hope on this mysterious act of incarnation by which God remained what He was and became what He was not. And as the tie is Divine, so it is *redeeming*. FOR brings us 'far-ben' into the mystery of sacrifice, propitiation and atonement, for it links us to an act of grace by which God in His Son *gave* Himself. Not only does it tell that God reached us, but it instructs us in the further mystery that God took our place in all that self-identification and substitution can mean. With this tie is interwoven the scarlet cord of atonement and sacrifice that draws the soul from a state of guilt to a state of grace, from death to life. And it is a tie that has at its heart the steel girder of God's gracious and sovereign *purpose of love* for the soul. Here Paul claims FOR himself the love of God and the offering of that love as if none else had part or share in it. 'Who loved *me* and gave Himself for *me*', registers an experience that not only brought to him life from the dead, but that everlasting security that is the very essence of eternal life to the soul. To be made to see in one's unworthy self the object of everlasting love and all-availing sacrifice, is to find oneself caught up in the sovereign purpose of God, and see one's own destiny as secured in the councils of the Eternal. We repeat that the tie laid bare in the spiritual relationship FOR may seem flimsy and unreal to the man who merely examines it as doctrine and decries it as dogma, but it is, in the spiritual experience of men, the tie which gives hope, quickening and security, that is indeed the basic strand of the spiritual life.

2. Next in our order we have the tie that lays bare the *Principle of the spiritual life.*

It is the word BY. 'I live,' said Paul, 'by the faith of the Son of God'.Every life has its own principle of existence, and survival hangs upon obedience to that central principle. The principle of the Christian life is *faith*. As it is necessary for a new- born life to breathe as a condition of survival, so it is a necessary principle of the new-born soul to exercise faith. Immediately the soul comes to life, it lives by faith. The *environment* of faith is indicated by Paul when he says, 'The life I now live in the flesh, I live by the faith'. So faith has to be exercised in the old environment of the flesh with all its unholy desires and appetites, with all its weakness and frailty. Yet faith has to overcome the promptings and lustings of the flesh in obedience to the law of the new life, just as an aeroplane overcomes the law of gravitation and rises from the earth in obedience to the higher law of aerodynamics. Why God should leave the man of faith 'in the flesh', surrounded by its temptations and weighed down by its corruptions, we may not in this life be able fully to understand, but we know that faith yields to the pull of the unseen and eternal and rises above the flesh. The *springs* of faith ensure that it cannot fail to exercise its power and live according to its own principle: it is 'the faith of the Son of God' of whom Paul could say 'He loved me and gave Himself for me'. Faith strikes its roots down to the only reality in a universe of shadows, and entwines itself round the Son of God. There it finds stability and security that withstand the promptings of the flesh. And as that faith strikes down to the nether springs of Christ's love and sacrifice as matters of personal interest and experience, faith is fed and revived and strengthened. The life of faith is not, therefore, the bare and drab existence that it is too often presented to be; it is a life that is brought by faith into living contact with the springs of all joy and revival, the love of Christ and the sacrifice of that love. And so the Christian goes on living – and living the life that is life indeed – on the principle of faith.

3. The third link mentioned by Paul lays bare the *Nature of the spiritual life*.

It is contained in the word IN. 'I live' declared Paul, and then added by way of amplification and exposition, 'yet not I, but Christ that liveth in me'. That is the very essence of the Christian life – an indwelling Christ in the presence and power of the Holy Spirit. The gracious function of the Holy Spirit at regeneration is to beget Christ in us, and His function in sanctification is to cause Christ to exercise His life in us in such a way that we can say with Paul 'For me to live is Christ'. And as the Christian life develops, and the Christian grows in grace, his nature comes more and more under the dominion of Jesus Christ, and Christ more and more exercises His crown – rights over the empire of man's soul. Only thus is the man entitled to the name Christian, and only thus will the world call him the Christ-one. It has to be noted, however, that though the sceptre of Jesus Christ is raised over the whole of nature claiming every acre of its territory for Himself yet it is so done that human personality is not destroyed. 'I live,' cried Paul, and his further explanation is not really a withdrawal of that exclamation. The 'I' that constituted Paul's distinctive personality continued to live, even though it had been so transformed that it 'put on the Lord Jesus Christ' and made 'no provision for the flesh'. There is no outrage on the sacredness of personality by the operations of grace, and no disintegration of human personality in union with Jesus Christ. But there is such an identification with Christ in His character and grace that the man is transformed to the image of Christ and his personality is regulated and governed by the will of God. In this respect he can truly say 'I live' and yet, with equal truth declare, 'Yet not I, but Christ that liveth in me'.

4. Our final link-word, and the one which Paul first introduces into the sentence, stresses the *Claims of the spiritual life.*

It is the word WITH. 'I am crucified WITH Christ' was Paul's opening cry. For it probably was the experience he was most conscious of, inasmuch as it was the reality nearest the surface of his life. Every kind of life makes its own demands, and the creature can be said to live only as it responds to these claims. Life – biologically considered – may be said to be merely an answer back to life. The Christian life makes its own peculiar demand on the man who professes it – so peculiar that it is unique in the whole realm of animate being – it demands *crucifixion*. And crucifixion is apparently death. But such is the implication of being saved by the Cross, that life evermore becomes a crucifixion, a crucifixion that works death to the old nature as it liberates and invigorates the new nature to possess its possessions. The Cross of his redemption so wrought in Paul that he could exclaim 'I die daily', and the Cross is evermore the lot of the Christian. Had this been the whole truth, it would present so forbidding an aspect of the Christian life that men might be excused from embracing it. But it was only half the truth, for Paul's exclamation was: 'I am crucified with Christ'. It is the *fellowship* of the Cross that transforms its crucifixion into a life of peace, and joy and holiness. Apart from Christ, the Cross would only mean the prolonged anguish and pain of self-immolation and self-sacrifice – as those who separate the Cross from Christ find –

but 'with Christ' the Cross is a transforming power, a healing balm, and the talisman of victory for the soul, for it brings us into the knowledge of His grace, into the fellowship of His sufferings, and into possession of the power of His resurrection. It was this experience that gave to Paul his most triumphant boast: 'But God forbid that I should glory save in the Cross of the Lord Jesus Christ, by whom the world is crucified unto me and I unto the world'. It is the response that the Christian dare not refuse to give, save at the peril of his peace, his purity and his power.

Group 5

The Church

THE CHURCH THE BRIDE OF CHRIST

There are three similitudes used in the N. T. to describe Christ's relationship with His Church. These are the Church as Christ's Building or Temple of which He is the Foundation, giving stability, or the Chief Corner Stone giving cohesion. Secondly the Church as the Body of which Christ is the Head, giving vitality and unity in diversity, making it not an organisation but an organism. And then there is the somewhat less familiar one of the Church as the Bride of Christ, of whom He is the Bridegroom, giving to the Church an identification with Christ that reaches its complete fulfilment in the Age to come, the Age which is to be the climax of history. There is a gradation in these similitudes: the Building pointing to Zion restored; the Body pointing to the Race restored to the image of God; and the Bride, undoubtedly the highest, indicating all that is personal and possessive and abiding: the restoration of the Redeemed to the glory of their Redeemer.

The Bride-Imagery was applied in the N. T. first of all by John the Baptist (Jn 3:25-30), but the metaphor was steeped in O. T. association, having been used by the Prophets to designate the relationship between God and Israel. Hosea speaks for all the prophets when he says in the name of God: 'I will betroth thee to me for ever'.

The fact that it could be used of Christ's relationship to His Church elevates Christ to the place claimed exclusively in the O. T. by Jehovah, thus ascribing to Christ Deity in the highest sense. It bears the significance of taking up and fulfilling a divine relationship to the Church that under the O. T. was claimed, but never realised because of the waywardness and unfaithfulness of His Church. Christ is thus taking up the promise and blessing of the O. T. and accepting the responsibility of bringing it to complete and perfect fulfilment in Himself, and very particularly in His death, resurrection and ascension. This indeed was involved in what Mark records of Christ's words in defence of His disciples who were being charged with a lack of the abstinence that characterised the disciples of John the Baptist: 'Can the children of the bride-chamber fast while the bridegroom is with them? But the days will come when the bridegroom shall be taken away from them; in that day they shall fast' (Mk.2:19-20). The words 'taken away' are indicative of violence; the bridegroom is to be wrested away from their fellowship, and as such it constitutes the first recorded reference to His violent death that Christ had made to His disciples.

Thus the symbol of the Bridegroom is applied to Jesus by His own authority. Indeed He has placed Himself at the heart and centre of the symbol.

But it is significant that those of His parables which use this symbolism place a passage of time – a period of delay and separation – before the personal union of the Bridegroom with His Bride, and so the mutual joy of the Wedding Feast, that marks the end of an era and the beginning of another. For this reason, the Bride, and Bridegroom symbol is not now very popular, as it puts the goal and summit of the Church's glory in the unforeseeable future, marked by what is known as the Second Coming of Christ – the one far-off divine event to which the whole creation moves. And this future belongs to the Church as the Bride of Christ.

Now we must ask: What does this imagery contain for us? Underlying it all there is the familiar biblical idea of Covenant. The relationship common to both O. T. and N. T. is that of Covenant. And marriage, in the social relationship, is the highest expression of Covenant. In the marriage formula the question is put 'Do you promise and covenant to be....'.

The question arises at once: Why should the Bible make such frequent references to the divine-human relationship as that of Covenant? May it not be because God's very substance is an expression of Covenant? God in Himself is a Fellowship: a Fellowship of Three Persons who can enter into contractual relationships that can only be called Covenant, each Person fulfilling an office that bears on the self-manifestation of the entire Godhead. This becomes our highest conception of Deity – a Fellowship in mutual participation and manifestation.

But since that Fellowship can, in its very nature, be shared, and was shared within the Being of God before any creature came into being, it becomes clear that this sharing was the supreme purpose of the creation. God created beings with whom He could share that Fellowship that was eternally His.

When man was created, it was in order to enter into God's Fellowship, and the fact that he had been made in God's image rendered him fit to respond to that Fellowship and participate in its blessings. And the biblical position is that God made this Covenant with man. And when man on his side had failed to maintain the character that fitted him for that fellowship, God made known that its complete fulfilment would be undertaken by Himself. Thus it is that Christ is spoken of as the Mediator of the New Covenant, new in the sense of manifestation; as the One who was to operate and guarantee it. And He operates it for His Church that He has bought back into a Fellowship that is as close and personal as that of a bride to her Bridegroom.

It is therefore evident why the symbolism of marriage and the conjugal relationship it involves should be applied to the Church. Hence the Church became in His symbolism the Bride of Christ – the one in Covenant with Him as Bridegroom and Lord.

It falls to us then to trace very briefly the main features of that relationship between Christ and His Church that can be characterised by a marriage covenant.

1. First of all we come face to face with the Covenant Mystery of Redemptive Love

It is commonplace to assert that marriage on the human plane is based on love – love without conditions. But this is *Redemptive Love* bestowed while the Church was still forlorn and lost. To us this will always have the element of mystery in it, but one text of Paul's puts it simply 'Christ loved the Church and gave himself for it'. He gave Himself – poured Himself out – at the behest of love to the unlovely and unlovable. No wonder it stands written in letters of fire 'For God commends his love towards us, in that while we were yet sinners Christ died for us'.

We are here in the presence of electing love, and we can see it only in its operation and results. The Bride is bride of the Bridegroom's choice – the choice of love. That love had in it the quality of all true love – that it is not general but personal and individual. It was this that Paul felt when he spoke of the Son of God who 'loved me and gave himself for me'. He found himself at the heart of this love and this sacrifice, as if there were none other to share it with. So it is not shared love among individual members. The identity of the individual is not lost in the mass. Christ's love to the Church – His redeeming love – is love to the individual, distinct, personal, intimate. It thus preserves human personality which is deepened and enriched in the fellowship of the Church. This is love that led to ownership and possession. This is the distinctive fact about the Church – there is close communion, but all its members remain persons whom Jesus loved and redeemed individually. I find myself at the heart and centre of His love and sacrifice, as a Bride does in her husband's love.

2. This Covenant relationship finds expression in regenerative grace

The objects of Christ's redeeming love were unresponsive and unloving. But a miracle happened that amounted to nothing less than a new creation – a new heart and a new spirit given. In other words redeeming love created responsive love, as the Church freely testifies; 'we love Him because He first loved us'. We said that the Bride was bride by the Bridegroom's choice. But we now say that she is bride by her own free choice. There are few verses in the Bible more meaningful for the Christian than the one that says 'He made them willing in a day of His power'. This power was conjugal grace and love in operation – and grace brings all the resources of God into contact with us at the point of our need.

It is of our own free will that she is now the Bride of Christ, and free will is will made free by the grace of the one who loves. And so the Church lays herself in all she is and hopes to be on the altar of His redeeming sacrifice – her response is complete and entire: the response of conjugal love.

It is significant that when Christ expresses His disappointment with His Church, it is in the realm of her love to Him. Think of His complaint against the Church at Ephesus. He commends the Ephesian Church for three qualities: her work, her labour, her patience, and yet she is found wanting at the heart and centre of her life. 'But I have this against thee, that thou hast left thy first love'. The Church at Ephesus toiled on, but she lacked her first enthusiasm, her bridal love had gone cold.

Of another Church, the Church of Laodicea, Christ complained that her love was luke-warm, and added: 'because thou art neither hot nor cold I will spue thee out of my mouth'. She made him sick – no emotion, no enthusiasm, no urgency, no passion in her love.

Thus a loveless Church is a grief to her lover and redeemer – her distinctive quality is gone – her response to His love.

3. This Covenant relationship finds expression in vocational loyalty

Christ's redeeming love to the Church has found recognition in a sense of vocation. Because she is His Church, sensitive to His love, she recognises her vocation: it is the call of His love to yield Him loving service. Her partnership with Him implies community of aims and interests. This is basic to marital partnership – both parties must have common aims and interests if they are to pull together, and if they do not pull together they will pull apart. There is no neutrality possible – not a case of each going his and her own way. That is not wedded life.

The Church is Christ's representative in the world. She bears His name, and she learns to understand His will for her. There is no mistaking of the direction in which she must go. His objectives are her objectives.

So we are workers together with Him – in a willing partnership. He is enthroned in glory, but we are the members of His body, and all our members – mind, heart, soul and strength – must be engaged in pursuing His interests.

This is the trust that He has committed to His Church, ere He left to heaven's scene. 'All power is given unto me in heaven and in earth, go ye into all the world, and preach the Gospel to every creature, teaching them to observe all things whatsoever I have commanded you, and lo! I am with you all the way'.

It is not easy to escape from this muster of all's – no way out, but perfect obedience.

The All of unlimited Power – our resources.

The All of unbounded endeavour – our field of service, all the world.

The All of unswerving obedience – our marching orders.

The All of unceasing Presence – the guarantee of our success, the unfailing partnership.

The Bride cannot opt out of that without destroying her marriage contract. He has given us His programme, and He expects of us loyalty and obedience. If once the Church steps aside from this manifestation of His will and purpose to serve her own interests, she can no longer claim His presence and support. From her He expects what He gave on her behalf – the loyalty that He gave to her complete salvation – the obedience that He gave even unto death to achieve it. This He expects from His Bride the Church – if He 'for the joy that was set before Him – her redemption – endured the Cross, despising the shame'. Ought she not to find her purest joy in going forth without the camp, bearing His reproach?

This may indeed resolve into a call to His Church to suffer for Him. There is a strange phrase of Paul's: 'that I may fill up that which is behind of the sufferings of Christ for His body's sake which is the Church'. The meaning would seem to be that Paul envisaged his own suffering in the proclamation of the Gospel as contributing to the building up of the Church: as Christ suffered unto death to redeem her, so Paul would fain believe that his sufferings in the Gospel would set an example that would upbuild the Church.

This labour is no servitude. It introduces us to the sphere of true Christian liberty. Paul and Silas were in chains in the inner stocks of the prison at Philippi, and they sang praises to God that compelled others in that prison to listen. It introduced a totally new spirit into suffering that compelled attention.

So it is that when many servants of Christ are persecuted and thrown into prison they have no sense of deprivation. For this see Paul's prison letters: they breathe the air of perfect liberty. In their loyalty to Christ they are able to surmount their bonds.

Thus the service of Christ introduces us to a spiritual liberty in which we can exercise all our faculties, all our gifts, all our resources – nothing lies unused. As the entire life is laid upon the altar of service we are drawn into the fellowship of Christ's sufferings – the Christ who once suffered for us, now suffers in us for the good of His body the Church.

This is the Christian vocation and we are less than Christian if we shun it. It was to Christian slaves that Paul opened up the opportunity of *adorning* the doctrine of God their Saviour in all things.

4. This Covenant relationship envisages the prospect of a final fulfilment

The marriage union in its true setting is the state of complete fulfilment for two lives. It is what God brought them together for and they come to recognise that some deeper purpose is being fulfilled in their union. In short, marriage has a definite end in view.

Similarly the Church is the fulfilment of Christ's purposes of grace and glory. In a way we cannot understand the Church is the fullness of Him that filleth all in all. That is to say, the Church is moving towards a state in which it can be seen as the Body of Christ – the Body of which He is the Head, the ruling and life-giving Head, and the Church is the fulfilment of all the Head plans and purposes: who puts into operation all His purposes towards the intelligent universe of which He is Supreme Ruler and Lord.

So the Church justifies her title – the Bride of Christ. In her as the Body of Christ the intelligent creations in Heaven have glimpses of the mind and heart of God never seen before, and never to be seen elsewhere. Redemption is the master stroke of Divine intelligence, the manifestation of God's nature and character as seen nowhere else. And the Church is that redemption completed, a glorious Body worthy of its glorious Head. How can we put this then as logical presentation? Is it something like this?

God had a purpose in the creation of man in His own image – a far-reaching purpose stretching beyond the natural creation – but that purpose would seem to have broken down in sin, rebellion, disobedience, that arrested and marred all.

But there appeared One to step into the breach – who was true man but more than man – and His errand was to take up that purpose of God and fulfil it completely. It carried Him by way of Bethlehem and Calvary to the Eternal Throne, and there will come a day when that purpose will be seen perfectly fulfilled in redeemed mankind – a new race, the Body of Christ, His Church. We have reason to believe that Christ's relation to his Church in incarnation, atonement and exaltation has some reference to the whole moral universe and not to mankind only. Paul tells us that it was the divine purpose that 'unto the principalities and powers in heavenly places might be known by the Church the manifold wisdom of God', or as the R. S.V. puts it 'that through the church the manifold wisdom of God might now be made known to the principalities and powers in the heavenly places' (Eph 3:10). That is to say it is a further declaration of God's glory in a unique and amazing fashion to the whole of His moral universe.

In that day the eternal purpose will be seen filled in full as He the Head will present His Church 'a glorious Church, not having spot or wrinkle, or any such thing; but that it should be holy and without blemish' (Eph 5:27). In that day the Bride will be seen as worthy of Her Bridegroom. And Christ will be admired, wondered at – in His saints (2 Thes.1:10). As the angel said to John 'Come hither, I will show thee the bride, the Lamb's wife'.

We know that in the here and now, when a poor pilgrim of earth becomes conscious of his sin and unworthiness and laments over his condition before God in groaning and tears, the angels reach for their harps and put it into music, for there is joy in the presence of the angels of God over one sinner that repents.

But when the Church sings her welcome safely home song, the angels listen in rapt amazement, for they cannot join in. The song is: 'Unto Him that loved us and washed us from our sins in His own blood, and has made us kings and priests unto God and His Father, to whom be glory and dominion for ever and ever. Amen'. (Rev. 1:5-6). They are not sharers in that redemptive experience personally, but they learn much from its glorious accomplishment. 'Which things the angels desire to look into'. (1 Pet. 1:12)

That is the Bride at home, the principal guest at the Marriage Supper of the Lamb. 'Blessed are they who shall sit down at the Marriage Supper of the Lamb' (Rev. 19:9).

LYDIA, THE MOTHER OF EUROPEAN CHRISTIANITY
(Acts 16:14-15)

This chapter contains the record of how Christianity first came to Europe. When at Pentecost the Gospel had burst through the barriers of Judaism, the disciples were carried on its outward surge to other nations and peoples. Three of them, Paul, Silas and Timothy, were guided west in the direction of Europe.

The guidance itself is interesting to us. Luke, who had joined the company at Troas, refers to it as 'assuredly gathering that the Lord had called us to preach the Gospel to them also': it was the gathering together of threads – several threads of different kinds and textures – to form a cord that pulled them towards Europe. These threads are now quite visible to us, and very interesting they are.

There was, first, the strange providence of closed doors. The small company of evangelists had left Palestine to go eastwards with the Gospel, perhaps towards the ancient and highly civilised nations of India and China. But we are told that their journey came under a sudden arrest: 'they were forbidden of the Holy Ghost,' says Luke, 'to preach the Gospel in Asia'. What exact form this took we do not know, but it was God's 'no' to their plans, and it had the effect of leading them to turn North, through Bithynia, towards the shores of the Black Sea. But there again the same hand of arrest was laid upon them: 'The Spirit suffered them not.' The road east and north having thus been denied to them, they turned west. This was the turn of the tide of Christianity westwards. What it was to mean to us in the west we can never estimate. Had it instead moved eastwards, we in Europe would have been left for long centuries under the blight of paganism, and the light of the Gospel might only now be coming to us from the distant east.

And so the small band journeyed west until they reached the sea, and when they could go no further they halted at Troas, the Troy of classical literature. From there they looked across the Aegean Sea to Europe and to the mountains of Macedonia, and waited for further guidance for their journey. It was then that the second thread was added to the cord that drew them west. It was in the form of a midnight vision. Paul saw in vision a figure, whom Luke calls 'a man of Macedonia', beckoning to them to come over and help them.It was the culture of ancient Greece, now corrupt and bankrupt, waving the flag of distress to Christianity. And the disciples, joined by Luke who was Paul's physician, were not slow to follow: 'immediately we endeavoured to go into Macedonia,' Luke says. In two days they landed at the port of Neapolis – the modern Kavalla – and headed for the city of Philippi, some ten miles inland, which was a Roman colony and so linked up with the trade routes of the far-flung Roman Empire. Paul, strategist and statesman that he was, saw the possibility that this opened up for spreading the Gospel along the trade routes of Europe. Their arrival at Philippi passed unnoticed: there was no deputation to welcome them, and stranger still, the Man of Macedonia, so urgently beckoning them to come, was nowhere to be seen: he had disappeared into thin air!

A similar occurrence, by the way, is still met with in the experience of many ministers of the Gospel. Congregations send them a call to come to them with the Gospel, and when they arrive the supporters are almost as thin on the ground as the Man of Macedonia was!

But the disciples felt that God's guidance could be trusted, and they waited in Philippi for further developments. In this way the third thread was to be woven into the cord. True, nobody in Philippi seemed anxious for a new religion: they had plenty religions of their own. Information, however, reached Paul that women – some of them Jews and some God-fearers from the Gentiles – were in the habit of having weekly meetings by the riverside for worship and spiritual fellowship. Paul decided that this was the open door they were waiting for, and on the Jewish Sabbath he took his small band out to the place of meeting by the river, and when he saw these pious women gathered together in worship of the Living God, I think he realised who the man of Macedonia really was: it was a band of spiritually minded women praying for light and hope and peace. That was in very truth the spirit that clothed itself in the Man of Macedonia of Paul's vision. And so the Gospel on the continent of Europe began in a sort of Mothers' Meeting, a foregleam of what the mothers of Europe were to mean in spreading and sustaining the Church of Jesus Christ in the ages to come. And the first convert on European soil was a woman, Lydia. Could it be that the Man of Macedonia was not a man at all: it was a woman, Lydia?

Since Lydia was the first European convert, the one who rocks the cradle of European Chritianity, may it not be that the manner of her conversion affords a pattern of what was to follow, a prototype of the millions of conversions in the continent of Europe, the first sheaf of a harvest that would be gathered in from the soil of Europe.

Let us look, then, first of all, at the nature of Lydia's conversion: 'whose heart the Lord opened:' a case of an opened heart.

Lydia was a person of some standing and a householder in Philippi. She was a woman of business interests who came to Greece from Thyatira in Asia Minor to carry on her business of selling purple, whether purple cloth or purple dye, or both, we cannot say.

She was not a Christian, but she was a woman of spiritual instincts and religious habits, a devout woman who needed religion to keep her soul from being swamped in material concerns. She was in the habit of consorting with other women, like-minded, to a place of prayer by a stream that runs through the outskirts of Philippi to this day. The flowing stream seemed to symbolise their longing for cleansing and refreshing, but it could not slake their inner thirst, it may only have accentuated it. It is said that those who are dying of physical thirst hear in their dying hours the murmur of running water, sometimes the noise of a waterfall, but it does nothing to slake the burning thirst within, it only intensifies it.

So Lydia was given to worship and outward ablutions and washings. But with it all her religion was external, on the outside of life. It involved prayer, worship, outward ceremonies for cleansing, doing certain things and not doing other things. It was sincere, but a mere habit rather than a satisfying possession or power in her life. So many religious people are in that condition.

But God was now to put religion at the heart and centre of her life. Only the religion that Paul brought could do that, for Christianity works from within outwards. It is Christ dwelling in the heart by faith, enthroned in the heart, controlling all feelings and emotions, unifying all scattered hopes and longings and aspirations, giving meaning and purpose to all the duties and devotions.

To be a Christian then meant that Christ must dwell within, a Living Presence within the heart, sweetening and cleansing all the streams of life. And that is what happened to Lydia at the riverside. The water that she now received to slake her thirst was to remain in her, a well of water springing up into everlasting life. Not external, but a hidden fountain within, independent of her surroundings, not merely satisfying her own thirst but causing to flow out of her life rivers of living waters.

That was to be Lydia's religion evermore, the religion of the open heart. And I believe that despite failings and declensions, the Christianity of Europe was, at its best, a religion of heart rather than of head.

Let us glance now at the Agent of her Conversion. There are two sides to every conversion, the divine and the human, God is in it and you are in it.

First, the divine side: 'whose heart the Lord opened.' So deep an experience is surely of God, for He alone can touch the springs of life and stir the human soul to its utmost depths. Throughout the Bible, God is constantly spoken of as the One who deals with the heart of man, and deals with it so radically that He can make it anew. Ezekiel the O. T. prophet presented this divine promise to the callous, hard-hearted, indifferent people of his own day. 'And' says God, 'I will give them one heart, and will put a new spirit within you. And I will take away the stony heart out of their flesh and I will give them an heart of flesh'. I suppose this is the first record of a heart transplant we have in all literature, and in the hands of the Supreme Surgeon it was a perfect success. The heart of stone, cold, unfeeling, unnatural, is excised, and a new heart of flesh, natural, sensitive, feeling, is given to make us what we ought to be, the men and women we ought to be.

Conversion, then, is a divine operation, deep-seated, radical, at the centre of life, the giving of another heart. This is truly of God.

But there is also the human side of conversion.

It is said of Lydia that 'she attended to the things that were spoken of Paul'. It could equally well be put that 'she applied to herself the things that were spoken of Paul'. From the human viewpoint that puts it in its right setting. Lydia applied to herself what Paul had told her about Christ and His salvation. As he spoke she found herself at the heart and centre of what he was saying. It isolated her from the crowd, took her apart, and spoke to her personally, as she sat by the riverside that day. What a difference it makes when we apply to ourselves the Gospel that is being presented to us, when we find ourselves at the heart and centre of God's love, God's mercy, God's salvation. It brings light to our understanding – a new sort of light that sheds its radiance within. It brings awakening to our conscience, and a conviction that grips us and refuses to let us go. It brings feeling to the heart in a love that is shed abroad by the Holy Ghost. And this finding ourselves where Paul found himself in his early Christian life when he spoke of 'the Son of God who loved me and gave himself for me' is the meaning of personal religion, and the will is won over to make us the free and willing bondslaves of the One who died to set us free.

This sort of conversion takes us over completely and all the centres of life – of thinking, of feeling, of willing – come under Christ's control and He raises His sceptre over the whole empire of our manhood and womanhood, till we cry: 'For me to live is Christ.'

That was Lydia's conversion, and by the grace of God it may be ours.

Let us give a last look at the evidence Lydia gave of her heart conversion, of the new spirit put within her.

Luke here tells us that 'when she was baptised and her household, she besought us saying: if ye have judged me to be faithful to the Lord, come into my house and abide there. And she constrained us'.

Lydia's conversion was followed by an act of public obedience: 'she was baptised and her household.' No half-measure about that, not when the Lord God gives a new heart and puts a right spirit within it. Her business instincts, even, told her that it must be all or none.

But Lydia was not the soft or merely sentimental type, even when her religion was a heart religion. There was a robustness about her character that called the disciples to pass judgment upon the reality of her religion: 'if ye have judged me to be faithful to the Lord.' She wanted to base her hospitality and service to the apostles, not merely on the sense of gratitude to them, but of fidelity to her newly-found Lord. It was to come from a higher source than that of mere gratitude to the messengers. It was for the Lord that she was offering her service.

And this found expression in the large-hearted hospitality she pressed upon them: 'Come into my house and abide there.' When the Lord opened Lydia's heart, she opened her house and made it a home for the messengers of Christ her Lord. And so it remained, I am sure, a haven of refuge in the heart of a heathen community for all who knew and loved her Lord.

And what a boon it was to the infant church at Philippi that there was one home, one woman, one loving heart, who could give shelter and sympathy and understanding love to those who were accepting Christ. As an infant needs a home and a mother if he is to survive, so the infant church at Philippi needed it and Lydia supplied it. And so she became the mother of European Christianity, the nursery of the young Christian life in a large commercial city.

This church at Philippi grew into a very large community, as the foundations of the early church which have been excavated have shown. This excavation suggests a building perhaps as large as St Paul's Cathedral. To that church Paul sent his warmest and most affectionate letter. Truly Lydia's love and care had not been in vain. It never is. Christianity will never die in a community as long as a home is found to nurse and shelter the young disciples of Christ in their midst.

Ere we leave the scene, we may note that the two first converts in European soil were taken from different strata of society, at different ends of the moral scale, Lydia and the Jailor of Philippi. How diverse in character, how different their conversion, as if to show that Christ suffered for all, none too good to need Him, none too bad to have Him.

But it does not end there. Lydia and the jailor soon meet in loving service. You remember that our last glimpse of the converted jailor is in the open courtyard of the jail, with a basin of water, washing the bruised feet of the disciples whom he had thrust in the inner stocks, and doing it with all the tenderness of a woman's hands. What a triumph of grace in Lydia's open heart and open home, and in the once harsh and callous jailor, now on bended knees washing the feet of the disciples of Jesus.

THE RIVER AND ITS SOURCE

Our Comfort in Troublous Times

The closing book of the New Testament consists largely of pictures, unveiled to the eye of prophecy, of 'the things which are and the things which shall be hereafter'. And these pictures have the quality which belong in our own times to aerial photography. Received on the lofty heights of prophetic vision, they share with those examples of aerial photography the qualities of a comprehensive survey, accurate proportion and true perspective. In other words they let us see things as they appear from the high altitudes of the spiritual world, showing us the forces that operate in human lives in their real importance and true proportions. Thus they correct our false emphasis and wrong perspective. There is appropriateness, we think, in the fact that, towards the close of his revelation, John should be given, as it were, a panoramic view of Heaven and earth, in which the great saving relationship of God with this world is strikingly portrayed. That great saving force that operates from God in the world below, here and elsewhere in the New Testament referred to as 'the water of life', is depicted by John as the most outstanding object in the expansive landscape of Heaven and earth, and is suggestively described as 'a pure river, clear as crystal, proceeding out of the throne of God and of the Lamb'. There are several things in this picturesque description of Gospel grace and blessing that call for special attention, for they reveal qualities of God's grace in the Gospel that can be seen and appreciated only from the high altitudes of the Heavenly world.

I

John's vision saw the grace of God in the Gospel as a River. A river is surely a natural thing in a landscape, and yet John was not accustomed to associate the blessings of the City of God with a river. The Jerusalem he knew had no such river running through its borders. True, it had a half-stagnant pool like Siloam, an intermittent fountain like Bethesda, an elaborate artificial construction like Solomon's aqueducts, and it had a poor puny stream like Kidron, turbid and polluted, but it had no river, certainly no 'river of living water', to bestow its manifold blessings upon its inhabitants. In sharp contrast with the badly watered earthly Jerusalem, the Heavenly Jerusalem had a River; not a half-stagnant pool but a living stream, not an intermittent fountain but a constant flow, not an artificial construction but something that fitted into its environment as naturally, as beautifully as a river always does. So, we learn, is the Grace of God that flows to this world in the Gospel of His Son. Though it comes from Heaven above, it is, as it were, perfectly at home in this world of men; though it is so supernatural, it is as perfectly natural as a river that is never out of place in its surroundings. And how manifold are the blessings it has brought to the world below! Where would Glasgow be without its Clyde, or London without its Thames, or Perth without its Tay? This is truly the River whose streams make glad the City of God, bringing the resources of Heaven to the impoverished, beleaguered children of earth. How splendidly detached a river may seem from the human turmoil and upheaval of the land through which it passes! How little is its course affected by the wars and rumours of wars that throw the stream of human life into disorder! It and the 'everlasting hills' from which it has its rise seem the abiding realities in the world of nature. It is said that when King Charles quarrelled with his Parliament, he threatened to remove his Court from London; at which one of his ministers replied: 'As long as your Majesty leaves us the Thames we shall not do so badly!' If London were shattered and levelled to the ground what of that? If the Thames were left, another London would rise on its banks as stately as the old. Similarly if the River of Divine Grace is left to us, another civilisation may rise on its banks more glorious than the old, and perhaps more worthy of God and His gracious purposes towards the world! The one hope of spiritual survival for the world is that it pleased God to send the flowing stream of His Grace to us as a River that is wholly independent of the ebb and flow of human fortunes. That is the channel of all our blessedness, and its continuance is the source of all our hope for ourselves and for the world.

II

John, from his vision, is able to give a description of the River as to its appearance and its quality. In appearance it was 'clear as crystal', or rather 'gleaming like crystal'. A placid river, sparkling in the noon-day sun, is ever a pleasing sight, but it must be particularly arresting in its beauty when seen from the skies. Such was John's impressiom of the River of Grace. And in quality it was equally excellent. for it was 'a pure river' or more correctly 'a river of pure water'. Purity scarcely belongs to any water, never to a river. Jerusalem had its Kidron, but how defiled it was! Glasgow has its Clyde but how polluted it has been! India has its so-called 'sacred' rivers, but they are shockingly unclean. The truth is that no river can, strictly speaking, be called pure. It is coloured by the soil through which it passes, or as frequently happens, polluted by the city through which it flows. Yet here was a River, beautiful in appearance, 'gleaming like crystal', and pure in the whole of its course. Such is the Grace of God in this world – fair and pure. As the flowing river reflects the light of the noon-day sun, so the grace of heaven reflects the glory of the God from whom it flows. Grace, even in its setting in this world, is beautiful, and God meant it to be attractive. It was so as it appeared in His Son Jesus Christ, and it is so, today, in the Gospel where 'as in a mirror'we behold the Glory of the Lord. From the heights of Heaven John saw its attractiveness, and we believe it is still among the things 'which the angels desire to look into'. And it is pure, and remains pure no matter what soil it passes through. It borrows nothing from its environment, and it owes nothing to its surroundings. Its stream flows through defilement and pollution unspeakable, but it gathers no contamination; it cleanses, but it does not itself become foul! So the Divine Life can be kept clean no matter under what conditions it may have to live. It is not a life for which the world is too strong, and which is sure to break down at some point or other in face of continued opposition. There was a 'Church of God' in Corinth, the foulest city of the ancient East – a clean stream flowing through that polluted city and gaining none of its pollution! And if God can keep that stream pure in such a polluted world, He can keep your life and mine clean in any surroundings. More, He can keep His own grace clean in our soiled and sinful lives, a pure river flowing through the swamps of our nature, and flowing out from our lives in all its purity into the lives of others! This is truly not the least comforting message of our text to those who may have reason to wonder if the grace of God can work savingly through them. It is a pure river, and remains pure no matter what it passes through! A River so natural in its setting is, beyond all question, supernatural in its cleansing efficacy and abiding purity. For this we thank God and take courage.

III

From the exalted heights to which he was lifted, John was privileged to do what even the most devoted admirer of nature is seldom privileged to do – follow the River to its Source. Even those intrepid explorers that have hazarded their lives to penetrate the great waterways of the world to their source, may have been disappointed at the insignificance of the trickling spring from which a great river took its rise. But John experienced no such disappointment! With holy awe and wonder he saw the veil lifted from the Heavenly Source of Gospel Grace and Blessing, and it was 'the Throne of God and of the Lamb'. That revelation gladdens our hearts and gives us new understanding and fresh confidence. God is behind this Gospel – *but it is God in Christ*. God's sovereignty is behind it, for it flows from His Throne, but His sovereignty is exercised through the Lamb. God's everlastingness is behind the Gospel, for it flows from the Rock of Ages, yet it is the Rock smitten and cleft in Calvary's sacrifice. God's almighty power is behind this message, but it is a sceptre that goes out of Zion and that takes its saving potency from the efficacy of the blood of the Cross. What light this throws upon much of the Gospel dispensation that may have been mysterious to us! How often we have wondered why this River should have chosen a course that took its cleansing stream to us ' Why, after having flowed East, did it turn West to Europe and America? To all these questionings of mind or heart there is but one answer, and it is perfectly satisfying: it flows from the Throne of God and of the Lamb! Or we may ask how it is that the Gospel stream has survived to this day. How has it not lost itself in the desert or dissipated its waters in the sands? Having cut its bed in the flinty rock, and gone through arid sands and marshy wastes, it comes to us out of the dark and barren centuries, and it flows on! Why is this? Because it has behind it the two abiding realities – God's Throne and God's sacrifice in His Son! That is the momentum wherewith it has reached us, and shall yet reach into the ends of the earth – it flows from the Eternal Throne through the Eternal Sacrifice! If we follow the River of Blessing to its source, there are few problems of the Christian life but will find solution, and our souls shall bow in adoring gratitude and wonder that our blessedness should have its rise in the Majesty and Mercy of God, in the Glory and Grace of the Lamb!

In troublous days when men are asking in dismay: 'If the foundations be destroyed, what can the righteous do?', let them find confidence where the Psalmist found it: 'The Lord is in His holy temple, the Lord's throne is in heaven.' And from that Throne comes the stream of Gospel Grace into His Temple below, and in its course and in its flow it is independent of human wisdom or strength and unaffected by human turmoil or strife. Let this be our comfort in troublous times.

THE INTOLERANCE OF THE CHRISTIAN WITNESS

Toleration is generally regarded as the hallmark of a mature and fully developed civilisation, the distinguishing feature of a culture that is both broad and deep. Christianity is, therefore, regarded as, *par excellence,* the religion of toleration, and any section of the professing Church that shows the slightest sign of intolerance, or that protests against practices and beliefs that seem to it inconsistent with a Christian profession, is regarded as having thereby put itself outside the pale. Frequently the Free Church of Scotland is constrained to raise a witness against disloyalty to the truth on the part of those who pay it lip homage, and to expose practices that undermine the purity enjoined upon the Church of Christ in its worship and discipline. In consequence it is often treated with suspicion, and at times with open hostility by those who profess to cherish a like precious faith. This is done in the name of the tolerance that is supposed to be the mark of genuine Christianity, and above all, in the name of the positive witness which is supposed to comprise the whole duty of the Church of God in the world. It is well, then, to examine these positions and find out if they are true to the New Testament witness and to the practice of the Apostolic Church.

I

Let us, first of all, investigate the claim that Christianity is supremely the religion of tolerance and that the civilisation built upon it must be marked by a broad tolerance in thought and life. With the New Testament open before us, it is very difficult to recognise this spirit of toleration as belonging in any true sense to the Church of Jesus Christ. On the contrary, it could be claimed that Christianity, judged on the human level, owed much of its potency and dynamic to its implacable intolerance. When it first entered the easy, indulgent, rotten world of its day, with its multitude of religions that suited every taste and indulged every vice, it came as a challenge to all the accepted values and standards of life and at once opened relentless war on all that would not measure up to God's full demand upon the mind, the heart, the soul, and the life of man. In this it thought it was truly interpreting the mind of its Lord, who declared that he came not to give peace but a sword. This intolerance was applied in the realm of conduct to distinguish between what was animated by the Spirit of Christ and what was governed by the spirit of the world, in the realm of thought to pose the two great opposites of truth and error; in the realm of loyalties to deal with the ultimates of love and hate, of acceptance and rejection, of fidelity and compromise. Thus the Church of Christ in its first impact on the world owed not a little of its vitality and its transforming power to its open and unrelenting intolerance of all that was not in accord with the mind of Christ, and its insistence that the whole empire of mind and heart and life be brought under the sovereignty of the Divine Lord. We cannot see that its vocation can have changed, or that its vitality and strength can derive from any other attitude to the world than that of a stern refusal to be 'called the son of Pharaoh's daughter'. If this be so, must we not recapture and reassert the intolerant note in the mission and message of the Church in order to present God's challenge to the unrighteousness and ungodliness of men?

II

In this context of toleration we are frequently told that, in the interests of harmony and peace, we must put dogmatism aside, cease to insist on denominational distinctions and recognise the contribution that every branch of the professing Church is making to the discovery of truth. To insist on our own 'insights' is inevitably to cause disharmony and division. Indeed, the placing of special emphasis on any distinctive doctrines of the faith is to be deprecated as tending to cleavage and disunity. Too precise a statement of belief is also to be discouraged as bringing to light disharmonies that had better be submerged. In this respect theology has to answer for a great deal as the greatest divisive factor in the ecclesiastical life. If thinking deeply on the verities of the faith is to underline differences, it is better not to think at all! In this spirit of mutual tolerance a common Creed, a clear statement of belief to which all must subscribe, is emphatically ruled out. Christianity must be expressed in terms of its lowest common denominator with other religions, and an assortment of vague generalities, capable of a multitude of interpretations, is to do service for the basic faith of the Church. When one comes face to face with the tragic consequences of this indifferentism in matters of faith, one realises somewhat more clearly why Paul was so insistent on holding fast 'the form of sound words', why he pledged his converts to fidelity to the precious deposit of truth he committed to them, why the Church was urged to 'contend for the faith once for all delivered unto the saints'. It was because its deposit of doctrinal truth constituted the foundation laid by prophets and apostles on which the Church of God was to be built. It was because this broad field of truth formed the soil out of which the Christian life was to derive its strength and substance. It was because 'the truth as it is in Jesus' was to light the steps of His pilgrim people till the Eternal Day should break upon them. To diminish this deposit by one jot or tittle was to pilfer God's truth and prove unfaithful to the Divine trust. To carve and pare this body of doctrine was to do injury to the living body of Christ which is His Church. There was, therefore, good cause why Paul should passionately urge his young disciple: 'O Timothy, keep that which is committed to thy trust, avoiding profane and vain babbling'.

III

It is in this spirit of toleration, too, that we are urged most frequently by our fellow evangelicals, to cease protesting against situations inside and outside the Church and be content with proclaiming the Gospel. This is what is termed a positive witness. Now, while every Church must have a positive witness if it is to disclose to the world the truths for which it stands, we cannot for a moment agree that its responsibility to the truth ends there. We have the example of the Master Himself and of His Apostles in their exposure and denunciation of error side by side with the proclamation of positive truth. Only in this way can our hearers be instructed to distinguish between the false and the true. Failure to do this, due largely to a spurious charity and fear of division, has led in the past to spiritual disaster and to the very divisions that we tried to shun. We have in mind, to give but one example, a certain youth organisation that we have been in contact with in Scotland which has been in recent days practically split from top to bottom, so that the patient upbuilding of several generations seemed in danger of being overthrown. This had been brought about by the admission into its membership of those who were not, as it turned out, in full sympathy with its doctrinal position. It is very clear to us now that this situation came about by the policy over a number of years of presenting 'a positive witness' only, and ignoring doctrines that were silently and subtly sapping the foundations of faith. That this policy was adopted in the interests of harmony and tolerance there can be no doubt, but in the end it proved more disruptive than the faithful exposure of false doctrine would have been. And yet many of its long-distance friends would have the Free Church today adopt the same policy which could not fail to have, in the long run, the same disastrous results. If Apostles, in declaring the whole counsel of God, shunned not to expose and condemn 'damnable heresies', no more must we if we are to inculcate in our members an intelligent and a vigilant faith that will stand in the day of testing.

Thus it is, that Christian intolerance, which applies the will of God to every situation in life, produces the conditions under which true liberty thrives, and a mere licence is not confused with freedom. And if the will of God is to be asserted and His law applied to human government and human conduct, we must give heed to the apostolic injunction: 'Reprove, rebuke, exhort, with all long-suffering and doctrine.' And this, by the will of God, we will continue to do.

THE PSALMS IN PUBLIC WORSHIP

The Book of Psalms is accepted by all Christians as the classic *par excellence,* even in the canon of Scripture, of the devotional life, but it has been all too common to give lip homage to the excellence of the psalms, and to lay them aside as not quite adequate to express the praises of the woshipping people of God in these latter days. For that reason it may not be out of place to consider here the claims of the book of Psalms to exclusive use as the hymn-book of the Christian Church. It is to be understood that we are here referring chiefly to congregational praise, such as was introduced into the public worship of God by our Reformers. In the centuries immediately preceding the Reformation there was practically no congregational song in the Church, apart from the choral singing of monks and nuns. The voice of the people was not heard in the worship of God till the Reformation stirred hearts and touched the springs of praise, and then the Reformers turned instinctively to the Psalms, prepared metrical translations in the language of the people, and encouraged the practice of congregational song. In this, as in many other reforms they were but going back to New Testament principles and to the practice of the Apostolic Church. That the Psalms held a place of honour in the early church may be seen in that of 283 quotations from the Old Testament that appear in the New Testament, not less than 116 are from the Book of Psalms. As we have already indicated, the Book of Psalms was the only hymn book of the early church, and the very fact that it alone of the books of the Old Testament has not its counterpart in the New, would seem to indicate that it not only belongs to both Testaments but that it was designed of God to be the hymn-book of the universal church. That being so it is only right that we should pass under review its claims to meet the spiritual needs of men universally, and its sufficiency to give expression to the praises of the pilgrim church of God in all the world and through all the ages.

I

The Psalms are pre-eminent in their unveiling of God as Creator of the ends of the earth, and the Covenant God of His people. The transcendent majesty of Jehovah and His immanent presence with His people are the two great thoughts that ring through the Book of

Psalms, giving to it height and depth that have not been paralleled by any other book of praise. Inasmuch as the Psalms call upon us to 'sing praise with understanding', so the glory of God, His nature, His character, His purpose, is proclaimed in the sublimest strains of inspired poetry that appeal to the intelligence and understanding of people of all climes and all ages. And God's government in the world is but the manifestation of His nature and character so that amidst earth's turmoil and sorrows we can give thanks 'upon every remembrance of His holiness'. Yet to the Hebrew psalmists God's omnipresence was as real as His omnipotence and, though His throne was above the flood, His presence was within the flood, restraining, guiding, over-ruling, comforting. How conscious they were of the shadow of His wings, the scrutiny of His eye, the sound of His footfall, the pressure of His hand all-comprehending, all-pervading, all-embracing! What comfort they found in the holiness of His character, the righteousness of His rule, the justice of His law, the tenderness and compassion of His grace, the certainty of His judgment! His holy character was the sheet-anchor of the universe and the haven of refuge of the weary and oppressed soul! How readily the Psalms come into their own in times of national peril, in hours of personal sorrow and perplexity, amidst the clamour of the world's hatreds and strife, because they reveal a God whose character is eternally relevant to man's deepest need and the unfolding of whose purpose gives meaning to the tangled skein of the world's history! Little wonder that men fall back upon them where there is anything serious on hand, for they fit into every human situation and present God as the answer to every human problem!

II

The Psalms are unrivalled, too, in their utter fidelity to man's true nature and condition. Elsewhere we may find a false optimism regarding man's inherent powers or an equally false pessimism regarding man's position in the universe and his final destiny. The Psalms harbour no illusions about man. They strike a note of realism that surveys man's position as a creature of God and a child of His purpose, yet a rebel and a sinner in the presence of His Maker. Man's dignity as 'made a little lower than the angels' is not allowed to obscure his position as a transgressor of the central law of His own being and in revolt against the law of his God. Man's sin is throughout related to God as a personal affront, an act of defiance, for which every man shall give account of himself unto God. It is this placing of sin in the light of God's presence that gives to the Psalms their peculiar insight into the nature of sin and the feelings of the penitent sinner that is absent from any merely human composition. What may be resplendent righteousness in the eyes of men can be folly of sin in the eyes of God. The man who can, with truth, say 'They that hate me without a cause are more than the hairs of my head ', can add in the next breath, with perfect consistency, 'O, God, thou knowest my folly, and my sin is not hid from thee'. Thus there is no grovelling subjection at the feet of man when there is abject prostration at the feet of God. Where else is the balance between man's dignity as a creature of God and his condition as a sinner before God so exquisitely preserved? Certainly nowhere outside the inspired volume. Thus the Psalms that foster reverence towards God foster humility and dependence in man.

III

The Psalms must be accorded a unique place in the praises of the church because of their portrayal of Christ as Redeemer and Lord. The objection has frequently been raised that the Psalms belong to the Old Testament dispensation and are therefore not adequate for expressing the praises of the New Testament church. Here it is apparently forgotten that the New Testament church throughout its entire course used only the Psalms in worship and apparently found no difficulty in reconciling them to the New dispensation. It is also forgotten that our Lord Himself not only used the Psalms in His private devotions, but made them His textbook both before His death and after His resurrection in instructing His followers in the mystery of His Person and work. It is not surprising, therefore, to find that the Apostles made similar use of them in their earliest preaching after the Resurrection. It is, therefore, obvious that the Old Testament Church and those who had known Christ intimately in the days of His flesh had no difficulty in recognising Him in the Book of Psalms. It is often pointed out that the Psalms have a serious inadequacy in that they, at least, merely pointed forward to the coming of Christ, while the New Testament outlook is that of realisation and fulfilment. This is to ignore the very significant fact that prophecy in the Psalms, as elsewhere in the Old Testament, had the vision of redemption as accomplished fact. The Psalmists, in words so graphic that they might in very reality be eye-witnesses, portrayed the humiliation, sufferings, death, resurrection and exaltation of Christ, and in almost every instance the matter was dealt with as history rather than as the mere fore-telling of events. The truth would seem to be that as the New Testament writers behold by faith the finished work and the living Lord, so the existence of a like faith, given the vision of revelation and the certitude of inspiration, enabled the Old Testament writers to behold the incarnation and redemption as events that had taken their place in world history as they already had their place in their own spiritual history. Thus it is that the Psalms view the Lord as having passed through the bitterness of death and risen triumphant over principalities and powers. And it cannot be forgotten that Christ in the days of His flesh sang the Psalms as expressive of His own inmost experiences, and gave fulfilment audibly on the Cross to many of their prophecies. In such a case, it was the Author singing His own songs, and singing them, need we add, with an understanding and significance that no other could give them! In truth, as we read the Psalms in the light of the Gospel narrative we come to realise how accurately and fully they represent the inner thought and heart of the Divine Sufferer, so that we can say that if the Four Gospels are His biography, the Psalms are His autobiography. For that reason no man can say that the Psalms do not constitute fit material for expressing the praises of the New Testament Church.

IV

One thing more remains to be said: it is that the Book of Psalms deals with the depth and variety of spiritual experience as no other hymn book does. It is with this in view that Calvin called the Psalms 'an anatomy of all parts of the soul', and Athanasius 'a mirror of the soul of everyone who sings them'. They do, indeed, seem to touch the spiritual experience of man at every point and give expression to the deepest yearnings and the loftiest hopes of the soul. Augustine states with profound emotion what the Psalms had been to him at the time of his conversion. 'How did I then', he said addressing God, 'converse with Thee when I read the Psalms of David – those songs full of faith, those accents which exclude all pride!. How did I address Thee in these Psalms, how did they kindle my love to Thee, how did they animate me, if possible, to read them to the whole world, as a protest against the pride of the human race? And yet, they *are* sung in the whole world', he adds, 'for nothing is hid from their heat'. It matters not what our experiences may be; we discover that they find adequate expression somewhere or other in the Psalms; it matters not where we may be, we find that the Psalmist has been there before us! In this, the Book of Psalms is absolutely unique.

We feel, therefore, that there are good and sufficient reasons why we should accept from the hands of the Church the hymn book that God's spirit has given to her, and in doing so we are confident that we may well exclude from the public sanctuary all the productions of men. They are, at their highest, but second best, a mere shallow stream that receives thoughts and aspirations that trickle into it from the ocean of the Divine Song Book. Indeed we agree with the saintly Hooker in asking: 'What is there necessary for man to know which the Psalms are not able to teach?'

THE TEMPLE AND ITS PILLARS
(Sidelights on the everlastingness of Service)
(Revelation 3:7-13)

Very much of the symbolism of the Book of Revelation is unintelligible to us until we understand the precise circumstances under which it was used or the local conditions that gave it point and meaning. For example, we learn that there was a practice in ancient Greece, and perhaps further afield, of adorning the heathen temples by pillars that were outstanding examples of the architectural art of that day. Furthermore, we know that many of these artistic columns were gifted to the temple by some wealthy citizen in honour of one of the great national figures of the day, and that the pillar sometimes took the form of a statue of the person in whose honour it was erected. The valour of some soldier, or the wisdom of some statesman, was thus fittingly acknowledged by the gift of a marble pillar of elaborate design to the temple of a favourite god or goddess. In such cases the donor was permitted to have his name and designation inscribed on the base of the column. But since popularity was as fickle in those days as in our own, it meant that great personalities rose and fell in popular esteem pretty much as they do now. And this, in turn, meant a reshuffling of pillars in the temple: the monument to the hero now discredited was taken away to make room for a statue of the man of the hour! We believe it is to this practice that the message to the Church of Philadelphia makes reference when it says: 'him that overcometh will I make a pillar in the temple of my God, and he shall no more go out; And I will write upon him the name of my God, and the name of the city of my God, which is new Jerusalem, which cometh down out of heaven from my God; and I will write upn him my new name.' Certainly in the light of the details above given, the message to the Philadelphian Church receives new point and takes on new significance.

I

The message indicates, first of all, the Place that is given to the faithful in the Temple of God. 'I will make him a pillar in the temple of my God,' is a statement into which we can read much regarding God's purpose and plan. Christ is the architect of His Father's spiritual Temple. He is building it in the power of His Holy Spirit, and He pays attention not only to its stability, but to its beauty and glory. While He quarries all the stones from the common rock of fallen human nature, and makes each of them fit for its appointed place in the building, He expends special pains on some who are to be pillars of strength and beauty in His Father's House. These receive more of the hammer and the chisel than the others, and come under the special skill of the Master Builder. And when His work in them is completed,they shall be worthy of His craftmanship and worthy of the place of eminence they receive in His Father's Temple, giving strength and beauty to the entire building, and co-ordination and unity to all its parts. And when God shall enter His Temple, each polished stone shall reflect His glory and each pillar shall show forth His image. In that day the whole intelligent universe shall gather round to worship God in His Temple, to behold His glory in His saints and admire Him in all them that believed. While that is the final prospect for the redeemed Church of God, it is well to bear in mind now that amidst the upheaval and turmoil of our day, the Builder, by many a strange providence, is still preparing pillars that He shall donate to his Father's House as special examples of His Divine workmanship.

II

We are next directed to the Promise that the message holds out to the saints at Philadelphia. Bearing in mind the frequent placing and displacing of pillars in earthly temples, we see at once the significance of this promise given by the divine Architect to those who shall be made pillars in the Heavenly Temple: 'And they shall go no more out.' This, we take it, refers not so much to their security but to the permanence of their labours. It is not 'the perseverance of the saints' we have here so much as the everlastingness of their service. Their place in the Temple of God is forever. Their spiritual function shall not cease, nor shall the value or effectiveness of their service ever diminish. It were easy to indicate the several respects in which this holds true. For example we believe the *labour of God's saints shall never lose its fruitfulness.* Their toil was the sowing of precious seed and the living grain will go on yielding its harvests long after the sower has gone to his rest and reward. What harvests are being reaped today from the labour of such saints of God as Paul, Augustine, Luther, Calvin, Knox, Chalmers, Spurgeon – they are the pillars in the spiritual temple and they shall go no more out! Or it may be made to mean that *the characters of the saints wll never lose their influence.* God has gifted to the church men and women noted for saintliness of character: Stephen, Polycarp, St Bernard, Madame Guyon, MacCheyne, Duncan. These, and characters like them, made deep impression on the world of their day, and the fragrance of their character lingers on centuries after they are gone. They are the everlasting possession of the world of Christ, pillars in the House of their God, and they should go no more out. We think, too, of men *whose example will never lose its inspiration*. These were men who were prompted by the Divine Spirit to break new ground, to leave the highway of life and go in to the byways, to gather in souls for Christ. These were men and women of Christian initiative and enterprise, such as George Muller of the Orphan Homes, William Booth of the Salvation Army, Elizabeth Fry of Prison Reform, Jerry McAuley of the back alleys of New York. They blazed the trail for thousands of others and we believe their life and labours will remain a source of inspiration to the very end of time. Our text suggests to us, too, that there were men and women in the Church of God *whose prayers will never lose their efficacy*. Christ's greatest gift to His church was perhaps the gift of great intercessors – men and women who wrestled with God in persevering, believing prayer. Their names cannot be mentioned, because they, for the most part, carried on their gracious ministry in secret; but the Church of God owes more to their prayers than it can tell. And we believe their prayers are still a living force around the throne, waiting a more abundant answer. Truly they, too, are pillars in the House of God and they shall go no more out. We thus see that everlastingness is written upon the lives and labours of the saints insofar as these contributed to the buildng of the Temple of God amongst men.

III

The message next directs us to the Privilege that is accorded the Donor of those pillars. As the donor of a pillar to the heathen temple was permitted to write his name and designation upon its base, so the Lord Jesus claims the privilege of writing upon the pillars He has gifted to His Father's House 'the name of my God, and the name of the City of my God, which is new Jerusalem which cometh down out of heaven from my God; and my new name'. We note that the privilege is of the highest order. He is permitted to write upon them the Name of His God. Higher He could not go. Their own names are sunk and forgotten in the new relationship that is theirs, a relationship so close that their lives are hid with Christ in God! The distinctive thing about them is that they were men and women of God and that God was not ashamed to be called their God. Furthermore, they are to be designated as belonging to the City of God, the new Jerusalem which cometh down out of Heaven from God. Their heavenly citizenship is thus acknowledged. While labouring with both hands for God's Kingdom in this world, they are colonists of Heaven who receive their instructions and inspiration from above. The saints to whom Paul wrote were both 'in Corinth' and 'in Christ Jesus', or as he elsewhere designates them, 'the saints in Christ Jesus who are at Philippi'. There you have, as some one has put it, their business address, and their home address! And there is reserved for the 'overcomers' of our text a further distinction: He writes upon them His 'own new name'. It is difficult to arrive at a definite conception of what that new name is meant to represent. We remember that when our Lord called His disciples to Him He gave each of them a new name, indicative of what they were by His grace to become. Simon He surnamed Peter, a Rock. And the new name, Peter, enshrined all that grace was to do in and by the fickle, impulsive, unsteady Simon! May it not well be that this distinction is in reserve for all the saints, and that he will give each of them His 'own new name' as a secret token of what grace has wrought for them and in them and through them! This would surely add to the glory of their redemption and to the perfection of their felicity.

IV

We now note the people for whom this distinction is reserved, and to whom this great promise is given: 'Him that overcometh.' This startles us by its unexpectedness; it is a designation that sets upon our own normal calculations a restraining influence. It cuts athwart many of our foolish notions regarding eminence in the Kingdom of Grace and of Glory. It holds out the highest distinction in the Father's House to those most conscious of their own weakness, whose life is a constant battle against the world, the flesh and the devil. That battle may be waged in obscurity, most often on the floor of their own hearts, and so hot is the conflict and so uneven the contest that they might well be tempted to give up the struggle. At times it does not seem worth while to carry on this interminable struggle any longer! But Christ here assures them that it is the only thing in the world that is worthwhile! To them is given the greatest promise of His Grace, and for them is reserved the highest distinction in his Kingdom of Glory. Let them continue the conflict till the Master Himself gives them honourable discharge and enables them to say 'I have fought a good fight, I have finished my course, I have kept the faith; henceforth there is laid up for me a crown of righteousness, which the Lord the righteous judge shall give me at that day; and not me only, but unto all them also that love His appearance'.

IN THE MIDST OF THE GOLDEN CANDLESTICKS

(A Study in Mutual Relations)

It used to be said that Luther was strong on the prepositions of the Bible. I suppose it was because they indicated those vital relationships that ensure the life of the soul. Most certainly the Church is maintained in life through those living relationships by which her worship and obedience ascend to God, and His grace and presence descend to her. Many of the well-known similitudes and figures of Scripture are designed to convey this vital truth, none more so than the arresting figure, familiar to the Revelation, of Christ walking in the midst of the seven golden candlesticks. Here is the perfect illustration of those mutual relations that ensure for the Church the life that is lived for God because it is lived in God.

I

It is significant that Christ, in addressing the seven churches of Asia, spoke of Himself as walking in the midst of the seven golden candlesticks. The figure contained those elements of admonition and comfort that wavering or disheartened Churches most needed. It conveyed to unfaithful Churches the warning that they were constantly under the Divine scrutiny, and that nothing could escape the searchlight of His eye, which was 'as a flame of fire'. Any flickering of light, any dimness of shining, any wavering of testimony, any concealment of truth, any coldness of love, was instantly observed and correctly judged by Him Who walked in their midst. The defects of their witness might for a time be concealed from the eyes of men, but He walked in the midst to examine and search out and assess the quality of their shining. No gardener ever looked with closer scrutiny at the flowers he had planted, or searched more anxiously for the fruit of his toil and skill than did He Who gave their place to these candlesticks and imparted to them their light. That is an aspect of the Real Presence of God with His Church that all of us, and especially those who look for it in a mechanical use of sacramental elements are very ready to forget.

Notwithstanding its searching nature, the similitude had its message of comfort. It was not an inactive scrutiny, a critical examination and nothing more. It was a *walk* of fellowship and grace in which He sought to replenish the diminishing oil and trim the flickering light. It may often be that an over-fondness blinds the eye to defects in those we love, but His perfect love can never be charged with this human infirmity. See Him walking in the midst of the golden candlesticks, and you may observe Him now and again bending earnestly over a candlestick, trimming its wick, refilling it with oil, and uplifting its light! He has taken upon Himself this responsibility of seeing that the lights are kept burning and clearly shining. He has not left the oversight of His Church and people to others, to eyes less kind or hands less skilled. Not only is His eye ever open to observe the first signs of flickering light, the first dimness in our shining, the first token that the secret oil of grace is running low, but His hand is ever ready to replenish and cleanse, to revive and restore. It is no small comfort to His people that he Who dwells in light inaccessible and paces the golden streets of the New Jerusalem, delights to walk in the midst of the seven golden candlesticks, to see reproduced in them the gold of the Heavenly City fashioned and burnished by His own hand, and to see them shine with heaven's light and transmit its uncreated rays! No small comfort, indeed, for it is their salvation and their security.

II

This illustration depicts, however, a dual relationship. He who walks in the midst of the seven golden candlesticks has something to get, because He has something to give. Not only has He lighted those candles, but He has seen fit to walk in their light and be seen in their illumination. 'Ye are my witnesses that I am God', He said to His people of old, and the witness of His Church is still His chosen way of making Himself known to a world that lies in the darkness of ignorance and unbelief. That He should have made Himself thus dependent upon the fidelity of His Church is one of the mysteries of His grace that never ceases to surprise, and at times to appal, His people. Their infidelity to this sacred trust is an obscuring of Him! The decaying love of Ephesus, the heresies of Pergamos and Thyatira, the deadness of Sardis, the self-complacence of Laodicea, were not only unbecoming and wrong in themselves, they were hurtful to Him in that they obscured the light in which He chose to reveal Himself. As the vine is dependent upon the branches for its fruits, so the Lord is dependent upon His people for the revelation of His grace.

But the Lord's relationship to His people has in it this further fact – that He *walks* in the midst of the golden candlesticks. Not only does

He unveil the reality and grace of His nature and character in the faithful witness of His Church, but He also reveals His walk, the path of His sovereign will. While it may be true that God's ways are often in the dark and His footprints may not be discerned by the wisdom of men, yet it is equally true that the witness of His Church sheds light upon the ways of God, both in Providence and Grace, so clear that He who runs may read. To study God's dealings with the Church throughout the ages is to be able to see His walk – the path on which His sovereign will is being executed, the highway of His eternal purposes. God's *walk,* both in Providence and in Grace, is illumined by the corporate witness of His Church, and the pages of her history in the world is but the unfolding of His mind and purposes.

Thus it is that God, in the condescension of His grace, has made the knowledge of Himself and His ways dependent upon the witness of His people. And the Church is fulfilling her mission in the world only in the measure in which she reveals God and justifies His ways to men. And in the fulfilment of that purpose the Church is most truly one. He who walked in the midst of the seven golden candlesticks gave unity to their light, inasmuch as they all revealed Him. The scattered churches of Asia Minor separated by distance and differing development, formed a unity in their testimony to Him. In so far as their light was focussed on Him and served to reveal His character and His will, they were most vitally one. Herein is the real unity of the Church: not a unity of organisation, or of method, or of order, but of witness to Him. There may be seven or seventy Christian Churches, but there is only one Christ seen in their combined light. If it has pleased God to scatter His Church and make her light shine through different branches and denominations, we know that it is His will that the world should see in the combined light 'no man save Jesus only'.

Knowing, therefore, that He who walketh in the midst of the seven golden candlesticks has a purpose of mercy concerning us, let us give the more heed to the admonition: 'Let your light so shine before men that they may see your good works and glorify your Father which is in heaven'. The privileges of grace contain at their heart the responsibilities of faith. If we are 'a chosen generation, a royal priesthood, an holy nation, a peculiar people' it is that we may 'show forth the praises of Him Who has called us out of darkness into His marvellous light'.

THE CHRISTIAN HOPE FOR HUMANITY

(A Bible Study of Man as he Was, Is, and Shall Be)

It has been said long ago that man is the proper study of man, a saying to which we would give unqualified consent were there no Revelation of God given to man for his contemplation. But, next to the study of God, man should take pains to study himself. For this the Bible is the best textbook, because it shows man as he really is – man at his best and man at his worst; sometimes, man at his best apart from God, and man at his worst with God. And truly no study seems more necessary at the present day, when we are being stung into consciousness that all is not well with man. We have a new awareness that man at his strongest apart from God is poor, weak and helpless, a misguided creature bent on his own destruction, a prey to forces within and around that plan his overthrow. It is easy in days of disillusionment to give way to despair concerning humanity, just as in days of ease we may have betrayed an inordinate pride and confidence in human progress and enlightenment. The Bible alone can correct both this facile optimism and despairing pessimism, because the Bible alone faces up to the facts of man's Fall and Redemption, man's failure and triumph, man's bankruptcy in self and the resources available to him in Jesus Christ, his Saviour. No passage in the Bible puts this complete aspect of man's birthright, man's failure, and man's glorious destiny more clearly than that striking passage in the Epistle to the Hebrews chapter 1, where the writer refers to the unfolding glory of man in the eighth Psalm, and exclaims: 'Thou hast put all things in subjection under his feet — But now we see not yet all things put under him. But we see Jesus who was made a little lower than the angels for the suffering of death, crowned with glory and honour; that he, by the grace of God, should taste death for every man'. There we have a three-fold presentation of man's condition: man as he ought to be; man as he is now is; and man as he, by the grace of God, can be. These deal in turn with man in God's creative purpose, man in his own sin, and man in the recreative grace of the Lord Jesus Christ. Only the inspired Word of God could give us this comprehensive view of man's history and man's destiny, and it is only in the light of that revelation that we can study man without facile optimism or dark despair. For it is in that revelation alone that man appears in the hopefulness of the grace of God bestowed upon us in Jesus Christ, His Son.

I

This arresting passage directs us, first of all, to a study of man as *he ought to be,* and as he was in that purpose of God brought to light in the creation of a soul in His own moral and spiritual image. 'Thou madest him a little lower than the angels; thou crownedst him with glory and honour, and didst set him over the work of thy hands.' The natural consequence of this moral glory was man's investiture with material authority: 'Thou hast put all things in subjection under his feet'. It was the dominion of Reason over Instinct. Man bore this resemblance to God that he was created a rational being, endowed with intelligence, and possessing a mind that was cognate to the Divine Mind. The animal creation, on the other hand, was given the guidance, not of reason but of instinct: it was blind guidance, merely, that drove it irresistibly on along the way of self-preservation and self-propagation. How high is reason above mere instinct! So lofty is man's dominion over the animal creation! But we must not forget that it was the dominion of Conscience over Will and Desire, since man was created a moral being with power to reflect on his action and to test whether his conduct was right or wrong. The animals have no such controlling voice within, no court of appeal to which they can bring their actions for approval or disapproval. Their wills follow the line of desire and gratification. Let us remember that it was conscience, as God's representative within the soul of man, that elevated him to his place of authority. In a word, it was the dominion of Spirit over Flesh. This was the distinguishing mark about man – God breathed into his nostrils the breath of life, and he became a living soul. Thus it is that, though in the composition of his physical frame he has kinship with the animal creation, in his spiritual nature he has kinship with God. And as spirit has dominion over matter, so man as a spiritual being was fitted to have 'all things in subjection under his feet'. How readily man forgets that he derives his authority over nature from his spiritual being – from the spiritual qualities that we designate Reason, Conscience, Soul! God would not have us forget this, lest we desecrate this inner shrine and fall to the level of the animals that perish.

II

Our text encourages us to consider *man as he now is*. Alas! It is a tale of failure, and frustrated endeavour, and unfulfilled promise on man's part. In spite of the fact that man's Creator 'left nothing that is not put under him', the reality is that 'We see not yet all things put under him'. This fact is as self-evident to-day, after the passage of the centuries, as when the writer to the Hebrews told it forth. There are still many 'things' that do not accept man's dominion, because man has broken the central law of his creation. It is because man is a sinful being that his dominion is imperfect and incomplete.

It were easy to point out the incompleteness of man's dominion. For example, the *forces of nature* are not yet under him. Sin has broken man's authority over nature. Though it be true that we have got nature to unlock many of its secrets, and we are able to harness the wind and bridle the flood, yet man's utter helplessness when brought face to face with many of the forces of nature is more impressive than his authority to curb them! Man is dethroned from his place of dominion, and too often his weakness and ignorance make him the helpless victim of those mysterious forces he was meant to dominate and control.

Then there are the *forces of disease*. Here his failure to obtain dominion has been as spectacular as his successes. Sin has broken man's fellowship with God, and, out of touch with the fountain of life and healing, man has become a prey to disease and pain and death. The stream of spiritual life that should flow to maintain him in perfect health of body and spirit has been arrested by sin, and the gates have been opened to all manner of disease. And as long as these vast armies remain uncontrolled we must agree that 'all things are not yet put under him'.

Most striking of all, the *forces of evil* are not yet put under man. It is in this realm that he must register his direst failures. His spirit, that was to exercise authority and control, has been maimed, fettered and degraded by sin. And the result for man has been impotence and failure within and without. Dark forces within his own breast make of him their prey. He is caught in the grip of passions and hatreds and jealousies and evil desires that are too strong for him, and his spiritual nature is brought into bonds, dethroned and debased. And his impotence to control the forces of evil in the world around him is but the reflection of his failure to control the same forces within his own breast. It requires no words to underline and enforce this truth in calamitous days. When war and passion and hate threaten the utter ruin of humanity, we readily agree that all things are not yet put under man's dominion. The testimony of Scripture is, here at least, amply verified in man's own sad experience.

III

The object of our text, however, is not merely to remind man of what he was in God's creative purpose, or what he is in his own sinfulness, but rather *what he may become* through the regenerating power of the Lord Jesus. How swiftly and majestically the text swings from what man is to what Christ is! 'But' – and the *buts* of the Bible are often hinges by which we swing from feeble self to Almighty God – 'but we see Jesus who was made a little lower than the angels for the suffering of death, crowned with glory and honour; that he, by the grace of God should taste death for every man'. When we see Jesus thus, we see in Him what man by grace can become! In Christ we see man *rescued.* He – man's Saviour and Deliverer – was 'made a little lower than the angels', and in thus descending to our weakness, He took hold of our broken humanity, and in laying hold of it, He rescued it from its fallen and debased condition. In the mystery of the Incarnation there is much we do not understand, but there is in it the fact that is the foundation of our hope for fallen humanity, that God took our nature into such intimate relationship to His own that they became indissolubly bound in One Person, and *that* the Divine Person of the God-man, Christ Jesus. In this act of condescension fallen man was finally and effectively rescued.

In Jesus we see man *redeemed.* The Son of God stooped to assume human nature 'for the suffering of death', in order that 'He, by the grace of God, should taste death for every man'. Whatever else that may mean – and it means so much more than we can comprehend – it surely means that when Christ died He tasted in that one cup all the ingredients that can enter into your death or mine. And His purpose in thus tasting death was clearly redemptive – it was FOR man: a death that redeemed man from the curse and guilt of sin as it had rescued him from its blight and power.

In Jesus we see man *enthroned.* When we see Jesus 'crowned with glory and honour', we see in Him man's forerunner, the earnest and pledge of man's exaltation and enthronement. Man, rescued and redeemed, has thus his enthronement pledged to him by the ascension of his Kinsman and Redeemer to the place of centrality on Heaven's Throne. To see Jesus 'crowned with glory and honour' is to see man an heir of glory yet to be revealed, man exalted far beyond his dignity in creation, man made by grace an heir of God and joint-heir with Christ.

What other antidote can there be to a baseless optimism or an overwhelming despair? Are we disposed to pride ourselves on man's attainments? 'We see not yet all things put under him.' Are we ready, as we may reasonably be in days of brutality and suffering, to despair of man's future? 'We see Jesus crowned with glory and honour' and in Him we see man rescued, redeemed, enthroned! This is the Christian Hope for humanity, and we rejoice that its anchor is within the veil!

IS THE BIBLE THE WORD OF GOD?

This raises a question of vital importance to every one of us. For if God speaks anywhere it is of supreme importance that we should hear and understand what He says. And apart from the Bible there is no word of God that we can adequately hear or understand. It is true that God speaks elsewhere – in Nature, in Providence, in the moral consciousness of man – but it is often so faint an echo that we are not always able to interpret its meaning or its relevance to us. In the Bible God addresses us in human speech and through human personality, so that His word makes direct contact with us and makes an immediate appeal to our understanding and our moral consciousness. For that reason we claim that the Bible is the source of our religion, since all we know of God – of His nature and character and purposes – we learn from the Bible. But we don't, for that reason, make the Bible our God or the object of our faith. We are not Bible-worshippers, even though we accept the testimony of the Bible and are dependent upon it to know God and His purpose for us. Our question 'Is the Bible the Word of God?', assumes, therefore, vital importance, and it is right that we ask it and press for an intelligible answer.

The Word as Revelation

It is well to ask ourselves, first of all, what we mean by the Word of God. On the purely human plane it is very simply answered. A word is the expression in speech of a thought in the mind and is therefore a vehicle of communication between mind and mind. As far as the individual speaking is concerned, words are his means of self-disclosure and contain, more or less adequately, a revelation of his thoughts and feelings and will. In like manner it can be said that a word of God is His self-disclosure and that His words may be expected to be an adequate revelation of His mind and heart and will. Now it is this revelation that is behind the Word of God in the Bible. Self-revelation is a quality of the Divine Being, and it is as natural for God to reveal Himself as it is for the sun to shine. And as the sun in shining imparts its light and warmth and energy, so God communicates Himself in His self-disclosure. But we are not, therefore, to conclude that it was necessary for God to reveal and communicate Himself to us, and certainly there was no such necessity in our case when we had fallen from God by rebellion and becme enemies in our minds by wicked works. The fact remains, however, that God was pleased to give a revelation of Himself to mankind and that He willed that it should, for the most part, come to us through human personalities whom He had selected and prepared both to receive it and to transmit it. There were three ways in which the special revelation of God might be given, in the spoken word, in the written word, and in symbolic action, and of these the spoken word is by far the most common. The written word was employed in the giving of the moral law at Sinai, symbolic action was frequently employed and this took the form not only of natural events but also of events in which God broke through the natural order and spoke through miraculous occurrences. The spoken word by which God made His voice heard and understood in the inner consciousness of man whom He had called to this office was God's normal way of communicating His mind and will to the world.

Revelation Recorded in Scripture

The Bible as Divine revelation contains the three forms we have mentioned. It contains a transcript of the written word, a reproduction of the enacted deed, and a record of the spoken word, all three combined constituting the revelation that God saw fit to communicate to men. Since it was God's will that this special revelation should have finality and bear a deep relevance to the needs of man everywhere, He caused a record of it to be made, both to perpetuate it and to make it communicable to all men and all ages. As this revelation took place in human history, it had at each stage a special relevance to the age to which it was given, and was therefore in its unfolding progressive. This has several implications that it is well for us to face. Basically it means that the Word of God to each generation to which it was given was in very truth the word of God to that generation. While it often contained truth that looked forward to coming generations in the form of the prediction of events yet to come, it nevertheless had, even in the case of prediction, the effect of pressing home the truth, by way of warning or encouragement, for the age to which it was given. It means, moreover, that God generally 'accommodated' His revelation to the level of perception of the people to whom it was given. His word to Israel at each stage of its history was the word best suited to Israel's situation. This 'accommodation' does not imply, however, that the truth at any stage was compromised, or that the word given at one stage had to be amended or corrected at a later date. Though the revelation was not full as to its extent, it was perfect as to its nature, and the truth communicated at each stage became a stable foundation for the further truth that was to follow. To outgrow the alphabet or the multiplication table is not to say that these are discarded; rather do they become the foundation of all further literary or mathematical studies. Thus the light of revelation was growing, though not, it is true, without periods of eclipse, and it reached its meridian splendour in Him who is for all time the Word of God. It was meet that the truth should reach finality in Him who is indeed the very centre of history and the contemporary of every age, who in the things of the spirit is the Way, the Truth and the Life. This does not imply that Christ came to revise, far less to correct, the truth already given. He was conscious Himself of having come not to destroy the Law but to fulfil it, and His whole life and teaching clearly indicate that He was putting spirit into the letter of the revelation and giving substance to its shadows. So the way of revelation, that had passed from stage to stage in the course of the centuries, had as its destination Jesus Christ. And when He came He took His hearers back to where the Old Testament had left them, and it is impossible to understand His message till we understand the Old Testament that coloured His thought and speech. That revelation, then, in its historical and progressive unfolding, is recorded for us in the Scriptures.

The Scriptures the Word of God

Do the Scriptures, therefore, claim to be the Word of God?

They certainly claim to *contain* the Word of God. When we bear in mind that God has spoken elsewhere than in the Scriptures, we have to be clear on how much we are to understand here by the Word of God. There is a Word of God that is special and unique because it contains that revelation of Himself that is needed by sinful men if they are to be saved. The Bible contains, undoubtedly, that word of God which is necessary for salvation and which is found nowhere else. But the Bible also reproduces the revelation that God gave of Himself in other ways, such as creation and providence, and reproduces it in such a way as to remove its distortions and give it a new clarity. For that reason the Bible contains history, politics, social customs, natural philosophy and much that is the product of personal research and historical study. It is true that all this is given from a new angle – the viewpoint of Scripture – but it is nevertheless true that in a general way God has republished in the Scriptures the truths of natural revelation and cleared them of misconceptions. So the natural and the supernatural, the general and the special forms of revelation, are found side by side in the Scriptures. For that reason we say that the Scriptures *contain* specifically the Word that is able to make us wise unto salvation.

But we also affirm that the Scriptures claim to be the Word of God as well as to contain it. This claim means that though the Bible contains what is special and unique revelation from God, and what is natural revelation republished and restored to its original purity, the two forms of revelation reveal but the one God and therefore constitute but the one revelation. Thus the special revelation and the natural revelation in which it has its setting go together and constitute God's saving revelation of Himself to us. The entire Book is one consistent revelation of the God of Redemption, and therefore all its parts stand or fall together.

It is customary nowadays to speak of the special revelation and its natural setting under the figure of a child in the cradle, and the argument is then applied: What though the cradle be ageworn, decrepit and motheaten, it is the child that matters! In this way all in the Bible that may not be regarded as partaking of special revelation – such as its record of creation, its history, its biography – can be disposed of as outworn and outmoded, leaving the Divine revelation intact. We can only reply that a cradle so decrepit and outworn is a strange resting place for a Child on whom the destiny of millions of men depend, and that in any case after the passage of so many years the bottom must have gone out of it and the child is surely by this time fallen out, that, in fact, we are left now only with a handful of sawdust! In other words, truth in a setting of falsehood, of superstition and forgery is unworthy of the God of Truth, and is to a reverent mind unthinkable. Thus we conclude that the contents of Scripture, whether natural or supernatural in nature and scope, are alike of God and constitute His word to the children of men.

The Scriptures and Inspiration

The implication of all this is that the Bible claims to be the Word of God in the words of God. This involves inspiration.

What is inspiration? The word itself is scarcely used in the Bible, though the idea underlying it is everywhere. Nor need we expect a definition of inspiration there, since the Bible is not a scientific textbook whose affirmations are definable and provable by the scientific method. Its appeal is rather to experience and to the moral and spiritual consciousness of spiritually-enlightened men and women. The classic passage on inspiration is in 2 Timothy 3:16 where we have the statement: 'All Scripture is given by inspiration and is profitable....', the Greek construction having the force of 'all Scripture seeing it is given by inspiration of God, is profitable....'. Even in this translation there is the difficulty that the very word 'inspiration' suggests an operation of *inbreathing* which is not supported by the original text. When Paul here claims that all Scripture is 'God-breathed' he employs the figure of the forthputting of the creative breath of God as in the original creation of the world. This would suggest that the Scriptures are the product of the creative breath of God just as the material creation has been, and that the God whose breath brought the first creation into existence as a manifestation of Himself has also wrought this second creation as a higher and fuller revelation of His nature and character.

On the mode of inspiration, Scripture is largely silent, and it is profitless to speculate. The passage in 2 Peter 1:21 is the most adequate explanation given to us; it says that 'the prophecy came in old times not by the will of man, but holy men of God spake as they were moved by the Holy Ghost'. Here the operative word is 'moved' and it means 'carried along as by the wind'. The verse gives us the human and the Divine side of the Scriptures. 'Holy men of God spake;' of this there can be no doubt, for they left the imprint of their character and training and personality upon the writings. But the action behind their writing was Divine, for they were borne along by the wind of the Spirit, sometimes a gentle breath, sometimes a veritable hurricane. but always a wind in which they breathed as freely as a bird in the air, carrying them to a destination that was Divine. Thus there was nothing forced or mechanical about the operation, as if they were robots instead of men, nothing in the way of mere dictation, though God could have employed this method of communicating His will had He so ordered it. As it is, God made use of differences in personality, in temperament, in training, culture and experience, to make men the kind of messengers that He needed for the purposes which He had in view. If it had been writing to mere dictation, a child could have done it, yet we can safely conclude that no child could have written, say, the Epistle to the Romans! How that Epistle could be at one and the same time the words of Paul and the Word of God we cannot understand, though Paul himself was fully conscious of the fact.

As to the extent of inspiration, the passage before us clearly teaches that inspiration extends to 'all Scripture'. Thus there are not degrees of inspiration, though, of course, there are degrees of usefulness and of profit to be derived from the inspired record.

The Authority of the Scriptures

It remains to be discussed how the Bible proves its authority as the Word of God. Authority can be judged by the historical test, the moral test or the spiritual test. Under the *historical* test the Scriptures have authority as giving truth in the realm of history. The historical facts of the Bible are subject to the same tests as secular history, and under the most scientific scrutiny Bible history has authority unsurpassed by any section of secular history. This is even more remarkable where the Bible gives history in advance in the form of prediction, whose fulfilment has already, in many cases, passed into the experience of men as history.

There is the *moral test* by which the Bible reveals its authority as giving truth in the realm of conduct, directing men from the paths of iniquity into the paths of righteousness, and becoming a discerner of the thoughts and intents of the heart.

There is supremely the *spiritual test*, under which the Bible reveals its authority in the realm of faith. Only to faith does the Bible reveal its treasures, and only by faith can its full authority in men's hearts and consciences be felt. The man who is willing to spend an hour with the Bible investigating what it has to say about his sin and his destiny will not fail to feel its authority, as the Spirit in the Bible speaks to his spirit and reveals to him the will of God for his salvation. For this reason the uneducated man, even the illiterate, may know assuredly that this is the Word of God, when the scholar and the savant may not attain to any such conviction. To make scholarly research and scientific investigation the basis of spiritual conviction would be to introduce into the spiritual life a tyranny that would fetter and degrade the spirit of man. 'The heart knows a reason which reason does not know' is a saying of Pascal's which is applicable to the Bible and its authority over the souls of men. Thus to attempt to prove the testimony of God by the testimony of man is completely to upset the Divine order. In the sphere of faith the Spirit witnesses with our spirits that this is the Word of God and that it is the final authority for our spiritual beings.

THE BIBLE AND THE NATION

Our theme here is the Bible and the Nation. Since it is perhaps, more comprehensive than the other themes of Bible Week, we can perhaps take toll of them all in placing the Bible securely at the heart of the Nation's policies, life, culture and hope.

The Bible has a message for the Nation as it has for individuals. It is a guide to human living, to character and conduct, and it offers its guidance to individuals, tribes, churches, nations. It brings the nation to its bar of judgment and it offers the nation its only hope of healing and survival. 'I will heal their land' is God's promise in the Book, and a land can be sick: politically sick, economically sick, socially sick, morally and spiritually sick; and its disease can sap its energies, frustrate its efforts, and drag it down in inertia, lassitude, ruin.

There are symptoms today that our nation is sick: the will to work is paralysed, the vision of spiritual ideals is lost, the sense of God is gone.

How can the nation be healed and restored? We think there is only one way back: it is back to the Bible. Queen Victoria was not far from the heart of things when she described the Bible as the secret of England's greatness. We believe ardently that the Bible is the source of national greatness.

Why is this so? Can we give a reason for this faith that is in us concerning the Old Book? What is the Bible's relevance to the Nation?

1. The Bible is the Supreme Judge of All State Policies

We are not concerned here with politics: but we are anxiously concerned with *policies.*

More, God is concerned with the policies of the Nation, and the Bible makes it clear that in the matter of State Policy 'righteousness exalteth a nation, while sin is a reproach to any people'.

The Bible has this valuable thing about it: that its outlook is supra-national. It has a world outlook and places all the nations in the majestic pattern of God's creation and providence. It relates to the Eternal Throne, man to His Maker, and every soul to the Judgment Seat of God.

Thus the Bible places the Nation in the setting of history. It is unique in its capacity to set the nations of the world in the larger pattern of history.

And the Bible deals with all history as the unfolding of God's plan. That is the meaning of history, and the Bible alone gives the religious view of history – God's view. It is the unfolding of God's redemptive plan, and the Bible sets the redemptive purpose of God within the living stream of world history.

And the Bible indicates that the Nation that does not fit in with God's plan must perish. The nation that does not serve the voice of God is disowned and thrust into dust.

The Bible thus shows very clearly that God takes to do with Nations, that He judges, rewards and punishes nations here in time. Many of the most pungent words of warning uttered by the Prophets of old were given to Nations, and many of the most solemn denunciations pronounced by God were to Nations. To more than one Nation has God said 'I will put my hook in thy nose, and my bridle in thy lips'. The prophets taught that the very sufferings that came on the nation came from the righteous hand of God whose hatred of sin is such that He will severely punish His own people that offend and will rather have them vanquished by their godless foes than aid them in a wrong cause.

The Nations were under physical laws: they were also under moral law: as they sowed, so would they reap. The Bible's solemn woes were pronounced in turn upon Edom, Sidon, Egypt, Assyria, Babylon, and God had many messengers of destruction at His behest. Yesterday it was disease, famine, drought; tomorrow it will be atomic bombs. The prophet Nahum warned his day that 'the Lord has his way in the whirlwind', and in the name of God he said to Nineveh, the largest city of the ancient world, – four times the size of modern London – 'I will make thy grave, for thou art vile'. In 606 B.C. Nineveh was sacked and overthrown and levelled to the ground. It is now a rubble heap.

It can happen still, for there are no favourites with God. One by one the giant nations of the ancient world – Babylonian, Persian, Grecian,

Roman – were weighed in the balances and found wanting. *Our* nation today needs the reminder that Daniel gave to Nebuchadnezzar, the tyrant and dictator of the world of his day, 'But know, O King, that there is a God in Heaven'.

Thus the policies of the Nation must come under the scrutiny of God's Word. You cannot have one ethic for the individual and another for the Nation. What is wrong for the individual is much more so for the nation. So we who are Christians must bend every energy to bring the policies of the nation into line with the revealed will of God, to mould the machinery and policy of the nation to reflect the will of God and serve His purpose.

For ourselves we need it as the only means of survival – the forces preying upon us, communism, stark paganism, are spiritual and malignant.

For the sake of others we need it – moral leadership is needed among the nations of the world as perhaps never before. If we provide that leadership, I believe we shall stand and prosper. If we fail in this day of opportunity, we shall crumble into dust as others have done. Bible history and secular history alike show clearly that God casts off nations because of moral decay and spiritual apostasy. The Bible's message is relevant to the Nation today: it strikes a note of warning: let us not presume upon the favour of Heaven: we may be cast off. It was within the purpose of God to permit a national disaster, such as the captivity, to befall Israel with a view to their purification by such painful disasters, and to the strengthening of their moral and spiritual fibre.

2. But there is another way in which the Bible brings its message to bear upon the Nation: it brings the challenge of God to Society: it demands social righteousness.

The Bible is the *Touchstone of Social Morality*. What after all is the Nation, but the people that make it up! A nation cannot rise higher than its people, for a nation is what its people make it. The State of itself is unable to preserve order or promote justice – unless order and justice are established in the hearts of its people. The Nation is the people, the people bound together in the social order, in their daily contacts and cooperation.

The Bible sets the standard for social righteousness. How the prophets of God exposed the sins of the social order of their day, and how relevant their rebukes are to our own day! Read Amos, Hosea, Ezekiel, Isaiah, and you will see how fearlessly these men of God rebuked the social evils of their day – hypocrisy, falsehood, perjury, impurity, lawlessness, Godlessness. The O. T. develops a social responsibility. The O. T. makes it clear that it was the design of God that there should be no destitution in Israel. The Hebrews were commanded to show such kindness to their poorer brethren that the temptation to theft, springing from want, should cease.

While the O. T. Mosaic Law is full of warning against greed and wealth, it does safeguard the right of property. It affirms that he that giveth to the poor lendeth to the Lord.

The Bible develops a social conscience – a sensitiveness to what is right and wrong. It enlightens, educates, and purifies public opinion. And the Bible does it as nothing else in the world. It does it as a graceless culture never can. Education as a factor in the field is disappointing. Mass education but processes the mass-mind. Cinema, radio, television, literature often poison the wells, and the fruit of it all is this superficiality of thought, this vulgarity of taste, this emptiness of life that we have with us today. Political socialism is held out as the great educator, and it has done much to uplift the submerged classes of society. Let us not forget that in its origins it was the product of Christian ideals, inspired by Christian men. Today it is built on an illusion – the illusion that man is fundamentally good, kind, altruistic, and that he will act according to law. This may be true of a colony of ants, or a hive of bees, guided unerringly by instinct, but it will not do for a human society moved by hell-born passions and often controlled by devil-inspired intelligence. To combat these you need something stronger than idealism and sentimentality. You need the stern Law of God, and that you find in the pages of the Book.

We must keep the Bible in our schools, it is the well of culture undefiled, it is the true educator and developer of the human heart.

Thus the Bible rears safeguards for the defence of Society. It fences off things sacred from things secular. It announces and applies the Law of God – engraven on the Old Testament and applied to daily life in the New. That law is relevant today, as it will be eternally relevant, for it is founded on the Character of God and finds its echo deep down in the moral nature of man.

In short the Bible produces a spiritual culture that pervades and inspires all thought and all life. Men and women who drank deeply at this source were truly educated and possessed a culture which the secular thought of tyranny cannot inspire. Secularism has introduced false values which serve to disrupt society and the nation and we need to get back speedily to the Bible. For we are living on the spiritual capital of our fathers, we are living on the Bible-reading of our ancestors, we are content with the by-products of Christianity, wholly divorced from faith in God. The Bible is what we need: it brings its ethic into all relationships, and holds out the Kingdom of God as the only workable society and the only basis for satisfactory relationships.

3. The Bible's message bears on the Nation in another way – it is the custodian of the Family Sanctities.

The Family is the unit of Society, the cell of the social order. And the Bible gives the only satisfactory and intelligible explanation of the foundation and meaning of the family. It has its origin in God who is not a solitary Being, but a Trinity in unceasing fellowship. And father, mother, child is a trinity that has its roots in the very nature of God.

The Family is thus the unit of society, and in its unity, discipline, cooperation it is the pattern of what the larger family – the nation – ought to be.

The unity of the Family is the foundation of National unity; the cohesion of the family is the mortar that binds together the Nation. Divorce is in itself a national disaster, for it must lead to national disintegration. The cooperation of the Family is the training school for the larger responsibilities of life, and the larger the family the bigger the scope for that give and take that is so valuable a training for the rough and tumble of life. The discipline of the family, its wise restraints, its call to personal self-denial, builds up the character for its place in society and the nation.

And the Bible is the charter of the Family, the Heavenly Father is the pattern of the earthly father, and the Christian Home is the nearest thing to Heaven.

4. The Bible's message to the individual is basic to its influence over the Nation.

The Bible is largely the record of God's encounters with specific individuals, and the far-reaching effects such encounters have had upon the human story.

For us the Bible solves the problem of how the individual is to maintain and exercise his liberties and yet be the true servant of society and the nation. To maintain the balance between individual liberty and responsibility to the State will never be easy; it can be done only by 'rendering unto Caesar the things that are Caesar's, and unto God the things that are God's'. The State is ever ready to infringe on the liberty of the individual: to become dictatorial, authoritarian, totalitarian. Only the recognition of God as King of Nations can curb its claims.

The Bible secures for the individual his great fundamental freedoms – freedom of thought, freedom of conscience, freedom of worship. These are the liberties of the human spirit and the foundation of all liberty.

'THE SAINTS' EVERLASTING REST
Revelation 22:4

The Book of Revelation in its unveiling of the future contains much that is dark and mysterious. Amidst its thunder and lightning, its vials and trumpets, we often falter and stumble. Now and again we come to a green glade where the light streams down and we are glad to rest and be refreshed. Is it too much to claim that at the words of our text 'And they shall see His face' we have at last come into the open, to bask in the sunshine of an eternal day? It certainly presents to us a vision that is not dimmed by the mists of earth, and extends to us a promise that is to be our staff and our song in the house of our pilgrimage.

1. Let us see here the Crown of Revelation

We recognise that through all God's dealings with men there runs His purpose to make a revelation of Himself. What are Creation, Providence, the Gospel, but vehicles of Divine revelation, channels through which God is communicating to us the revelation of His mind and heart and character? But at their best they are but partial revelations, inasmuch as they utterly fail to reveal *all* that God is. Even the Bible, that is the fullest and clearest and highest revelation of God, is but a partial revelation – not because it is not perfect as far as it goes, but because it is not complete. Holy men of old had wonderful glimpses of God and their experiences are enshrined in the pages of the Book.

The 'God of Glory' revealed Himself to Abraham, to Moses, to David, to Isaiah, and to many other ancient saints, and yet the cry of the Old Testament is 'Verily thou art a God that hideth Thyself!'. In the New Testament the revelation of God reached its fullest and brightest; and yet one of the most privileged of its saints left it at this: 'Now we see through a glass darkly'. As we follow the footsteps of a self-revealing God through the whole of the Book, we find it is the experience of saintly hearts and the clear testimony of the Word that the revelation is incomplete – and it would remain for ever incomplete had not this promise been given: 'They shall see His face.' That is the grand climax to which Revelation is moving, that is the noonday light that streaked the dawn with its early brightness. If this had been left out of the Bible the Book had been left unfinished – nay, it would have been written in vain. Revelation does not receive its crown till this becomes an accomplished fact – 'They shall see His face.' This is the full, perfect, complete revelation that God promised to give of Himself when first He began to make Himself known to men.

2. We see here, again, the Goal of Faith

Faith is the Divine method of spiritual life for us here below: it is taking God on trust, believing Him when we can't see Him or feel Him or understand Him. And faith is a wonderful principle of life – it has accomplished much as the dynamic of holy and fruitful living. But it is not perfect, it is not final, it is not God's best for us. If faith were told that it was a way of living that was to remain for ever, it would collapse! Faith is kept living by the anticipation of better things: it hopes for something greater! And what is that greater and better thing that faith looks and waits for? It is sight. Faith would be ready to give up in despair were it not assured that one day faith would be swallowed up in sight. So faith cheers itself along the road by singing hopefully, 'I shall yet see; I am trusting now, but I hope, I expect, I believe I shall yet see.' See what? 'Oh, a thousand things and wonders innumerable!' 'Yes, yes, but one thing I *must* see – His face!' Faith will have fallen far short of its goal unless it will see His face. Oft it saw gleams and glimpses of His face by the way that sustained and strengthened it. But it was 'through a glass darkly'; now it must be 'face to face'. And so faith struggles and toils and fights in the good hope that it will see His face. If this were not promised, faith would say it were not worth while to carry on. In the eleventh chapter of Hebrews we see a great army of God's saints marching on to this goal – lured by the prospect that they shall see His face! This is the face that brought the saints through fire and flood, the Face that they crossed the Jordan to see! And faith *will* reach its goal, for it stands written, 'They shall see His face'.

3. We have here also the Zenith of Knowledge

It is part of the discipline of the spiritual life that our knowledge should remain incomplete. Now 'we know in part' and we understand but dimly; often we trust when we don't understand at all. There are mysteries in Heaven above and earth beneath that we would fain unravel. There are problems of thought and heart that baffle us. There are experiences in life that are dark and mysterious and disturbing. How often are we as birds that beat their wings against the bars of their cage; we seem so helpless before the dark providences of our own lot – the why and the wherefore of suffering we cannot tell. Now, indeed, we know in part – but we shall see His face! And then we shall know even as we are known! In the radiant glory and grace of His countenance we shall see all, and know all, and understand all, and – blessed thought – we shall joyfully accept all. This is the final reach of knowledge: 'They shall see His face'; and in the light of His wisdom and grace and love all will be lighted up, every difficulty solved, every mystery cleared, and every baffling thing made plain.

4. Lastly, may we not say that here we have laid the Copestone of Sanctification?

This is the completion of the great work of making the soul like Christ. It *was* a work – an uphill work often and very slow its progress seemed! Through prayers and tears, in conflict and agony, His people have sought the Lord to 'perfect that which concerns them', yet they ever seemed to fall immeasureably short of their desires. Their condition remained so unlike their position! But 'they shall see His face', and that vision will imprint His image perfectly, indelibly, and for ever upon their souls! They but look – and they are transformed into the same image from grace to Glory, from earth to Heaven. It is not merely that Glory has begun – the dawn of Heaven has already run to noon! This is the light in its meridian splendour! All else were twinkling stars that sent their beams of light into the darkness of their night; but this is the Eternal Day, and they are all 'light in the Lord'. 'But', says the Apostle of Love, 'we know that we shall be like Him, for we shall see Him as He is!'

What is the goal of your own life, the crown of your expectations? Is it that you may 'see His face'? If so your life is lived on a different plane from that of other men: you have different hopes and expectations, different joys and sorrows, different desires and longings. There is strength in your life, and there is hope in your death, and there is glory everlasting in your destiny. Toil on in the work of faith, the patience of hope, and the labour of love, believing you shall have your full reward when you shall see His face!

THE THEOLOGY OF MISSIONS

It has been well said that argument on behalf of Missions is either needless or useless: needless in the case of those who have any knowledge of the will of God in Christ, useless in the case of those who have no such knowledge.

This is an attempt to show that missions like every other Christian activity have their roots in Christian theology. It is there that they have their warrant, their inspiration and their reward.

And Christian doctrine has its roots in God. It is there, therefore, that we must go for a study of the theology of Christian missions.

1. In God's Nature
2. In God's Authority
3. In God's Purpose
4. In God's Provision
5. In God's Promise

1. In God's Nature

Our God is a self-revealing and self-communicating God, the only living and true God, and His nature and character form the sheet-anchor of all missionary effort.

God has revealed Himself as the only God, the true God, and He is therefore the God of the whole earth, and every other God everywhere is false. What is true of God at one place and in one country is true of God always and everywhere.

Now since self-revelation is a quality of the Divine nature, it cannot be God's will that some should know Him and others should not, or that some should have false views of Him and false attitudes towards Him. A true God must will to be truly known to all men, and in this no race or nation has a special monopoly. It is His will that all men, irrespective of race or nation or culture, should come to His knowledge. The very character of God thus carries with it the missionary obligation and idea.

It is significant in this connection that the Unitarian view of God never produced a mission of any note, and even where it has started, actuated by an urge from without rather than from within, it has proved incapable of sustaining the effort.

It is equally significant that those who found in the study of Comparative Religion an approximation to God in the gods of heathen tribes and pagan nations, have not favoured aggressive missionary effort, except on purely humanitarian grounds. The Reformed position is that God alone is true, and the gods of the pagan world are false. They are not approximations to God but contradictions of God, and are obstacles to faith and not aids to it. What other religions at their best are seeking after, is what Christianity possesses: knowledge of the true God and an experience of peace with Him.

2. In God's Authority

Without doubt we have the authority of God Himself in His word for the missionary enterprise. In the Church of Scotland Assembly of 1796 Dr George Hamilton, the leader of the moderate section, advanced this argument when Foreign Missions came to be discussed: 'To spread abroad the knowledge of the Gospel among baboons and heathen nations seems to me to be highly preposterous in as far as it anticipates, nay, as it even reverses, the order of nature. Men must be polished and refined in their manners before they can be properly enlightened in religious truths. Philosophy and learning must, in the nature of things, take the precedence. Indeed it should seem hardly less absurd to make revelation precede civilisation in the order of time, than to pretend to unfold to a child the Principia of Newton ere he is made at all acquainted with the letters of the alphabet'. He concluded: 'These ideas seem to me alike founded in error, and, therefore, I must consider them both as equally romantic and visionary'.

It was to this sophistry that Dr John Erskine of Greyfriars – fresh from a baptism of the Spirit at the Cambuslang revival – responded: 'Rax me that Bible' and began to read the Great Commission. But it must not be forgotten that the entire life and teaching of Christ led up to the Great Commission. Though He belonged to one race and one nation, He thought in terms of the world and spoke of Himself as the Saviour of the World. The bread He would give was His flesh, which He gave for the life of the World. He was the Light of the World. If He were to be lifted up He would draw all men towards Him.

And let us not forget that the teaching of Christ and of the entire N. T. had its roots in the O. T. The God of Israel was the God of the whole earth, and Israel's programme was a missionary programme that embraced all peoples, because the Lord to whom it testified was One in whom all the families of the earth are blessed. Both psalmists and prophets rejoice in the transfer of the theocentric relation peculiar to Israel unto all mankind when the 'Desire of all nations should come'.

The teaching given throughout His public ministry reached its consummation in the 40 days of the Resurrection period – during this period this was the one theme that was uppermost in His mind – that was the one great burden on His heart. His redemption work was finished, and He longed to have His disciples proclaim the glad tidings everywhere.

So when the Great Missionary Command from the Mount of Olives broke upon the ears of the gathered disciples, it did not seem strange or alien to their thought. He who had a right to command did give the command, and the command coming from Him, called for one thing only, unhesitating and unquestioning obedience till the task was finished. Nor did the amazing sweep of the Programme daunt them. Many minds have commented on these Alls. 'All power – the All of unlimited Power. Go ye into all the world – the All of unbounded Grace, teaching them to observe All things -the All of unreserved obedience. And lo I am with you all the way – the All of the unceasing Presence. It is difficult indeed for anyone who calls himself by the name of Christian to escape from the sweep of the net – so all-embracing is it.

3. In God's Purpose

In so far as God has revealed to us His purpose for His creation, we cannot fail to discern the missionary programme as an integral part of that purpose. It is here that there are several schools of thought that interpret that purpose differently.

To some the purpose of God is simply to rescue the perishing. They regard the world as merely a wrecked vessel, with its passengers and crew thrown out in the stormy seas: their duty is to save as many as they can before they perish. Compassion for the perishing is thus the basic motive in missionary enterprise.

But we think the purpose of God is capable of a more extended interpretation than this. That God has compassion on the erring and those that are out of the way, the Scripture explicitly states. But God has revealed a purpose of salvation that embraces men and women out of all nations and kindreds and tongues. Moreover He has made known His purpose to establish a Kingdom of Righteousness that embraces all peoples and shall continually be coexistent with the race. It is the revelation of this Divine purpose that gives the true urge and direction to missionary effort. It is the consciousness that God calls us to cooperate with Him in the fulfilment of these great and glorious purposes that clothes a missionary with zeal for the glory of God and a holy obedience to be found in His will.

Our compassion for the lost may be a compelling motive, but unless it is fed from the nether springs of the Divine will, it is liable to become exhausted. It is not the all - sufficient motive for the missionary enterprise, because it is merely man-centred. To be in the will of God is the Christian's first ambition.

To know that it is His will to save men from all nations invests the missionary with a power that is not of earth. Dr Henry W. Frost, at one time Director for North America of the China Inland Mission, tells the story of a lady who called on him at his office in Toronto one day. She was a Miss Kathleen Stayner of Toronto, a cultured woman from a well-to -do family. 'I have to confess that I do not love the Chinese. They are so ignorant and dirty'. 'Do you know, Miss Stayner, I do not think the question of whether or not you love the Chinese is the one to be considered: the real question is whether or not you love the Lord'. At this her eyes kindled and she exclaimed 'Oh, yes I do love Him'.

4. In God's Provision

The Gospel is the glad tidings of God's provision to deal with sin in its guilt, its pollution and its power. The atoning work of Jesus culminating on the Cross, and sealed by His resurrection is the Divine provision for sin.

Now the question arises: Is this atoning work adequate for all men? The next is: Is it operable or effective in the case of all sinners who avail themselves of it?

Has God revealed that there are some people who are excluded from its efficacy so that the offer may not be extended to them?

Have all people the same right or lack of right to be informed of the Divine provision?

Is there any hope for any people that they can enter God's favour in any other way?

These are all very relevant questions that relate to God's provision for man's fallen state. And to face them is to realise that fallen man everywhere ought to know of the provision made for his state.

It is true that no people or person will be judged on the basis of knowledge or privilege which they did not possess. But all will be judged on the basis of character, and in the last resort it will be found that they did evil, not because of ignorance, but because of their evil nature and character. It is sinful character that makes the unevangelised nations suppress the truth they know, or as Paul puts it, 'hold fast the truth in unrighteousness'.

But the Divine provision is applicable to them, the Cross of Christ has a world relevance, the sacrifice of Calvary is adequate to meet with sin everywhere, and our duty is to bring the sinner within hearing of the Divine provision.

It is a perversion of the doctrines of grace to make a limited atonement mean a limited responsibility, or to argue that since the doctrine of election lies behind personal salvation, it is futile to make the Gospel offer unless God in every particular case reveals to us the object of His secret purpose. It is our duty to tell all men that God has made provision for man's sin, that there is efficacy in the blood of Christ to wash away every sin, and that if they believe in the One who died and rose again they will prove the relevance and efficacy of that blood for them.

5. In the Promises of God

God has been pleased to put many a bright star of promise in the missionary firmament, lest we should be discouraged. They are promises given to Jesus Christ His Son, promises given to His Church, and promises given to His individual servants. These do not leave the issue in doubt. Christ *shall* see of the travail of His soul and shall be satisfied.

And these promises, like a rainbow of hope, span all nations and all people. God has done more than promised. He has revealed. He has lifted the veil from the future sufficiently for us to see a multitude which no man can number from all nations. This is for us truly realised eschatology as we see the New Jerusalem come down out of heaven from God. It is little wonder that the vision of the early Church was world wide.

So unbiassed a historian as Harnack says 'We may take it as an assured fact that the mere existence and persistent activity of the individual Christian communities did more than anything else to bring about the extension of the Christian religion'.

So the Church became a missionary society. The early Christians never thought to erect a formal institution or to sit down to compose reasoned arguments for Christianity: they set out to apply it everywhere.

CRIME AND PUNISHMENT IN THE BIBLE

As background to our study it may be profitable to trace, in brief, the history and development of penal law among the Hebrews. This is also necessary in order that we may be better able to place legal and penal references in their proper historical context.

Three stages in the development of Hebrew penal law can be noted.

(i) There can be no doubt that in the early stages the dominant principle is the jus talionis 'an eye for an eye'. In earlier times, however, the principle had its applicability, not as a norm for penalties to be judiciously inflicted, but as a regulative rule in private vengeance. It was for the individual himself to pursue his rights, and by universal custom he was entitled to do to the transgressor what the aggrieved had done to him. In the case of murder the blood relative had not only the right but the sacred duty to avenge the deed.

(ii) A second stage can be noted when in Hebrew law compensation could take the place of revenge pure and simple. This was a great step forward, for it was at this stage that ceremonial law began to take the place of revenge. At an early stage it will be found that Hebrew custom demanded such a mode of settlement for all cases of bodily injury, as Exodus 21 indicates: 'And if men strive together, and one smite another with a stone, or with his fist, and he die not, but keepeth his bed; if he rise again and walk about upon his staff then shall he that smote him be quit: only he shall pay for the loss of his time and shall cause him to be thoroughly healed' (v.18). This early usage, however, did not sanction blood-money, except in cases of accidental homicide. Numbers 35, lays down the rule: 'You shall accept no ransom for the life of a murderer who is guilty of death' (v.31).

(iii) The third stage that can be recognised is when by general law the duty of revenge was taken over from the individual and rested upon society at large. Revenge now became lawful punishment, regulated by the general interest of the community. At a still later stage statute determined the kind and measure of the penalty, and the constituted authorities – generally the elders, accepted the duty of seeing it carried out.

But in the Hebrew view the object of the punishment is not completely attained even when the claims of compensation or retribution found expression. Grave crimes, and especially murder, defile the land, and its guilt lies upon the whole people. It is this sense of the divine wrath that has to be met and the blood of the slayer alone cannot appease the divine anger and cleanse the land (Num. 35:33-34). Evil had to be removed from the midst of the people by a more general punishment as we shall later see.

As soon as there began to be a properly constituted authority, it took blood vengeance into its own hands, and converted it into a death penalty. There was, however, the distinction enforced between murder and manslaughter and at every sanctuary there was the right of asylum as well as at the appointed Cities of Refuge.

Coming down to the Biblical text, we are not over-embarrassed by wealth of material. The only parts of the O.T. not immediately connected with Jewish law are the Pentateuch, and the closing section of Ezekiel (40-48). Jehovah is source of all law, and Moses the medium through whom it is revealed to Israel. And so the formula: 'And Jehovah said unto Moses: Thou shalt say to the children of Israel'. The prophets were also regarded as media of the Torah, and the priests at various festivals issued instructions that were legally binding, though they were mainly by way of interpretation of the law in reference to specific cases. As a consequence of the ascription of the origin of the law as from Jehovah, the Hebrew historians do not directly and explicitly record the introduction of a new law or a changing of an old one. Only Ezekiel in his ideal sketch of the future kingdom – the restored nation- gives a constitution that may be regarded as different from that already codified.

The N.T. has but incidental reference to Law and its enforcement in civil cases. Our Lord's parables make reference to existing modes of exacting punishment and Paul and Peter have references to the duty and power of the civil magistrate. These pretty well exhaust the biblical references on which we are to base our conclusions as to the Bible's approach to crime and its punishments.

That the Bible took cognisance of crime as such is very apparent, and that it associated crime with punishment is also very apparent.

The common Hebrew word '*awon* is used variously for offence, for guilt, and for punishment – 55 times for crime, 155 times for guilt and 7 times for punishment – suggesting that these three facts are so interrelated as to be inseparable – crimes, guilt, punishment.

In the N.T. the Greek word δικηζ has also a two-fold meaning: its primary meaning of judgment, and a secondary meaning of punishment, suggestive of the same inter-relation, the nexus between them being the root idea of justice.

As in Hebrew the words *hata* (*n.het*) were used alike for offence against God and offence against man, so in Greek αμαρτιαζ is used in the N.T. in this two-fold sense. These words are used in the main for what may be called crimes against the person, human or animal.

This reference is implicit in the Jewish conception of law. In the O.T. consciousness Jehovah was behind the law, and so the spirit of the law expresses His will and character. It can be seen that the divine character determines the spirit rather than the precise details of the legislation. It had reference to man only secondarily as made in the image of God. It was this relationship to God that gave sanctity to human life: 'for in the image of God created He man' was the reason given for the command 'whoso sheddeth man's blood, by man shall his blood be shed' (Gen. 9:5-6). A sin against a fellow-Israelite was regarded as a sin against God.

We see then that crime, whether against God's character or against man's life, and punishment are so inter-related that they are regarded as inseparable. They are but two parts of a whole. The N.T. accepts this view. Paul in Romans 1:32 speaks of 'the judgment (or decree) of God that they which commit such things are worthy of death'. Christ in the close of the Sermon on the Mount, brings together man's judgment and God's: 'Ye have heard that it was said by them of old time, Thou shalt not kill; and whosoever is angry with his brother without a cause, shall be in danger of the judgment – but whosoever shall say, Thou fool, shall in danger of hell fire' (Matt. 5:21-22). Whatever the personal interpretation of these words they undoubtedly imply that the earthly sentence is but a reflection – even if a pale one – of the eternal one. And the particular offence in mind is one against the person of man, and so against the character of God.

This connection of crime and punishment was early expounded in the case of Cain's act of murder. The curse of God was pronounced upon the murderer's person and at the same time protection was given to Cain's life from the violence of men's vengeance. Clearly crime was not to be punished by crime. God was not to condone violence, and indeed it is the fact that 'violence filled the earth' that is given as the cause of the flood.

When we examine the sentence pronounced on the occasion of Abel's murder we have some difficulty in arriving at its precise interpretation. 'Whoso sheddeth man's blood, by man shall his blood be shed, for in the image of God made he man'.

The particular reprieve here is not easy to grasp. 'Whoso sheddeth man's blood, by man shall his blood be shed' – is this a charge to man to execute the death penalty on the murderer? What is the reference of 'For in the image of God created he man'? Is it a comment on the heinousness of the shedding of man's blood, since man had been made in the image of God? Or is it authority given to man to dispense justice for his brother in virtue of the fact that man was made in God's image and so is charged with the authority to dispense justice in the name of God?

Though this may not be clear, the overall reference is sufficiently clear – it is a reference to man's uniqueness as made in the image of God, and any duty bound on this must have permanent obligation.

It is scarcely necessary to point out that the Sixth Commandment is fully consonant with this: its prohibition is designed to protect human life and declare its sanctity. Since the act of murder is a violation of this sanctity, it must be dealt with in terms of God's judgment already pronounced.

Thus far we have established the inseparable relationship between crime and punishment, not only in theory, but also in practice.

The objectives of Punishment

It is possible to elucidate the objective of punishment as presented in the Bible and to compare it with the avowed objectives of the present day.

Present day society reacts to an offence by the imposition of punishment, though in some situations that word is emptied of its ordinary meaning. The objectives of punishment are generally recognised as of four kinds – retributive, preventive, deterrent and reformative.

*1. **Retributive**.* This is the objective that merits the designation punitive. Behind it there lies the principle of justice that underlies all legislation. All true justice is punitive to vice as it is rewarding to virtue. This is basic to punishment.

*2. **Preventive**.* With regard to the well-being of the community the criminal is forcibly prevented from repeating his assault on the life of the community, and punishment in other forms is adapted to serve this end. Thus the community protects itself for a season at least by removing from the offender the opportunity to strike again. This, for example, is the aim of a prison sentence at one end of the scale, just as it is the aim of withdrawing a driving licence at the other.

*3. **Deterrent**.* This has reference not to the criminal himself, but to the community that has witnessed his crime and his punishment. In other words, it is a deterrent to potential criminals. Just punishment in this case is regarded in the light of its moral influence on the community.

*4. **Reformative**.* While this is the modern idea that fills the whole picture, it is not of the essence of punishment, except that it is imposed on the criminal against his will and probably against the interests of his nature. But it must be viewed as in the nature of medicine – perhaps nasty medicine – to a sick man, even when the sick man is not willing to swallow the medicine.

Of these four, which find prominent place in the Biblical conception of punishment? Without any doubt it is principally the first. The Biblical conception of punishment is essentially punitive and retributive. It is, in the religious context, the reaction of God's holiness to a man's unholiness, and that reaction can suffer no alteration, compromise or suspension. This establishes retribution as a dictate of justice.

That is not to say that the other aspects of punishment are entirely absent. But if retribution is not justice in order, the other forms of punishment are manifestly unjust.

*1. **Reformative**.* In the Bible this is called chastisement and it is a family word. God does not punish His children in the ordinary sense of the word, but He chastises them, physically, mentally, socially, spiritually. Punishment in itself is seldom effective in the direction of reformation, because it is applied from without and reformation of life and character comes from within. And this is the punishment that God applies to His people, as He declared through Amos 'You only have I known of all families of the earth, therefore will I punish you for all your iniquities'. The privilege of divine chastisement is given only to God's children.

2. *Deterrent.* This punishment is not unknown in the Bible. The protection of the moral order is here involved, and God presides over His moral universe. In Deuteronomy we are told the objective of punishment for idolatry. 'And all the people shall hear, and fear, and do no more presumptuously', and again 'And those which remain shall hear and fear, and shall henceforth commit no more any such evil among you'.

The destruction of the ancient Canaanites was of this order. It is not recognised that while the Canaanites were degraded beyond our imaginings they were also the channels by which venereal diseases were transmitted through the ancient world. They were vitiating the stream of life. God's concern was to keep His people untainted by this sin, for from them was to come the Holy Seed who should in body and soul be 'holy, harmless, undefiled, separate from sinners'.

Christ made use of this principle, for when He was approached regarding the fate of the Galileans whose blood Pilate mixed with their sacrifices and of the eighteen upon whom the Tower of Siloam fell, He replied in each case: 'Except ye repent, ye shall all likewise perish'.

3. *Preventive.* The great example of this is Capital Punishment viewed from the side of the community and society in general. Though this is not the whole, or even the major element, in capital punishment it is intended to protect the community and its life from assault.

I think that this is the image of Hell that the Bible presents very often. It is a place of eternal restraint. It would seem that moral evil cannot be destroyed or put out of existence. It is a spiritual reality that cannot be extinguished or annihilated. But it is to be put under eternal restraint so that it will no more ravage God's universe. The prospect held out by the Biblical revelation is that the moral universe will be swept clean, and evil put and kept under eternal restraint.

*4. **Retributive**.* The Bible's position is that punishment like all evil, must be considered in the context of eternal right and fundamental justice, the only context in which it can have any real meaning. Retributive punishment has thus its true place in the moral setting of right and wrong. Punishment in this context has several aspects beyond its primary object to mete out justice to the wrongdoer.

1. It may be to uphold the authority of moral law.

If the law is the conforming to absolute standards and not merely to social convention or communal custom, then it must be upheld at whatever cost. Ovid's line is well remembered: *'Justitia fiat, caelum neat'*

The punishment of sin is not an arbitrary experience, but the functioning of a necessary law. Not only so, but the penalty is a genuine child of the transgression. The wages of sin are pain in kind.

Since God is the supreme dispenser of the moral order it follows that He alone can dispense punishment for breaches of that order, and all who dispense it must act under His commission and with His authority.

When Paul says that the civil magistrate bears not the sword in vain, he is, in the practice of his day, referring to punishment by the sword, even to death itself. 'The powers that be', he says, 'are ordained of God – for he (the civil power) is the minister of God, an avenger to execute wrath upon him that doeth evil' (Rom. 13:3-4). This is the principle underlying the proposed legislation for the compensation of the victims of crime. Since it is the function of the State to maintain law and order, crime perpetrated is proof of the State's function, and for this it is now willing to assume responsibility by way of compensation. The action of the magistrate in Romans 13 above, is mainly punitive, for the upholding of the moral order. If punishment be merely reformative, the sword of the civil magistrate is a meaningless appendage: justice no longer decides the issue. When Paul tells us that the powers that be are ordained of God, he also tells us that 'whosoever resisteth the power resisteth the ordinances of God, and they that resist shall receive to themselves damnation' – that is God will punish them. It is obvious that this applies to constitutional government and constitutional laws only. Any order or law that is unconstitutional, i.e. outside the terms of the magistrate's appointment, is null and void.

Thus when punishment is removed from the sphere of justice, it ceases to be punishment.

2.   Punishment in the Biblical sense of it, may be dispensed to restore the order of the Law where it has been flouted and disobeyed .

Biblical justice has often been referred to as mere retaliation. But in Israel the law of retaliation was based on strict justice. It was a legally equivalent compensation in which the element of vengeance was not allowed to enter, on the principle that vengeance belongeth to the Lord. When Moses delivered, which is called his Song, to the children of Israel, he referred to the foes of Israel and their many misdeeds, but he did not incite to revenge, but rather cautioned in the name of the Lord 'To me belongs vengeance and recompense' (Deut. 32:35).

The Lex Talionis as given in Exodus 21:24-25, – 'an eye for an eye, a tooth for a tooth, hand for hand, foot for foot, burning for burning, wound for wound, stripe for stripe' was based on this conception of strict compensation: an eye and no more, a tooth and no more. When Christ substituted the Lex Evangelica for the Lex Talionis, He was not abrogating the old law, nor was He critical of it as is sometimes averred. What He did was to introduce a higher law for the Christian, based not on justice, but on grace.

3.   Only in the presence of justice can mercy be meaningful.

It has been said that 'mercy divorced from justice grows unmerciful'. It is highly doubtful if injustice can ever foster mercy, for mercy is meaningless except in the presence of justice.

Christ illustrated this in the parable of the unmerciful servant, who was forgiven his debt of ten thousand talents, and then shut his fellow servants in prison for a debt of a hundred pence. The assertion of justice was brought in when the unmerciful servant was eventually 'delivered to his tormentors till he should pay what was due to them'. Justice was the background against which mercy was shown, and when mercy was unjustly used or abused, justice stepped into the foreground and took sole control.

The evangelical interpretation of Calvary is the classical example of mercy seen in the setting of justice. The Cross thus viewed is the greatest example that the moral universe can afford of the open vindication of right, and the open condemnation of wrong in the public sentence passed on the sin-bearer and the sufferings that He endured unto death. The raison d'être of the Cross was in the very nature of God and of the moral universe He controls. Wrong had been done to that moral order and the principles by which it exists had been challenged. Sin had brought anarchy into the moral universe. Two moral problems had to find solution: how could the moral order of the universe be upheld, and the rebel brought to the place of amnesty and forgiveness? The Cross is the Divine solution. Calvary offers mercy on the basis of justice, justice done and justice seen to be done before the gaze of all the moral intelligences of the universe.

Thus we claim that the Biblical conception of punishment must be retributive because it approaches evil from the side of holiness and purity, justice and goodness. The punishment of evil is rendered certain because God is good, holy and just. No other conception of punishment will meet the exacting demands of justice. If a man is made use of to give a mere demonstration of law, to deter others from wrong, then he is grossly wronged in being punished if he does not deserve to be so dealt with. Reprieve for the sentenced criminal is meaningless unless he had been justly condemned to death. Even when mercy is in the forefront, justice is in the background, and it is assumed that the elements of justice are honoured when a way of mercy has been found.

Thus there can be only two views of punishment – the forensic and the medical. The one treats crime as wilful breach of law, the other as disease. The pathological view of crime is dominant today and so punishment has become merely therapeutic. But as we have seen this can degenerate into tyranny and injustice of the former kind. If a man can be forcibly treated for what public opinion or the State calls a disease, then the State can operate any form of brain-washing as a cure of the malady that the State does not like. This has been done in China in the name of justice for the crime of being deviationist or subversive of the ideological creed of the hour. Which goes to prove that no form of punishment is in accord with justice except the retributive, and that when another conception of punishment takes control, justice is in danger of being overthrown. But the subject can be discussed only in the context of morality, and morality is based on the eternal and absolute standards of right and wrong. God is the supreme expression of these standards. A thing is right not because God does it: God does it because it is right. To make contact with these absolute standards by which we shall be judged at the last, we must make contact with the will of God, and to make contact with the personal will of God we must go to the revelation that He has given in His word. The Bible alone provides us with the true conception of Crime and its Punishment.

Group 6

The Quest of the
Individual Soul

THE QUEST OF THE SOUL
(Luke 15:3–32)

The background to this chapter is interesting. These three illustrations were given by our Lord in answer to those who cavilled at His attitude towards the morally fallen and the social outcasts. 'This man receiveth sinners and eateth with them', one of the great tributes paid to our Lord by His enemies. They struck this blow to injure His reputation and assail His character, but like the blow that the blacksmith strikes at the red-hot iron – the sparks only serve to light up his own face – so this blow at our Lord lit up the grace of His character.

In reply He gave these three illustrations and they are spoken of as a parable. 'He spake this parable unto them' (v 3). In other words the theme is the same throughout – the salvation of a sinner from a life of sin and loss. But they look at this salvation from different angles.

The first two illustrations – the lost sheep and the lost coin – are clearly meant to go together, for the transition from the sheep to the coin is simply introduced by 'Either', indicating that the second does not introduce a new subject, but gives another illustration of the truth expressed in the first – the lost sheep.

But when He comes to the third illustration – the Lost Son – it is introduced by the words 'And He said', clearly indicating that we are dealing with the truth in a different way.

The sin and salvation of man is the ground-work of the Parable, and the theme is the quest of the soul that is being delivered and restored. The first two deal with the quest from God's side: God is the seeker. The last illustration deals with the quest from the soul's side – man is the seeker.

It is significant that on the Divine side of salvation, God is seen to be in it throughout: neither the sheep nor the coin take any part in the quest or the restoration. On the human side, in the case of the lost son, man is in it throughout, and the father takes no steps to seek out and recover his son.

I

Salvation from God's side

We are taught, first, that Salvation, from the Divine side, is altogether an activity of God. Both the initial step and the continuance are of God and the result is entirely God-produced. This is sin and salvation looked at from above. There are three things common to both illustrations.

> (a) A sense of loss.
> (b) The diligence of the search.
> (c) The joy of recovery.

(a) *The Sense of Loss*

(i)   A shepherd with a small flock of one hundred sheep in his charge knew each sheep, for he lived with them. And one went missing. When he discovered his loss, he took steps at once to recover it. For the time being his thoughts concentrated entirely on the one lost one – his sense of loss was acute.

(ii)   A woman has ten coins. We do not know or need to know how she came by them. Some think they were a marriage dowry from her husband, and that they were worn as a necklace. In which case, one would be seriously missed, as its loss would disfigure the ornament as well as raise sentimental feelings of regret. She too had an acute sense of loss. Now that is the first thing that is brought to our notice about God. In the departure of man from His communion He has a sense of loss.

This may well surprise us: that the God of the universe should miss the falling from His fellowship of one soul. But Scripture reveals that God made man for Himself, so made him – in His image and after His likeness – that He could have fellowship with His creature, and man could respond. And it is revealed that when man fell, God came after him with the cry: 'Where art thou?'. He missed the noble creature that had dropped out of His fellowship.

This is not to underline the importance of man in himself – after all it is one sheep in a hundred – it is only love that makes man important – it is the Divine sense of broken fellowship and of loss.

(b) *The Diligence of the Search*

In both illustrations there is active intervention from without.

(i) The Shepherd There is no concentration on the activity of the sheep; it has gone astray and the longer it is left the further it wanders. But all the shepherd's energies are concentrated on the lost sheep, pursuing her over mountain and through flood, 'until he find it'. He left his flock – ninety -nine – to concentrate on the one.

(ii) Similarly the woman, acutely conscious of her loss, swept for the coin so that no corner was left unexplored.

'Until he find it' – gives us the clue: the persistence of Divine Grace. The grace of God was the Divine intervention from without on behalf of fallen man. And grace allowed no obstacle to stand in the way, no barrier insurmountable, no suffering unendurable.

Salvation is the record of God's search for man, of God's intervention on behalf of man, of God's humiliation and sufferings in Christ for man's redemption. The so-called 'good' were not the objects of Christ's concern. 'He came not to call the righteous, but sinners to repentance.'

(c) The Joy of Recovery

There is more than discovery: there is recovery.

(i)   Having found the lost sheep – fatigued, footsore and weary, the shepherd laid his hand upon her, and lifted her upon his shoulders, and brought her home rejoicing.

(ii)   Similarly the woman retrieved the lost coin and added it to her cherished collection, restringing her prized necklace.

(iii)   And in the case of both the joy was shared. It was something that could not be hid. The loss and the recovery stood for values that were recognised by others, and others must enter into the meaning of recovery.

Is it not so with the salvation of man? His recovery is a pure act of God, and God views it with deep feeling: 'who for the joy that was set before Him endured the Cross, despising the shame'.

And the meaning of a soul's recovery in terms of eternal values is recognised throughout the whole moral universe of God. 'There is joy in the presence of the angels of God over one sinner that repenteth.'

Why? The angels recognise the value of a soul – they are aghast at the loss of a soul, they rejoice at its recovery. And they behold with wonder and awe the activity of God for man's redemption. 'Which things' says Peter, 'the angels desire to look into.'

We see in all this that the work is done by God alone – the sheep had as little part in its recovery and restoration as the coin: it was sought, was found, and carried home.

Salvation is all of God.

II
Salvation from Man's Side

Here in the story of the Lost Son we see that man is entirely in it. The departure was man's own: he was a rebel, a runaway, a traitor. And the return is viewed as man's own: the Father is entirely behind the scenes.

There are three steps in the return:-

(a) Self-reflection.
(b) Decision.
(c) Reconciliation.

(a) *Self-Reflection*

'When he came to himself.' Hitherto he was heedless, thoughtless, and senseless. He did not allow his mind to dwell on the facts. But he was jerked out of his thoughtlessness by dire need, by stark hunger. He faced himself within – came face to face with himself, and with the situation in which he found himself: the hopelessness of his condition impressed him.

That was the first step – a step inwards. And that is a man's own responsibility. God made us rational creatures, and He expects us to use the rational powers He has given to us to assess our own position. 'Come now and let us reason together saith the Lord' (Isa. 1:18). And that self-reflection led to conviction.

(b) *Decision.*

'I will arise and go'. Reflection on his state would not have altered his situation any. Shame and sorrow over his position would have made little difference. There had to be an act of will: he must exercise his will in the way of decision, and a decision to move in another direction – homewards – 'and go to my Father'. Of course there were factors that helped him to come to that decision. There was memory. 'How many hired servants of my Father's have bread enough and to spare'. There was the contrast with what he now was – 'and I perish with hunger'. And then the will came into operation, 'I will arise and go'.

The conviction was there, but that was not enough. Repentance is more than conviction – it is a decision to move in a new direction.

(c) *Reconciliation.*

True, his father's reconciliation took the initiative: 'he saw him a long way off – and ran - and kissed him'. And that reconciliation reached the heart of his son – made him most truly a son. This is confirmed by the fact that he omitted the words 'make me as one of thy hired servants'. And the restoration followed.

So reconciliation there must be before there is restoration. And without doubt God is the author of reconciliation. God has made the reconciliation – He invites us in to share it. And there must be this reconciliation before there is recognition and rehabilitation. (Cf David and Absalom – Ch. 46).

But in the restoration there is joy in which the son freely shared: there is public reconciliation and recognition.

The soul is fully and totally active in the processes that lead to salvation – the mind, the will, the heart, the conscience. And the joy of salvation goes as deep into the soul as the sense of sin has done. And the restoration, the acknowledgement, the witness – all put us on the road again.

In verses 7 and 10 we read 'There is joy in Heaven' and 'There is joy in the presence of the angels of God '. Do the angels know of the conversion of every soul, and if so how? Look at the illustrations of the parable. 'When the sheep was brought home and the coin recovered there was the disclosure by the shepherd and the woman to the neighbours – and she rejoiced in their presence and they joined with her.

Christ is the rejoicing one, but He communicates His joy to the holy and sympathetic creatures around His Throne, and let them share in it.

In summary we conclude:-

(a) Salvation is of God.
(b)The responsibility is all man's.

If your soul is saved, to God be the praise. If your soul is lost, the blame and fault is yours.

ASSURANCE

On the assurance of salvation Christian thought is sharply divided. Some hold that it is impossible to attain it and that it is largely presumptuous to ask or to expect it; while others have held that it is not only attainable, but absolutely essential to the very nature of faith and inseparable from a state of peace.

I believe there is a middle way between these extremes: that though assurance of salvation is neither essential to the nature of grace, nor inseparable from a state of grace, it is a condition, a state of grace to which any believer can attain, and a blessing which it is the duty of every believer to labour for.

The Assurance of Faith

'These things have I written unto you that believe on the name of the Son of God that ye may know that ye have eternal life, and that ye may believe in the name of the Son of God (1 John 5:13). Here we have three propositions submitted by John.

1. They who believe have eternal life.

2. They may be brought to a knowledge that they have eternal life.

3. That knowledge is not to supercede their living by direct faith on the Son of God.

1. They who believe have eternal life.

This, you remember, is the theme of John's Gospel, and it is reiterated with great urgency again and again in his First Epistle. It is the clearest and most unambiguous declaration of the way of salvation given to us in the N. T. John here speaks of it as: 'believing on the name of the Son of God'. Now that is John's way of placing Christ before us in all His sufficiency and glory as the Son of God: the *Name* stands for the person as interpreted by the Gospel. The Name is the expression of the person – a pointer to the nature and character and authority of the One that bears it.

And it is with a revealed Christ that faith deals: with Christ as interpreted by Himself and by the Spirit of the N. T. Thus faith is not a leap in the dark – a venture into the unknown - a gamble on the reality of truth given. Faith is the act of one who has examined the facts and is satisfied with the evidence.

Furthermore , faith is not belief in any proposition about Christ. Though doctrinal propositions are there, and are necessary for the guidance of faith, and faith accepts them as true, yet the ultimate and decisive act of faith is in respect to the Person of Christ. It is more than the assent of belief – it is the commitment of trust : it is more than *fides*, it is *fiducia*, the trust of the heart.

So faith deals with the person of Jesus Christ as interpreted by His Word and revealed by His Spirit. Nowhere can it be shown that the Apostles exhorted their hearers to trust the statements about Christ. Nowhere do they exhort their hearers to believe that God loved them, that Christ died for them, nowhere do they make that the foundation of their faith. Nowhere is it hinted that salvation consists in believing this.

To believe on Christ brings eternal life into our experience. When John says 'Whosoever believeth that Jesus is the Christ is born of God' he is dealing with the fruit of faith. He means that this faith is the effect and evidence of our regeneration – not the cause of it.

Thus the Gospel comes to us with an offer of Christ, and it is Christ we receive and not only His benefits. It is not a case of accepting justification – but accepting Christ who is of God made unto us justification. By this faith we pass from death unto life, from our side to His.

Thus saving faith, reaching out to Christ, and resting on Him must be distinguished from assurance that something has happened. It is not a logical proposition to which we give mental assent: e.g. God so loved the world: I am of the world: Therefore God loves me. Christ died for sinners: I am a sinner: Therefore Christ died for me. He that believeth is saved: I believe: Therefore I am saved. There salvation and assurance are found at the end of a syllogism. But that is neither saving faith nor the assurance of faith. Assurance does not come by process of logical reasoning. Yet assurance does come from direct faith in Christ. That is the basic factor in assurance.

2. That they may be brought to a knowledge that they have eternal life.

It is possible to have this knowledge, else John had written his Epistle in vain. His purpose, more than once expressed, was to assist his converts to attain this knowledge. It is clear from the Epistle that this assurance is attained by the coming together of certain rays: it is the result of combined evidence.

(a) There is this direct personal faith in Christ of which we have spoken. This alone channels eternal life into our experience. This is the faith that saves. But it does not always assure.

(b) There is the inward witness of the Spirit. This is subjective. Here the Spirit bears witness with our spirits that we are the children of God. *With our spirits* – with our spiritual nature, our inner beings, conscience in peace, heart in love, mind in light. The Spirit thus gives an inner illumination – seals the truth upon our spiritual nature, and gives the filial spark of love, trust, and obedience.

(c) There is the evidence of the Life. Here we examine our own lives in the light of what the Christian character should be. We look for the fruit of the Spirit as distinct from the works of the flesh. This has been spoken of as Evidential Assurance. When these three conjoin, when they meet and agree, that is the stable ground of assurance. Each separately is not enough. But these conjoining rays are to be set against a like number of other rays:-

(i) Direct faith alone. Here is the case of one who can look back on a past transaction – a day, an hour perhaps, when we made the first commitment. It is not enough to say that that transaction stands, and therefore you may be sure of your salvation, if you are not living now in the will of God and seeking to obey His commandments. That assurance is dead, and can breed presumption and disobedience, antinomianism.

(ii)It is not enough to derive our assurance from an inner consciousness of divine grace. An over subjectivism may well become mere mysticism – unrelated to the realities of life in conflict with sin and temptation. Mysticism of this kind may well prove a delusion – at any rate it alone does not provide an assurance that stands the strain of life.

(iii) It is not enough to base our assurance on our character and works of righteousness. This may breed a legalism that ends up in salvation by works. But when these three come together we have a

three – fold cord that is not easily broken – the committal of direct faith, the experience of peace and forgiveness and the life that manifests the founts of righteousness. Thus assurance is a living organism – direct faith the root, the marks of grace in the life the growth of the tree, and the witness of the Spirit the fruit.

3. Note the third proposition: that ye may believe – or go on believing – in the name of the Son of God.

No assurance that we may possess is to supercede or supplant a life of direct faith on the Son of God. The Christian can never afford to live on his past committal, or on his present feelings, or on his obedience of life. He must be looking unceasingly by faith to the Son of God. He must not change believing in his own salvation with believing in the life of Christ.

Conclusion

It is significant that there is a distinction commonly made between the assurance of faith and the assurance of sense, or as it is sometimes put the assurance of faith and the assurance of hope: the one is the direct act of faith, the other is the reflex act of faith.

The assurance of faith is thus an assurance regarding Christ; a confidence based on a certainty regarding Him. The assurance of sense is an assurance regarding ourselves, in that we are in a state of grace. By the assurance of faith we are assured of the truth of what God has said to us. By the assurance of sense we are assured of the reality of what God has wrought in us: the one is the root, the other is the fruit.

LOVE

A meaningful definition of love is difficult to arrive at, since so many feelings and attitudes and emotions go by this name. C. S. Lewis has written of the Four Loves - Affection, Friendship, Eros and Charity. But I cannot say that I found this classification helpful. In any case all those overlap one another, and scarcely one of them is found completely apart from the other three.

All are agreed, however, that love, in its true sense, is the deepest possible expression of moral personality: it is not an attribute so much as the spirit that animates or should animate all the virtues.

Our task here is simpler because we are thinking of love in the Christian context. It is something that is distinctive of the Christian life and has a quality that is not found anywhere divorced from the Christian experience. It has been said that Christian love contains the humility of the sinner and the devotion of the saved.

This places it apart from love as found in the thought and vocabulary of the non-Christian word. Christianity, indeed, had to rescue the world from polluting associations, and if it did not coin a new word it rescued one little used – agape -and stamped it afresh with the spirit of Christ.

And so we say that love is the fruit of the Spirit in the Christian character. As such it is distinctive and at its heart inimitable. It is an attitude of heart, a spirit that characterises every true Christian, and that finds expression in every relationship in life, raising human life to the level at which God meant it to be lived. Someone has said that 1 Cor. 13 – the Love Poem – depicts the character of a true gentleman.

1. Its Source

The entire Bible, both O. T. and N. T. , makes love the distinctive attribute of God in His relationship to His people. In the O. T. God Himself frequently unveiled this relationship as a love that was willing to suffer, and that was neither deviated by disobedience nor swayed by passion. To it alone was attributed the selection of Israel as a covenant people. 'Because He loved you' was the unanswerable ground of all His favours. Again and again Israel is told that it was God's love that made her precious to Him and not an intrinsic worth she possessed in His sight. There is very little indication of the universal love of God to be found in the O. T. and this is not to be expected since the O. T. was primarily given to the covenant Israel.

In the N. T. Christ spoke freely and to an increasing degree of the love of the Father to Him, and His love to His followers, and subsequently of God's love to His disciples. 'For the Father Himself loveth you' (John 16:27). Towards the close of His life He turned the thoughts of His disciples more and more to the love of the Father. This was taken up by the N. T. writers and John arrives at the equation 'God is Love'. In line with that equation of God and love John proceeds to say that 'he that loveth not knoweth not God, for God is love'. Without love, therefore, we are not on the same wavelength as God and cannot be in contact with Him.

To say that God is love, however, without a careful exposition of the term, is to open the way for all kinds of sentimentality. In modern usage the term too often connotes a mere indolent and indulgent good nature, which is almost diametrically opposed to what the Christian means in calling God love. Indolent good nature is the negation of love, because it signifies the absence of ethical concern. Indeed, it not infrequently springs from a self-indulgence which refuses to accept any moral restraints, which makes demands upon others, and none upon self, which puts the person himself always at the receiving end and has no sight of the rights of the one at the giving end. Love, however, as the Christian uses the term means the highest and most demanding attribute of personal beings, and finds its supreme example in the capacity of a God of love to give Himself to the uttermost.

The term 'God is love' is, on the other hand, construed to mean that God is nothing but love. That, of course, is based on a confusion as to the attributes of an infinite God. Because God is infinite, all of God is in every attribute. *Man* can divide himself between certain attributes – so much of each – so much compassion, so much justice, so much love, and there comes a point where compassion ends and justice alone operates. But God cannot be divided like that, because He is God and not man. So God is all justice, all mercy, all compassion, all love. In every situation in which God manifests His mercy, His justice, His love, God is there in all His attributes. The manifestation that each attribute takes depends on the particular situation that it meets.

Charles Wesley's often quoted phrase about Christ 'He emptied Himself of all but love' is an example of this confusion we have been speaking about. 'Nothing but love' is an impossibility for God as it would contradict His entire character. Found in man, it would be a negation of his personality. Found in God, it would be a denial of His essential goodness. God's love is the flowing out of all that God is – His righteousness, justice, His mercy and holy compassion are in sweetest harmony as they operate through the channels of love. This is the same as saying that God's love is an ethical quality – it is a holy love.

But love is a necessary attribute of God because He is a Trinity – a Fellowship of Persons whose very nature is a fellowship of life. That fellowship we call Father, Son and Holy Spirit would be impossible without love. The stream of life flowing in the Divine nature is flowing in love – the love of the Father to the Son, and the love of the Father and Son to the Spirit.

Now because God is fellowship of this kind, it is possible for Him to let His fellowship flow beyond Himself. He can communicate that fellowship. And when He communicates His fellowship He imparts His love. He can lift His creatures up into His fellowship and make them partakers of His love. And of course when He does this, He creates a responsive love in them. It is like taking a black ember, or a piece of coal and placing it in the middle of live embers – it soon glows. It cannot be there without becoming red hot.

So to be taken into the fellowship of God is to catch His love. And this was early recognised by the N. T. writers: 'We love Him because He first loved us'. 'Herein is love, not that we loved God but that He loved us'. Thus a Christian in fellowship with God is complete in that love that constitutes the Divine fellowship: his nature is transformed, affected through and through by God's love.

2. The Manifestation of the Divine Love

There is the love of the Creator for His creature, for the work of His hands:- it is significant that when God was about to create man we have the first hint of plurality in the Godhead: 'Let us make man in our image and after our likeness', because the creature man was to be lifted into the fellowship that is God. This Creator-love is often in the O. T. compared to a parent's love.

Among men we know what parental love is – a parent's love for his own child that bears his nature and image. This is often spoken of as a self-love – a loving ourselves in our children. Though it can be debased to this, it is not always so.

Parental love is capable of sacrificing self almost entirely, and has become the symbol of self-sacrificing love. God's love for His creatures that were made in His image, and still bear a likeness to Him is a patient, forbearing, long-suffering love. God found pleasure in His creation. The O. T. bears frequent reference to this love of God for His moral creatures, and for its manifestation in the provision made for their creaturely needs.

Though man has so often claimed independence of God, God has never for a moment ceased to provide for His creatures. He is a faithful Creator: His love still contains this ethical element of concern. He is not indulgent in His love. He does not look with a tolerant eye upon sin, since moral evil is fraught with pain and misery to the creature in all his relationships. It is the disintegration of God's workmanship. The surgeon's knife may be compared to the goodness and severity of God.

There is another manifestation of divine love that the O. T. contrasts rather than compares, with parental love. In Isaiah 49 we read: 'Can a woman forget her sucking child, that she may not have compassion on the son of her womb: yea, they may forget, yet will I not forget thee. Behold I have graven thee upon the palms of my hands'. This is love in contrast. He takes human love at its strongest and tenderest – a mother's love for her child. Then He contrasts His love for His people as He stretches out His hands and says 'Behold, I have done for thee what no mother has done for her child: behold I have graven thee upon the palms of my hands'. That is redeeming love – it involves identification, suffering, blood-shedding. If sin had not intervened, the Creator's love for His creature that bore His image would have satisfied us completely – we would rest in the faithful love of our Creator.

But sin has *marred* that relationship. It has not severed it: we are still God's creatures and He watches over us with faithful care. But we are creatures in revolt – we have claimed independence of our Creator. We became self-sufficient and unresponsive to His love and care. So God entered into a new relationship for us – that of Redeemer and Saviour. And this became a greater and deeper manifestation of His love than we had ever known before. To make contact with that love is to be transformed. Where do men make contact with that love?

Paul speaks of the love of God which is in Christ Jesus our Lord. Christ Himself had said 'No man cometh unto the Father but by Me', and again 'He that has seen Me hath seen the Father'. So there is no contact with this personal love of God except in Christ. All the Father's love is, as it were, composited in Christ, so that when we make contact with Christ we contact the love of God. It is therefore futile to speak vaguely of the general love of God as something that does not enter our experience, and that after all means little or nothing to us. A vague, general love is of no use to anyone: it is indeed not love at all. Love to be meaningful and real must be personal: only in this way can it create a personal response from us. A personal love is selective – it is the ground of our election among God's creatures and the election of this world in God's vast universe. There is one place where the love of God becomes intensely personal – at the Cross of Jesus Christ. Our personal involvement in what happened there is of a totally unique order. We are not spectators looking, we are actors and participants. And when God meets us there He is personal and active towards us. That is the aloneness which the Cross gives – the aloneness that lets us see the Atonement and the Atoner as entirely and completely our own. Thus each can speak of 'the Son of God who loved me and gave Himself for me'. There the love of God became intensely personal – we claim for ourselves what He has offered to all – we find ourselves at its heart and centre. It is that love that begets love in us.

3. What is Christian Love?

Christian love has been defined as the feeling begotten in our hearts towards God and towards our fellowmen by the penetration into our hearts of the sense of the love of God to us when He gave His Son to die for us. It is thus two-dimensional. It is vertical – Godwards and horizontal – manwards.

(a) Godwards. The love of God creates a responsive love in us. His love is shed abroad in our hearts by the Spirit that He has given us. It is a divine love that we give back to God.

It contains knowledge

'The eyes of your understanding being enlightened', we attain to a new knowledge of God, and in that knowledge He is loveable.

It contains experience

The experience of His pardon and peace. He is a God reconciled.

It contains access

We are called into His presence and fellowship. The fruit of all this is – that we love God – His love for us reflected back.

(b) Manwards. The horizontal reach of Divine love

As the love from God flows to its objects so the love of God in us overflows to others. That was Christ's picture of a quenched thirst, a personally satisfied soul. 'If any man thirst let him come unto me and drink. And whosoever believeth in me, out of his inner life shall flow rivers of living water' (John 7:37,38). And so John is insistent that he who loves God must love his brother also. To stem that spring is impossible – it will out. We are not creators of that love – we are aqueducts – channels by which the love of God flows to men, coloured of course by the terrain through which it passes, human and personal, but none the less divine.

Jesus added to Jewish thought in two directions:-

(i) He insisted that the commandment to love one's neighbour, did not limit one to a neighbour. Though it began at what was nearest to hand, it did not stop there. Cf the story of the Good Samaritan, where in answer to the question 'Who is my neighbour?', the answer is given anybody that has need of you and that you have opportunity to help.

(ii) He extended His demand to enemies. This was the new law of His Kingdom. The O.T. Law was 'Love thy neighbour as thyself' and the Jewish tradition added to it 'and hate your enemies'. Christ disavowed that tradition. This can be shown in giving him God's good news – in an evangelistic outreach, in overcoming his enmity by love for himself and endeavour for his highest good. That this can be done is one proof of the reality of Christianity.

4. What are the Characteristics of Christian Love?

God's love is not only the source of ours, it is also the pattern and exemplar of ours. 'A new commandment I give unto you' said Christ 'that ye love one another, as I have loved you'. That new commandment does not dispense with the others, but it animates them all - it pervades them with the Spirit that makes them work.

(a) It must be personal. If that is the quality of God's love for us, it is the quality of our love to God, and of our love to our fellows. The vague sentiment of goodwill, engendered by Christmas, the colourless feeling of general benevolence is not Christian love. God asks for personal

love, and he expects our love to our fellows to be personal. Cf 'Simon, son of Jonas, Lovest thou me, feed my sheep, my lambs'. It is personal love to Christ that enables us give personal service to our fellows out of love. This is the element of caring.

(b) That means that Love must be *Purposeful*. Love is credited with being blind: but blind as it may be to the faults and weaknesses of others it is not blind as to its purpose. It is enlightened and clear sighted love that acts on set purposes. There is thus a seriousness in love, a depth, a body that destroys a trifling flippancy.

(c) And that means the Love must be *Guided, Directed, Disciplined by Law*. So many people think that love needs no law, because it cannot go wrong. And so the reins are given to love to follow all its own behests regardless of consequences. That is not Christian love. Christian love is the fulfilling of the law. It is directed and controlled by the moral standards that God has given. Love has as its first duty – obedience. Christ has so directed: 'If ye love me keep my commandments'. God's law is written on our hearts and minds – an inward urge to obey

—on our minds in knowledge.
—on our hearts in love.

This introduces a moral sensitiveness into love, a sensitiveness that is part of its refining and purifying influence. When Augustine said 'Love and do as you like' he put it in the context of loving our fellows with the love of God – an ethical love.

(d) Christian love takes toll of the entire being. The O. T. command was 'To love the Lord our God with all our heart and soul and mind and strength' – our entire personality activated and stirred by love.

And that is Christian love wherever it operates: it grips the entire being, and brings it into service and obedience and sacrifice. It therefore makes large demands on us: it is a costly affair, or else it is not God's love. 'Hereby perceive we the love of God' says John, 'because he laid down his life for us, and we ought to lay down our lives for the brethren' (1 John 3:16). Thus love, true Christian love, can hold nothing back: it has no reserves – it goes the whole way. Because love is the spirit of Christ's command it penetrates the entire personality.

GOD'S GRACE AND MAN'S
A Study in Contrasts
(2 Sam. 13-18)

The grace of God revealed in Jesus Christ and operating in the salvation of men is altogether so Divine that in our human relationships it receives its clearest illustration only by contrast. In other words it is *the distinction and difference* between Divine Grace and any human grace that mark off the Grace of God as incomparable and unique. There is nothing analogous to it in the nature of man. As the Heavens are higher than the earth, so are God's ways in Grace higher than our ways. This truth finds striking illustration in the dealings of David with his rebel son Absalom. In the restoration of Absalom to the King's favour there was undoubtedly an expression of royal grace, but it was such grace as undermined the royal authority and fomented such further rebellion against the throne that David had to take refuge in flight. What were the elements of folly in the expression of David's grace, and wherein does it contrast with the grace of God towards the rebel children of men?

It was, first of all, *Restoration without Restitution.* In restoring his rebel son, David merely acted as father, and forgot his duty as king. He allowed his affection and indulgence towards his child to determine his action, while he neglected to bear his responsibility as king and ruler over God's nation. The result was that the rebel who had struck at lawful authority, using violence to usurp power and attain his ends, regardless of the anarchy it created or the bloodshed it might cause, was restored to a position of favour without requiring any restitution at his hands. Such restoration could only result in one thing, to confirm the rebel in his pride and anarchy and convince him that the royal authority could be defied and assaulted with impunity. David failed to realise that this act of his, in granting restoration without demanding restitution, had struck a blow at the foundations of his throne and had undermined law and order in his realm even more than the first open act of rebellion had done.

How different is the grace of God that reaches the rebel and restores him to favour in Jesus Christ! The Moral Ruler of the Universe, the Divine Lawgiver and Judge, must demand restitution before He can grant restoration, if the foundations of the Eternal Throne are to abide. And so there appeared in the fullness of time and in the guise of a servant One Who could contemplate His work and say: 'Then I restored that which I took not away'. Thus there had to be on man's side an act of full and complete restitution before there could be on God's side an act of restoration. And the restitution made in Jesus Christ was, in virtue of the dignity of His Person, so complete that not only did He satisfy justice and fulfil righteousness, but He magnified the law and made it honourable. And the Divine restoration is so complete that not only is the rebel reinstated in the Divine favour, but the sinner is adopted into the family of God. Here then we have a striking instance of human folly illustrating the wisdom of God.

In David's act there was the further folly of *Restoration without Reconciliation*. David's act, indulgent though it was, was imperfectly done. To the restored rebel he gave the instruction: 'Let him turn to his own house, but let him not see my face', and we read 'So Absalom returned to his own house and saw not the King's face'. When David thus restored his rebel son and refused to be reconciled to him, it had the effect of fanning the dying embers of rebellion, till the fires of revolt broke out again with devastating fury. And very soon the Kingdom was convulsed with a fresh uprising and David once again had to find refuge in sudden flight. Does not his folly serve as a foil to set off the wisdom of God's grace in dealing with men? He restores the rebel soul, but He reconciles before He restores! There are no half-measures and no reserves about the advances of Divine grace! God never restores and refuses to show the sinner His face in peace! Rather does He meet the sinner while he is yet 'a great way off' with the kiss of reconciliation. His call to restoration is always accompanied by an act of full and free pardon: 'I have blotted out, as a thick cloud, thy transgressions, and, as a cloud, thy sins: return unto Me; for I have redeemed thee'. And it is the experience of reconciliation that gives its melody to the Christian's praise: 'O Lord, I will praise Thee; though Thou wast angry with me, Thine anger is turned away, and Thou comfortedst me'. Thus restoration without reconciliation is as alien to God's grace as it is unsatisfying to man's heart and conscience. Only the folly of man acts so.

David was guilty of this further folly: he was satisfied with *Restoration without Regeneration*. Absalom was taken back by an act of clemency on the part of his father and king, who demanded no evidence of a change of heart. Absalom was at heart a rebel, and as a rebel he came back to his father's kingdom. His pride was not uprooted, his rebel spirit was not tamed, his nature was as perverse as ever. There was a change of position but not of heart. And the result was that the fires of rebellion soon broke out afresh. The grace of God regenerates when it restores. As it bestows upon us a new position, so it gives us a new nature. If it were not so, we would abuse the grace of God and consume it upon our own lusts. The God who 'hath blessed us with all spiritual blessings in heavenly places in Christ' has also 'chosen us in Him before the foundation of the world that we should be holy and without blame before Him in love'. Thus it is that those who are 'called in Christ' are also 'sanctified in Christ'; restoration is accompanied by regeneration and sanctification.

These observations, contrasting the wisdom of God's grace with the folly of man's grace, may serve to some little extent as a corrective to much loose thinking about the treatment that a Christian people should mete out to those who have plunged the world into the misery and suffering of war. It is seldom that we find this matter dealt with in the spirit of Jesus Christ or in the light of the grace of God. To face the situation on the plane of Christian behaviour would save us from the extremes of mere vindictiveness and of foolish indulgence. If we remembered that in God's dealings with mankind there could be no restoration without restitution, reconciliation and regeneration, we, as 'imitators of God' should translate that spirit into practice in our relationship with those who have maimed the world and desecrated what is hallowed in human life.

FOUR GREAT CONVERSIONS
Studies in the Art of Catching Men Alive

When the Master said to Simon: 'Fear not, from henceforth thou shalt catch men', He was not merely commissioning Simon for his life's task; He was restating the Christian's vocation and reaffirming a disciple's master-passion. All Simon's preparation and education, both in the knowledge of himself and in the unveiling of his Master's will, were directed to this end. Preparation and education there must be, since this most difficult and delicate of all arts takes toll of all we have and all we are. 'He that winneth souls is wise' was the dictum of one who was himself wise, and it takes no ordinary wisdom, as it takes no ordinary preparation, to master so complex and intricate an art. Grammarians, indeed, tell us that the word here translated *winneth* means at least four different things: it is used of activities as diverse as capturing a city, catching fish, winning affection and making a fortune, and it is probable that the wise man applied all four to the business of soul-winning. C.H. Spurgeon was in the habit of saying that a successful minister of the Gospel would be successful in any calling, since success in the ministry required qualities of mind and heart that would ensure success anywhere. This business of soul-winning, this *catching men alive*, as our Lord's words may be rendered, takes such an exacting toll of all our mental, moral and spiritual resources that only the wisdom that is from above is adequate to the task. The Book of Acts – the soul-winner's textbook – provides some striking examples of soul-winning that are set down as patterns for those who would catch men alive. It may be instructive to look at four of these in turn, the conversions of the Ethiopian Eunuch, of the Philippian Jailor, of Saul of Tarsus, and of Lydia of Thyatira.

I

The conversion of the Ethiopian Eunuch provides an example of the Spirit of God operating through *the enlightening of the understanding*. It is a vivid picture that the Book of Acts draws of that scene in the solitude of the desert. Along the caravan route there rides this swarthy son of Africa with a Bible open on his knee. As he draws near we can hear him uttering those great words of Isaiah's concerning a suffering Messiah, and words so instinct with life and passion seem strangely lifeless on the lips of this desert pilgrim. Philip breaks in upon the traveller's meditations with the arresting question: 'Understandeth thou what thou readest ?' It was a shaft prepared not by Philip, but by Philip's Lord. The answer was laden with helplessness and perplexity: 'How can I except some man should guide me?' Thereupon Philip went up and sat beside him – no small matter for a Jew in dealing with a Gentile, but the necessary qualification for a soul-winner who would lead the anxious and perplexed to the Saviour – and from this place of contact he 'began at the same Scripture and preached unto him Jesus'. It was no mere coincidence that Philip's preaching should *begin* there – where the Cross is uplifted in prophecy and the fact of sin-bearing revealed and interpreted. And this preaching of Jesus was to the Ethiopian the transmission of heaven's light, the illumination that he sought for in vain in the sacrifices of the temple, in the obedience of worship, in the pages of the Book, and became the light that led to peace and sent him on his way rejoicing. It is good that we should remember how the Holy Spirit's first approaches to the soul may come in enlightening the understanding, shedding illumination into the darkened mind from the Cross on which sin was borne and expiated. For this reason the soul-winner is often required to direct his message to the understanding, to remember that salvation is a Way, and to exert all his efforts in shedding light upon a plan that is the product of infinite intelligence and wisdom. In this aspect catching men is most truly like making a fortune – something that calls for planning and forethought, something that asks for the concentration of efforts to one end, the presentation to the understanding of 'God's easy, artless, unencumbered plan'.

II

The conversion of the Philippian Jailor introduces us to another aspect of effective Gospel work – that of *rousing the conscience*. Here indeed to win is to fish – for it takes the application of all the fisherman's art to draw and hold the sinner's conscience. The Jailor of Philippi had a rough awakening, an awakening suited to his nature and character. A Roman soldier, by nature and training rough, brutal, unfeeling, and filling a position that brought out all that was rough and brutal in a man, he had no respect for God or man, no sense of sin, no consciousness that he possessed a soul. It took an earthquake to do that! It was amidst this midnight upheaval – the earth underfoot reeling, prison doors flung open, and panic-struck prisoners all around

– that the question was proposed: 'Sir, what must I do to be saved?' There in the prison yard Paul uplifted the Cross bearing a Saviour clothed in the majesty of His three-fold office, the Lord Jesus Christ, and soon the rough barbarian, on bended knee, was washing the wounds of the saints with a hand as gentle and tender as a child's! The conscience roused, the man was 'caught alive' and made 'a new creature in Christ Jesus'. If we are thus to catch men we have to learn the art of dealing with slumbering consciences, with seared consciences, with awakened consciences, with wounded consciences, and with dead consciences. And the soul-winner frequently finds that where the mind is unable to grasp the message, the conscience is quick to feel its power, for conscience and not intellect is the true interpreter of Calvary and its sacrifice.

III

The third example of conversion is that of Saul of Tarsus, and it illustrates *the capture of the will.* Here to win is most truly to capture a city. Saul's will was resolutely set against submission to the faith. Trained in the theology of the Pharisees, versed in the traditions of the Jewish religion, schooled in the Law and the Prophets, he knew the right and pursued the wrong. He had seen the face of Stephen radiating the glory of the Throne, and that face had haunted him ever since. He was in the grasp of something or Someone he could not shake off, and he struggled with all the fury of a cornered beast to set himself free. Saul's was a stubborn, indomitable will that kicked against the goad and refused to yield to the hand that laid upon it its gentle but firm pressure. But the end came when the rebel threw up the arms of his defiance and cried, as he lay prostrate in the dust: 'Lord, what wilt Thou have me to do?'. The will was there surrendered, and henceforth obedience was the keynote of Paul's life, the master-passion of his soul. To win souls is to capture a city, and for the assault on man's defiant will, the soul-winner must be equipped with the whole armour of God.

IV

A further example of the soul-winner's art is illustrated in the conversion of Lydia; in her case *the winning of the heart.* Religious, dutiful, industrious, upright, she needed that her heart's affections be captured for the Heavenly Bridegroom. As she listened to the words that Paul had spoken – or, as we find elsewhere, 'she applied to herself the words that Paul had spoken' – the heart was opened by a sure and unerring hand, and its throne was offered, then and forever, to the Lover of her soul. Henceforth Christ dwelt in her heart by faith, and her religion evermore was the religion of the open heart. And the open-hearted Lydia becomes the mother of European Christianity, the first sheaf of a great and rich harvest! The Gospel of the grace of God applies its overtures of mercy to the human heart, captures its affections, and sanctifies and consecrates them to the service of God. It thus lets loose a power that accomplishes much in claiming the home and the family and the most sacred relationships in life for God and His Kingdom, and that lays it all upon the altar with but this one plea: 'We love Him because He first loved us'. The soul-winner that wins the heart – a man's, a woman's, a mere child's – for the Kingdom of God is most truly 'catching men alive' and rendering to his Lord a service that only love can give and love can requite.

Here are four classic examples of the soul-winner's art, four impressive illustrations of the workings of the mighty Spirit of God, and a recall to these first principles of Gospel operations would equip every Christian to be 'instant in season and out of season', and so 'do the work of an evangelist' in catching men alive.

TAUGHT TO PRAY
('Lord, teach us to pray': Luke 11:1)

T he disciples had been with Christ in a certain place, and had heard Him pray. What a prayer it must have been! How earnest, how heavenly, how divine! For the disciples it served as a glimpse into the inner secret of that life of unruffled calm and unwavering trust and majestic power: they saw in that prayer the connection between His public life of miracles and His private life of devotion. And feeling themselves but mere children in the art of prayer, they come to Him with the petition 'Lord, teach us to pray'. When we learn that our inner life of prayer is the measure of our outer life of power and strength, we, too, shall approach the Mercy Seat with this petition 'Lord, teach us to pray'.

Why need we be taught to pray?

How was it that the disciples just then felt awakening within them a desire to pray? Perhaps they saw as never before, the *privilege* of prayer. During their sojourn in His company, they saw their Master pray often and much, and now, beholding Him once again in prayer, they could not but feel impressed with the unique privilege of prayer. And a privilege prayer truly was to our Lord, for we know that He prayed in all His circumstances, in joy and in sorrow, in company and alone, and we read of Him getting up 'a great while before day' to pray, and 'continuing all night in prayer'. Now, when we remember that He had no sin for which to ask for forgiveness, no guilt to trouble His conscience, no want indeed which, if He exercised His divine power, He could not Himself supply, then we realise what a privilege He reckoned it to pray. And it surely is the great privilege of earth that men can pray. Prayer is the privilege of continual access to God through the rent veil; it is the privilege of standing as priests in the Divine Presence; it is the privilege of using boldness in the presence of God petitioning, reasoning, pleading with Him. Prayer gives us a right to take hold of God, of His faithfulness, His mercy and His grace. Thus the prayerless soul is a soul adrift from God in an abandoned world. Were we to understand the unspeakable privilege of being alone with God in prayer, how earnestly would we cry 'Lord, teach us to pray'.

The disciples may have felt too something of the *power* of prayer. As they watched their Master in prayer they realised something of the close relationship between the wonder-working life in public and the wrestling life of prayer in private. They saw prayer as a wonderful power and dynamic in the life, as a weapon that would prevail with God and with men, and they desired to possess it. When we realise that prayer was a weapon which the Son of God in His humiliation always employed, we realise something of the wonderful power of prayer. Alike in the personal life of faith and in the public life of service there is no power that can take the place of prayer; by it God fulfils His promises in us and through us, and hastens the coming of His Kingdom in our hearts and in the world. Thus it is that the disciples were never, to our knowledge, taught to preach, though to be men of God they must be taught to pray, for the prayer that gives power with God gives power with men, and makes us channels of blessing to the world. What a poor, starved, futile, life ours often is just because we do not keep open the channel of prayer between us and the God of Promise. Remembering that the coming of the Kingdom is waiting on the prayers of God's people, how earnestly should we cry, 'Lord, teach us to pray'.

We may infer from this request that the disciples realised too the *difficulty* of prayer. As devout Jews they were acquainted with the forms of prayer in common use, and were, no doubt, themselves accustomed to pray; but now when they heard their Master pray they felt that they could not pray, that, in fact, they had never prayed, and they cry, 'Lord, teach us to pray'. Prayer now appears to them in a new light: before it was a facile ceremony of mere repetition, now it is a heavenly service, and it becomes a hard and difficult task. And real prayer is ever a hard and difficult exercise, for it is the humbling and abasing of the soul before God's Throne – and that is not easy for proud and rebellious spirits: it is the exalting of God to His rightful place of sovereignty and power -and that is not easy for self-willed and self-sufficient souls. To realise the true meaning of prayer is to confess that 'we know not what to pray for as we ought'. With a mind so dark, a soul so dead, a spirit so earth-bound, we need to be trained by a master-hand; and we must ever come to the foot of the Throne with the humble plea, 'Lord, teach us to pray'.

By whom must we be taught to pray?

The disciples did not err when they brought this difficulty to the Master, for none else is sufficient to train men in the exercise of prayer. We realise this when we consider that we need Christ to *quicken* us to prayer. The disciples knew this, for those prayers they used before they met the Master were no prayers at all; it needed His quickening touch to awaken them to real prayer: it needed His heavenly hand to arouse the slumbering heart and His heavenly light to illumine the darkened mind ere there could be true prayer. It was so with Saul of Tarsus, for devout Pharisee that he was, he prayed often, in private and public, long, elaborate, laborious prayers; but it needed the arresting voice of the Lord Jesus and the heavenly illumination on the Jerusalem-Damascus road to put him to his knees, so that it could be said of him 'Behold he prayeth'. It is only the heavenly breath of Christ's own life that can make our life like unto His life – a life of all-prayer. And since we know that He prayed often amidst the tears and trials and sufferings of His earthly life, He is for us the one true and skilled Teacher of prayer.

But again we need Christ to *sustain* us in prayer. Perseverance in prayer is so difficult to attain to that none but Christ can ever teach it; He is the perfect example of continued, unceasing, untiring prayer, for all through His earthly life He prayed. and He continues now to pray in heaven, where 'He ever liveth to make intercession for us'. And He waits to take His disciples into the fellowship of continuous intercession that they may learn to 'pray without ceasing'. As the arms of Moses, uplifted in prayer upon the mount, grew more weary than the arms of Joshua in the battle below, so the suppliant at the Throne of Grace has often to lament listlessness and weariness in prayer. We need to tarry at the foot of the Throne that we may learn to pray, and if God keeps us there without the expected answer, it is, perhaps, to teach us perseverance in prayer.

We likewise need the Lord Jesus Christ to give us *resignation* in prayer. Our Lord could offer up 'prayers and supplications with strong crying, and tears unto Him who was able to save Him from death', yet He learned submission in prayer to His Father's will. He who raised the earnest cry 'Father if it be possible, let this cup pass from me', did as earnestly add, 'not my will, but thine, be done'. None but He can teach us to accept God's will and be resigned to God's purpose while we pray. To pray without ceasing is hard, but is it not often the case that to accept the answer without rebelling is harder still? Since our will must be brought into harmony with God's will, nay more, since our will must be lost in God's will, ere we can pray aright, none but the Lord of all grace can teach us to pray.

How may we be taught to pray?

It may not be amiss to inquire if Christ has any familiar ways of schooling backward souls in the exercise of prayer. He does it commonly, no doubt, by the *spiritual convictions* of His Holy Spirit. The Spirit of God is called the Spirit of Supplications, because that is an important office He executes within the hearts of men when 'He maketh intercession within us with groanings which cannot be uttered'. And the Spirit teaches us to pray, often, by discovering to us our need, by revealing to us our weakness and our wants, for prayer presupposes a discovery of our own selves and of our most urgent and vital needs. Thus it is that while we plead, 'Lord, teach us to pray', the Spirit may reveal to us our destitution and guilt and need, till we cry 'God be merciful to me, a sinner'. And thus too, it is that our prayers are so prayerless, because our souls are so unconscious of need. We know that the Lord often teaches men to pray by His *daily providences*. We cry 'Lord, teach us to pray', and straightway He brings us into the darkness of sorrow, into the fierce gale of temptation, into the hot furnace of affliction, till, under the pressure of our burden and suffering and sorrow, we are compelled to pray. In this connection it has been observed that Absalom's method of securing an interview with the unwilling Joab points to a discipline which God often uses to bring the wandering soul to Himself in prayer. In the light of the burning 'barley field' many a soul was able to see his way back to God, for He assures us 'In their afflictions they shall seek me early'.

The Lord at times gives wonderful *divine revelations* in the way of teaching His people to pray. Prayer presupposes not only a knowledge of self but also a knowledge of God, and it is in the measure in which we grow in the knowledge of God that we can grow in prayer. To see, however dimly and however distant, a personal God, is to see the possibility of prayer; to see the mercy of God in Christ is to see the hope of prayer; and to see the promises of God in the Gospel is to see the warrant of prayer. When God is revealed to the soul in His boundless sufficiency, when the sacrifice of Christ is seen in its infinite merit, when the grace of the Spirit is known in its inexhaustible fullness, the soul *must* pray. And the fuller the revelation the more real and spiritual the prayer, for prayer is worship and communion and fellowship.

Do we pray? If so, we shall find here a petition intimately suited to our deepest need, 'Lord, teach us to pray'. Are we prayerless? Then we can approach the Mercy Seat with this one short plea 'Lord, teach us to pray'.

THE UNREASONABLENESS OF UNBELIEF
(A Word to the Gospel Hearer)

It is a remarkable peculiarity of the Gospel records that they succeed in conveying not only the meaning and message of the written word, but on many occasions the tone of the spoken word and that inflection of the voice that must have conveyed so much to the original hearers. This is particularly true of the recorded words of the Lord Jesus Christ. At times it is possible to catch the note of an exquisite tenderness in His words, as when He said on a memorable occasion: 'Woman, has any man condemned thee?...Neither do I condemn thee, go and sin no more' (John 8:11}. At other times one feels the note of deep sympathy that throbs in His words, as when He said to Mary at the empty tomb: 'Woman, why weepest thou?'. Then there is the tone of hopefulness and comfort in which He said to Martha: 'Thy brother shall rise again'. And it is not difficult to detect the notes of grave admonition and stern finality in the words: 'If ye believe not that I am He, ye shall die in your sins'. A little more perplexing to us – on first thought in any case - is the note of surprise often expressed in Christ's words. Was there anything that could be an occasion of surprise to Him? It is definitely asserted that on one occasion 'He marvelled at their unbelief', and it is possible oft-times to catch this note of surprised feelings, of disappointed expectations, in the voice of One Who, though the Son of God, was also most truly the Son of Man. The occasion we have in mind most particularly at the present moment is that recorded by John, where the Saviour's words can – and probably should – be translated 'Ye search the Scriptures, for in them ye think ye have eternal life and they are they which testify of me, and ye will not come to me that ye might have life'. Here surely we have an expression of wonder and surprise, and it were well for us to ponder deeply the occasion for it, since it concerns the relation to the Gospel message of seemingly religious people more intimately than that of any other people.

Surprise at Spiritual Indecision

We note first, that this surprise was occasioned by a people's *Spiritual Indecision*: they are enquiring but not coming. 'Ye search the Scriptures' was not a charge levelled against them, but a true description of their attitude to religious things. They were a religious people, and they made it their duty to examine the sacred records of their faith. So far, good! But it was merely a mental occupation, an attitude of mind, and it came short of being a spiritual act of coming to Him; therefore does He charge them with this inconsistency: 'But ye will not come to me that ye might have life'. It apparently surprised Him that they should stop short just there – a mere mental enquiry without any spiritual effort! That anyone should care enough to enquire, to search for the way, and not move spiritually along that way towards Him, was what surprised Him! It was the spiritual indecision that refused to break off from the old moorings and launch out Christwards! It was the absence of that moral and spiritual resolution, of that urge deep down in the soul, an absence that leaves the soul where it was, without God and without life. This fact should cause many of us to pause and ponder. We are not irreligious, we are 'interested' in spiritual things, in fact we have the mental attitude of enquiry. We listen to a sermon with discriminating interest, and we sometimes go to the Bible to find out things. But we make no movement Christwards, we don't come to Him! It is all a mental interest, and there is no spiritual urge, no moral dynamic behind it. We rest content with this condition of mental enquiry, because the next step would involve a moral and spiritual departure. It means cutting away from the old moorings, snapping old ties, leaving familiar haunts, and familiar pleasures, and familiar sins, and this we have not yet decided to do! It is the fact that coming to Christ involves a severance of old ties and old associations, that it is a great breakaway, that stands between men and the duty of a solemn moral and spiritual decision. The Bible lays bare some startling cases of spiritual failure, but this is probably the sunken reef on which most of them have made shipwreck, that they declined to be broken away from the old life! For every one that has been hindered from coming to Christ by mental difficulties, there must be hundreds who are prevented by the solemn moral issues involved.

Surprise at Spiritual Unrecptiveness

The Saviour's surprise seems to have been caused too by His hearers' *Spiritual Unreceptiveness:* they were desiring but not receiving. 'Ye think that in them ye have eternal life' indicates a people that were actually in quest of eternal life, in whom there was a certain spiritual quickening, an awareness of the existence of the life eternal, and a desire to possess it. For this reason they searched the Scriptures, thinking that in this way they would discover the secret of the life everlasting. And yet alongside this diligence there was the stubborn refusal to come to Him that they might *have* life. In other words, they would not accept the life they sought after, and perhaps longed for! That is to say, they would not accept it on the conditions on which it was offered to them, and on the only terms on which they could become possessors. May it not be true that many of us are in this surprising situation? We would be possessors of eternal life because we are conscious that it is the only prize worth having. We have an awareness that we are children of eternity, that time does not exhaust our being or complete our existence, that we must meet our Master and present our account, that we are heirs to an eternal destiny. For that reason our attitude to the Bible is one of deep respect, even of reverence and awe, because in it eternal life is offered, and through it eternal life may be possessed. But we will not come to Christ that we may have that for which we search! We refuse to be receivers, and when it comes to accepting the gift, we decline to go so far in the matter. We are willing to be seekers of the way, but we refuse to agonise to enter it by the gate. Is it not because entering in involves the contest and the surrender that we shrink from? We, merchants of goodly pearls, would have the Pearl of Great Price in our treasure house, but we will not sell all that we have that we may obtain it! Was this not the issue which the Rich Young Ruler refused to face, or having faced refused to yield to? In spite of his great possessions he felt an aching void in his soul, and he desired 'to inherit eternal life'. Christ, with His true insight into every man's heart, put His finger on the great obstacle to the acceptance of eternal life: 'Sell all thou hast'! In other words, you must sell out, before you can take in! And the Ruler decided not to sell out; it was too big a transaction, 'for he had great possessions'. And the same note of surprise, of which we are speaking, appears in Christ's observation on this case: 'How hardly shall they that have riches enter into the Kingdom of heaven! It is a matter of surprise to the Saviour that men should remain spiritually unreceptive, desiring and not receiving!

Surprise at Spiritual Disobedience

Christ might well express surprise at this example of *Spiritual Disobedience*. Here were a people faithfully guided, but never reaching the goal. They were correctly directed in their quest when they examined the Scriptures, for of these Scriptures they had in their hands Christ said: 'They are they which testify of me'. It is as if he had said: 'You have gone to the right place for guidance to the goal of eternal life, and yet you will not come unto me that you might have eternal life. You are guided to me, but you will not come to me'. Christ found no fault with their diligence in searching the Scriptures; it was to emphasise this, perhaps, that our Authorised Version translators adopted the alternative rendering: 'Search the Scriptures'. The Scriptures, even of the Old Testament then in their hands, pointed the enquirer unerringly to the One Who would bestow life, and almost every chapter of the Book contained an index finger pointing to the source of life about to be revealed. But though the Jews had such an unerring guide to Him, they refused to come to Him. They gave outward obedience in searching the Scriptures, but they refused to give inward spiritual obedience by coming to Him. And this glaring inconsistency surprised Him! Many people in our midst are in similar circumstances. They are guided aright from the Book and from the pulpit, and the teaching they receive lays bare the Fountain of life. And yet we have as little spiritual maturity discernible as others. It is because more than direction is needed and more than accurate knowledge; obedience to the truth we know is needed, for that alone brings us to Christ. And spiritual obedience entails not merely a surrender of the old life to Christ, but also a building of the new life on Him. Christ in all that He is and has done and ever shall do is to become the sole foundation of the life henceforward. It is here that submission is refused, and the new life is still-born because of disobedience. Even the Rich Young Ruler must have felt the force of this, since he was given the direction not only 'sell all that thou hast', but likewise: 'Come, follow me'. Not only was he asked to pull down the old, but to build afresh a new life upon a new foundation. And the completeness of this obedience that Christ demands hinders many from final acceptance of Him. But there can be no half-measures, no compromise, and no lowering of His demands. He claims to be not only the direction, but the *way*, not only the teacher, but the *truth*, not only the means of sustenance, but the *life*. And He marvels at the disobedience of men that decline to come to Him the Way, the Truth and the Life.

It is only Gospel hearers, those acquainted with the truth, the religious-minded, that can occasion such surprise to the Saviour of men. They are those who are enquiring but not coming, desiring but not receiving, guided but not arriving! Are we such a people?

PEACE WITH GOD

I suppose one might define peace as a state in which our entire personality finds fulfilment. If that be so, true peace bears on all the centres of life, intellectual, moral, emotional, and volitional.

Intellectually we have peace when the mind reaches a certainty in which it can rest, works its way to a light that satisfies.

Morally we have peace when the conscience finds right and not wrong in active control, where it is satisfied that it is dealing with truth. *Emotionally* we have peace when the heart rests in an object, personal or impersonal, that it deems worthy of its trust and devotion.

Volitionally we have peace when the will is brought into harmony with a power that works its highest good, that releases it for service and free obedience.

Peace is thus not complete, or indeed real peace, until it reaches the entire personality and becomes relevant to every instinct of our nature. There is a partial peace that leads only to tension and conflict within – it is inadequate to deal with the entire situation – it serves but to intensify the dissatisfactions, the aching void, within.

It follows, almost by definition, that only God – the God who made us for Himself – can bestow perfect peace – a peace that sweeps our entire nature. The claim of Christianity is that it bestows that peace. That peace is found not in a theory or philosophy but in a person. Christianity is Christ, and Christ is our peace. 'For He is our peace'. (Eph. 2:14).

It is when Christ comes into a relationship with us that links Him to us and we to Him in faith, trust, love, and obedience that the peace of God becomes a reality to our entire nature. And this peace pervades our entire manhood and womanhood. It sweeps over our nature like a wave of the sea filling up every nook and cranny. It adapts itself to every situation and becomes splendidly relevant to our complex personality:

In our minds – it is light.
In our conscience – it is conviction.
In our hearts – it is purity.
In our wills – it is freedom.

That is what we mean by saying that the peace of God completely satisfies.

1.   To those who meet Him in the commitment of faith Christ is Light, a Light that illumines and awakens, and satisfies the understanding, that brings us into contact with the mind of Christ. Christ makes His first impact on the human personality as the Light that sheds its illumination upon life in all its mystery and difficulty and predicament. Christianity is perhaps the only religion that recognises the claims of intellect in this way. Other religions are mere taboos, mystery is their stock-in-trade, ignorance becomes the mother of their devotion. Not so in our Christian faith: it deals with Him who is the Light of the world. When a man is confronted with Christ he is confronted with a challenge to his thinking, to his understanding, to his thought-life. And in Christ light is shed on life as a whole, and not on part of it. Christ lets you see life from God's side – and that means life as a whole – life in all its bearings, its purposes, its meaning, its goal, its destiny.

What constituted life before is seen in its proper proportion as merely incidentals, something on the very fringe of life. But life itself is now laid bare, and its difficult heart-searching problems are faced. Where did I come from? Why am I here? Where am I going to? What is to be my destiny? Christ alone deals adequately with all these problems, shedding light upon them from God's side. Meeting with Christ is thus a Great-Awakening – the mind is alerted, the intellect quickened, the thought-life penetrated. and the radiance of God shed upon our earthly path and our earthly cares, till in His light we see light clearly. And a man thus empowered by Christ is able to bypass many of the superficial and oft supercilious questions of life with the honest admission: 'One thing I know that whereas I was blind, now I see'. And as the opening of eyes to the man born blind, as the light of day to those who dwelt in the gloom of night, so is Christ to those who make contact with Him by faith. So is Christ to those to whose faith He unveils Himself as the light of men. And this is the peace of those who were once blind and now see, the peace of those who see the great issues clearly.

2.   Christ is Peace to the Moral Nature of man, because He restores the lost harmony, because He brings into a man's nature a sense of reconciliation, because He leads to more than understanding, He brings conviction: understanding can be superficial – it need not be transforming – but conviction is rooted in our moral natures – it grips and holds and controls. Here are things that become meaningful to a man's conscience, here is something that conscience can interpret and assess.

For example, Christ makes it His business to deal with sin, the radical cause of dispeace within – conflict. He deals with sin as a factor in every man's life, as a factor that each man must face as his own great personal problem – the cause of his conflict and defeat. At such a time sin becomes real – no mere metaphysical abstraction – and you face up to God's judgment upon your sinful life. Christ is truth and as you deal with Him the searchlight of God's truth shines into your nature. You know, beyond all doubt, that you are a sinner and sin is no abstraction – it is something that alienates you from God, something that disrupts your own character, something that shadows your destiny.

It is at this stage that Christ flashes into your ken the Good News of the Gospel of Peace – that peace which flows from reconciliation, and reconciliation is made by God – a reconciliation that reconciles Him to you and you to Him, a reconciliation that conveys the assurance, the authority, the peace of Divine pardon to your conscience.

It is not pardon cheaply given – it is full and free – but not cheap. Its foundation was laid in suffering and sorrow and death by One of whom it was said that 'He was wounded for our transgressions, bruised for our iniquities, chastised for our peace, by whose stripes we are healed'.

Secured at a cost, but secured by the One who bestows it: it satisfied Him, it satisfies you, it accords with the moral principles that uphold the universe, it can bear the scrutiny of the last assize, it is the peace of God, and it is your peace. That gives peace to the moral nature of man – peace of conscience – the peace that flows from the consciousness that all is well between us and God – all is covered by our asking Divine forgiveness. As Christ reconciled you to the mind of God, so now He rconciles you to the character of God – to the holiness of God in His judgment of our sin.

3. Christ is Peace to the Emotional Nature of man because He provides a unifying centre for the emotional life – a centre that is clean and uplifting and inspiring. You see Christ is Light, He is Truth. But He is also *Love* – He opens in the swamps of a man's emotions a clean spring of love and gratitude and devotion. To a man whose life had been marred and soiled and corrupted He offers satisfaction with the added promise: 'The water that I shall give shall be in him a well of water springing up into everlasting life'.

We all know how disordered the emotional life can become – how it breaks loose, throws off the restraint of reason – of mind and of conscience, so that we ruefully say that a man acts foolishly because he is ruled by his heart rather than by his head. This is because the emotions are not properly centred. They are not coordinated with the rest of us – and in such a condition they can bring havoc, quick and terrible, to a life – to more than one life.

Why has Christianity become recognised as the religion of love – because it has recognised the true worth, the tremendous potentiality of human emotion, because it has laid emphasis on heart-religion, because at its very centre it presents the challenging question 'Lovest thou Me more than these?'. And when Christ becomes real to a man as Saviour and Lawmaster, He becomes real to a man's heart – He becomes the focal point of man's deepest emotions. He channels our emotions in one direction, He co-ordinates our emotional life into one supreme passion: He becomes the object of trust and devotion Himself. For in Him we make contact with the love of God – 'the Love of God which is in Christ Jesus our Lord'. It is easy to talk lightly, thoughtlessly, of the love of God, but it never becomes meaningful to us till we make contact with it in Christ Jesus our Lord. That is our point of contact that creates and awakens our responsive love to Him.

And when the redeeming love of God sweeps over a person's heart it is a cleansing stream, it purifies, it uplifts, it ennobles. When the love of God touches human love it cleanses and ennobles it. When it enters a human heart to abide there, it controls, it cleanses, it purifies and it satisfies.

And that is peace – true peace – to the human heart – in the cleansing stream of God's love.

4. Christ gives Peace to the Volitional Nature of man because He both liberates and empowers the will of man. We all know the dispeace, the hesitancy, the indecision that comes from a vacillating will, a conquered will, a will that is no longer able to assert itself, a will that is at the mercy of every wind that blows from within or without, that has lost its independence and its power of self-assertion. That is degradation, humiliation complete – it is the final dismantling of a human character.

But the Christ who is light and reconciliation and love is also Power in a man's life. He enters as Lord and Master. He presents His own will as our true inspiration and proper line of duty. In doing this, He liberates our will from all that enslaves it and enlists it in His most blessed service – under His yoke. And that is true freedom. To be without a master is to be still a slave. To have our will line up gladly with the will of our Redeemer is to be as free as a bird is in the air and a fish in the sea. To link our wills with His is to be empowered to decide and accept the life He would have us live.

This is Liberty – but not licence. And in that liberty there is peace – reconciled to the will of God. So you see what Christ's peace is – it is a great reconciliation to the mind of God, to the character of God, to the heart of God, to the will of God, giving light, conviction, purity and liberty.

Perhaps we understand now why Paul says 'He is our peace', and why elsewhere He speaks of the Peace of God that passeth all understanding keeping as by a garrison our hearts and minds – the peace of God is a military force – it keeps by strength – by force of arms – when all the odds would seem against us. Of course it passed all our understanding - it is completely unlike what we had reason to expect – it contradicts our fears, goes in the teeth of our calculations and expectations.

And it is the peace of God – and like all Divine things it is yours for the taking – it is yours in the supreme gift of His Son Jesus Christ – for He is our peace. Now Christian faith – saving faith -is just that relationship to Christ – that acceptance of Christ, that commitment to Christ – that brings the peace of God into our moral experience. Being justified by faith – being put right with God on God's own terms, we have peace with God through our Lord Jesus Christ.

THE GOSPEL FOR THE SPACE AGE

On a notice board of one of our city churches I noticed the other day:'The Gospel for the Space Age'. I wondered greatly how it was to be used by the minister. If he thought the gospel would have to be radically changed to adjust it to the Space Age. As if there was never a Space Age till now; if we were not in space, citizens of space, travellers in space, through all the thousands of years that have gone. As if the Bible and Gospel did not occupy the expanses of space.

In fact there is not a Book ever written that deals more authoritatively with what is going on in space, and what will yet go on in space as the Bible does. It speaks of the God who inhabits eternity and sits on the circle of the earth. It speaks of the other inhabitants of space as principalities and powers in the heavenly places. It speaks of a potentate whose domain is in space as the Prince of the power of the air. It speaks of the formation of a new heaven and a new earth.

It traverses the whole of space as under the sovereign control of the Creator and Preserver of all, and sheds its light upon what time and space mean in relation to its redemptive message.

But when I read the church notice board 'The Gospel in the Space Age', I thought instinctively of John 3:16 which deals with one of the planets in space, and illumines it by the redeeming love of the Creator who is also its Saviour. And whatever our preoccupation with other planets in space our concern as Christians is with our own, in which God sheds the light of His revelation. The task of the Bible is to relate the world to the Creator and Lord of the Universe. And the relation is that of love.

God's Love is Selective

'God so loved the world'. We do not know much of other possible worlds in space or whether any are inhabited by rational beings or not, but we do know that the Love of God has selected our planet in space as the objective of His love. This is of the nature and essence of love. If it had not the right and prerogative to select, it would not be love as we know it.

God's love is a personal love – which means that it settles on persons – on creatures who possess normal personality. But because it is personal love it selects the persons who are the objects of its love. Any vague impersonal general love is not personal love at all: we may call it benevolence, good will, altruism, but it is not love.

So because God's love is personal it chose this world out of all possible worlds of His creation. That is the distinctive thing we know from the teaching of Christ and the revelation of the Bible. God loved this world with a selective choice, as a free, personal expression of love.

But the selectiveness of personal love does not stop there. There are circles of selection within love. We read that Christ loved the Church and gave Himself for it. That was His further selection of divine love – within the world there was this that He loved well in personal love – His Church.

You remember how Christ in the Parable put it: one discovered treasure in a field, and because he valued the treasure and wanted it to be his own, he bought the whole field. Christ loved the Church and for her sake His choice fell upon the world.

But there is a further inner circle: Paul struck it when he spoke of the Son of God who loved me and gave Himself for me. He found himself at the heart and centre of God's love. And that is the marvel of love – it is personality – it is a being who can respond to that love and say 'We love Him because He first loved us'.

So you see the immensity of space causes us no worry: it does not in the least call for any change in our Gospel. On the contrary it magnifies the love of God, it enlarges our conception of a love that traversed space and made a selection of this world. You cannot readjust love. You cannot argue against it – it selects.

Divine Love is Sacrificial

Divine love must give or it dies. It is like a spring of water rising from the depths. It gurgles its way up and out. It must find expression, its energy is used to get it up and out. So must love – it expresses itself. This is true of human love. The verse suggests that the love is measured by its giving: the magnitude of the love by the fecundity of its giving: 'so loved that He gave'.

It is the nature of love's expression that startles us here – it is sacrificial. It gave its all – 'This is My Begotten Son'. In it love found a personal expression – it was in a Son. You remember in the Parable of the Wicked Husbandman – as a last resort the Master of the vineyard sent his son -'Perhaps they will reverence him'. So this is love's final expression – in His Son, His only begotten Son, the **One who was fully and eternally God.**

God's love found an ultimate and complete expression: He gave His only Begotten Son – He surrendered Him – He gave Him over to humiliation, and sorrow and sin-bearing and death. God spared not His own Son. He gave – and gave is a loaded word – it takes the whole Bible to unfold its content.

The validity of that deserves study. It is not spent – it is not a once-for-all gift – it goes on in inexhaustible love, for God still commends His love towards us in that while we were yet sinners Christ died for us. Commendeth – as if God had to draw attention to it – as something utterly unique. That love flows freely and for ever through His personal gift – the love of God which is in Christ Jesus our Lord. God is not finished with the world, for Christ is the Saviour of the world.

THE LAMB IS THE LIGHT
(Rev. 21:23)

We have the nature of Heaven's light and also the medium of its transmission. These are the two things that really matter about light: where it comes from and how it gets to us. For example it had long been thought that the sun was the source of our light here below: that the sun burning itself out created the light and transmitted it to us.

The Creation story was therefore ridiculed because it said that light came on the first day and the sun was placed only on the fourth day. It is now recognised that there is nothing at all unscientific about this statement. Under the wave or molecular theory of light the sun is not regarded as the only source of light. Light can and does exist without the sun.

So here we have the source of all light in the Heavenly world: 'The glory of God did lighten it'.

The radiance of God's character – the outshining of all that God is in His moral splendour and spiritual beauty – the sum total of all that a Holy God is, shining out in cloudless splendour – shedding its radiance from one end of heaven to the other: the glory of God did lighten it.

Then there is the medium through which it is transmitted. The Lamb is the light thereof. That determines how the radiance reaches us and becomes light – becomes illumination to us.

I. The Light of the City
II. The City in that Light

I. The Light in the City

The Lamb is John's name for Jesus Christ in His sacrifice and death and life beyond death. It is his name for the Christ he met on the banks of the Jordan, the Christ on whose bosom he was wont to lean, the Christ of Calvary and the Christ beyond the tomb.

Now this must mean that the Jesus of history, the Jesus who died on the tree of shame, is the medium by which the uncreated light of heaven is transmitted to His redeemed ones. Let us glance at the implications of this. Light stands for knowledge, understanding, revelation, interpretation. We often say 'I saw it in a new light', meaning 'I understood it differently'. Or, 'I have no light on it', meaning 'I don't understand what it means'. Now – this before us would mean that Christ in His sacrificial death sheds light on the historical world and so is the source of our seeing and understanding. In other words, the thing that happened on Calvary becomes our way of understanding what we meet on the other side. The divine, ineffable light of the uncreated God becomes illumination to us through the Christ who died for us. Coming through Him it is communicated in a way that enlightens and interprets.

1. It Illumines the Character of God
By that we mean His glory as a pure and holy Being who is the source of all life and goodness. Only in Heaven does His glory shine in undiminished splendour. But to us it is transfused through the One who died for us. So we see the layout of the knowledge of glory in His face.

2. It Illumines to us the Mind of God.
God's supreme intelligence – infinite mind. His thoughts are purposes we dimly see from below and fail to understand so often, because they transcend our capacity to understand. But there is the Christ who died for us. We read the mind of God in language we can understand – in our own language so to speak. In chapter 5 we read of the Sealed Book and of the Lamb in the midst opening it.

3. It Illumines the Heart of God
The Lamb interprets the holy love of God. Here below we make contact with the Christ proclaimed in the Gospel of the Cross. But there the Lamb that is in the midst of the throne shall lead us into the fountain head of love.

II. The City in that Light of Gems

It is the light that brings out the beauty of the gems.

(a) The Joy of the City

The wonder of personal redemption remains the eternal source for joy, and all – reconciliation, power, sanctification, glory – all is in Christ.

(b) The Fellowship of the City

The bond that binds us all in one is our common indebtedness to the One who redeems us.

(c) *Service in the City*

> Inspired by the love of Him who died for us, 'They shall see His face and His servants shall serve Him'.

(d) *The Security of the City*

> Safeguarded by the abiding value of what happened on Calvary, Christ is not light to you if you do not see things in the light of what He has done on Calvary.

THE TWO NIGHT SCENES OF THE NEW TESTAMENT
Simon and Judas – Similarity and Contrast
Luke 22:32 : John 13: 30

These two night scenes present us with the two experiences of repentance and remorse, the one leading to life, the other to death. Peter and Judas were both disciples of Christ and they present us with a fearful similarity and a clear contrast. We are studying them because they demonstrate both warning and hope: warning against trifling with sin, giving rein to the weakness and secret sin of our nature; and hope that if we have sinned, and sinned grievously, we can by the mercy of God be restored and reinstated in the service of Christ's Kingdom with a new and enlarged commission. The one was Judas, the other was Peter.

1. The Points of Similarity

They both sinned grievously, and on the surface their sin does not seem so different.

(i) *They both sinned against TRUST*

It is clear that both occupied positions of trust from their Master. It is no small matter that they were both disciples and so in the inner circle of fellowship.

Judas was treasurer of the small group, and husbanded their resources and catered for their needs. It is clear that he was very cash-conscious, as is seen from his conduct in the Bethany home, dissociating himself from Mary's deed of love in anointing her Lord 'against His burial', calling it 'waste', and quick to estimate its worth in money values. The explanation of his outburst, ostensibly on behalf of the poor, is given as 'He had the bag, and bare what was put therein' (John 12:6) where 'bare' has the more ugly meaning of "pilfered" (See R.S.V.).

Peter was one of the inner circle of three, with James and John, and was trusted with special privileges. There is a delightful touch of oneness in the command of the Master concerning the tax-money pulled out of the fish's mouth: 'That take and give unto them for me and for thee' (Matt. 17:27). Peter was to view the summit of Christ's glory on the Mount of Transfiguration and the depth of His anguish and humiliation in the Garden of Gethsemane.

(ii) *They both sinned against WARNING*

The vigilant eye of the Master saw the frailty in each, and gave them warning that should have cautioned them against coming peril.

Simon was warned that his loyalty would be tested when he would be 'sifted as wheat', to remove the living grain, and leave only the chaff, the outer shell of his religion.

Judas was warned that one of the twelve would betray their Master, one who sat at the table with Him, the one to whom He first gave the sop. Since the first morsel of the Passover bread was usually, out of courtesy, given to any stranger, Judas was identified as the 'stranger' at the table, and this was reinforced by the unspeakably solemn words 'Good were it for that man if he had never been born' (Matt. 26:24).

Simon had a similar warning, yet they both sinned against light.

(iii) *They both sinned against PATIENCE*

It was the patience of love. How patient Christ was with their frailties! He was patient with Peter's impetuous outbursts of superior loyalty, and did not attack it, but placed it in the light of Peter's subsequent conduct in thrice denying his Master.

It never seemed that Judas was treated with suspicion or cold-shouldered in any way. At any rate none of the other disciples saw any sign of distrust or coldness. Even when Christ said pointedly 'That thou doest do quickly', referring to the betrayal, they took it to be a request to buy something for the feast, or to give something to the poor. Rather did each of the other disciples strike his own breast and cry: 'Is it I, Lord?'. So weak were they at that bewildering hour that they felt it possible that they could do the foul deed! But it shows that Judas was not suspect. Even in the Bethany home, when Judas complains of the extravagance of Mary, Christ put the charge in the light of Mary's insight and love where it ought to shrivel to death.

It was the patience of grace and love. And yet they sinned against it all.

Sin is ugly in any setting: it is especially ugly against the background of Christ's trust and care, His patience and love. It is, perhaps, significant that none of the heathen religions depict a Judas, a traitor from the inner circle. It is only in the warm light and love of the Gospel that a traitor could find shelter. And yet it is in that very context that repentance for sin is born, for 'they shall look upon him whom they pierced and they shall mourn for him'. The Gospel is a savour of life unto life, or of death unto death.

2. The Points of Contrast

Where Peter and Judas differ. Both made a departure into the night, Simon to weep bitterly, Judas to commit the foul deed. Darkness is a great revealer, strange as it may seem. What we are in the dark is the determining disclosure. The difference was this.

(i) *Peter KNEW his Lord, Judas did not.*

Judas was three years in the company of Jesus, but he did not know or understand Him. An attempt is made to white-wash Judas: that his intention was good, to force the hand of Christ and bring on the crisis. But, alas, no white-washing will ever disguise the foulness of the deed.

Judas gave every sign that he did not understand his Master. He thought he knew Him but it was a superficial acquaintance such as you may have through reading somewhere about Christ or hearing about Him. Judas knew Him less and less every day he was with Him. When he planned the act of betrayal he said to his fellow-conspirators: 'Whom I shall kiss, it is he, hold him fast'. He seemed to have thought that Jesus would have made good His escape out of their clutches – 'hold him fast'. How little he knew of the power of Jesus to deliver Himself out of their hands. To Judas it was just an ordinary arrest.

Judas could make nothing of the Master, for their thoughts moved on different planes: Judas the grandeur of a throne and a golden sceptre; Jesus a cross of shame.

But Peter was not so. He did not know himself but he knew his Master. He had wonderful glimpses of His hidden glory. At one time he saw His holiness as he cried: 'Depart from me for I am a sinful man, O Lord'; at another, His majesty as he testified: 'We beheld His majesty when we were with Him on the holy mount'. Even when he tried to say: 'I know not the man', every instinct of his being told him it was a lie.

(ii) *Peter LOVED his Master, Judas did not*

Peter's love to his Master could never be doubted. His bitter tears in the night of his denial were the tears of wounded love – self-inflicted wounds.

And when Jesus on the shore of the lake that early morning of the resurrection questioned him about his love: 'Lovest thou me?' three times, Peter was grieved – grieved that his love could be questioned. His reply: 'Thou knowest all things, thou knowest that I love thee'. The undertones are: Thou knowest all things that happened to me and yet I appeal to Thy knowledge that I love Thee, and ever did since Thy call came to follow Thee.

Judas with enthusiasm joined the small band, attracted by the novelty and hoping for great things. A man of affairs, he became treasurer, had the bag and access to all that went into it. He loved position, and authority, and above all he loved money. In such a heart, there was little room for the love of Christ, and his love of personal gain seemed more and more futile and unattainable.

(iii) *Peter WANTED his Master, Judas did not*

Peter trusted his Master with the strong trust of faith. That is what the Master pled for him, that when he lost all else his 'faith fail not'. That life-line was not broken. And now as Peter went out into the night 'He wept bitterly', and nothing would dry his tears but his Master's presence. Jesus, who had His fingers on his pulse throughout, knew this, and in one of His first resurrection messages He included Peter by name: 'Tell my disciples and Peter'. He appeared to Peter on the first day of the resurrection – probably His second appearance – and what a meeting it was.It was too sacred for Peter ever to speak of it.

Judas went out into the night alone. He felt no link to the Master. The only thing he knew was that he 'betrayed innocent blood'. The money was like burning cinders, and he threw it down. And the New Testament draws down the curtain on this infamous life with studied reticence: 'that he might go to his own place'.

We all have our nights: let us not deceive ourselves about that. The question is how we act in our hour of darkness. Do we weep bitterly ? Or do we go out to destroy ourselves?

That is the ultimate difference between Peter and Judas: not how they got into the tragic situation, but how they got out of it.

Peter got out of it by the grace of God to become a stronger character, a more sensitive Christian, and a more hopeful and helpful disciple. Is that not what Christ had promised him? 'When thou art converted strengthen thy brethren'. Nothing is lost when grace is there, and where sin abounds grace can much more abound.

TAKE TIME TO BE HOLY

What does holiness mean?

1.   Holiness is the distinctive quality of God's character. It is something that belongs to all His attributes: something that marks each of them as Divine; e.g. Holy love, holy justice, holy compassion, holy wisdom. It is distinctive: for 'there is none holy but the Lord'. 'Thou only art holy'. Holiness in every creature is derived from Him.

2.   Holiness is what God requires of all His creatures. If His creatures are to be pleasing to Him they must be holy. Holiness alone gives us harmony with the Divine nature – a capacity to understand, to appreciate, and to respond.

3.   That Holiness God is willing to impart. God delights to share His holiness, and we can get it in no other way. It *must* come from God – the alone Holy – if it is to be there at all. 'I am the Lord who makes holy'.

4.   Holiness is the goal of Christ's redemptive work for us. Holiness is the goal of all God's work – this is the Divine consummation. The Son of God undertook His redemptive work in order to make unholy man holy. He lived to show us holiness in human life. He died to make holiness available. His sacrifice laid the foundation for our holiness. His blood becomes our cleansing offering.

5.   Holiness is the end of the Spirit's work in us. We are called by God to be holy. We are elected unto holiness. We are regenerated to give us a holy nature

6.   Holiness is *therefore* the first and great concern of every Christian. For service, God uses holy characters. 'If a man cleanse himself, he shall be a vessel unto honour, sanctified, meet for the master's use and prepared for the master's use'. (2 Tim 2:21).

No one can pass the judgment without it.

(a) *Holiness is all-pervasive*. It is not confined to any one part of us, it must enter every part.

(b) *Holiness is absolute in its demands*. It is intolerant of all that is unholy. Less than perfect holiness will not pass.

(c) *Holiness is progressive in its development*. It cannot stand still short of perfection – we must go on to 'perfect holiness in the fear of God'.

7. How to become Holy. 'Take time to be holy'. This is a case where you are building in time what outlasts time into eternity. But you must *take time*: it needs time – it is a growth – a progressive development. Character formation is the great business of time.

(a) *Look Christwards.* He is the source of your holiness. It is unto His likeness you grow. *Take time* to look to Him in meditation and prayer. Faith is an upward glance that beholds in Christ your pattern and goal. Faith recognises in Christ your Saviour and your Lord. Commune with Him and you drink in of His Spirit. It gives consciousness of sin.

(b) *Yield to the Spirit.* The Spirit is given to develop Christ in you. He is the Spirit of Holiness – the Spirit who brings the Holiness of God into your experience. *Take time* – to feel and understand His strivings within you. Listen to His voice. Obey His promptings: daily, hourly as obedience grows. Accept His convicting light. Do not resist, quarrel or grieve the Spirit.

(c) *Resist Sin.* You are active in your life of holiness. You co-operate with the Spirit of God. Take sides with the Spirit against yourself. Cf Paul: 'Sold under sin' – he was a prisoner of war in an enemy camp. Holiness means separation, a spiritual separation from all that is unholy. Death is the great separator – 'Reckon yourselves to be dead indeed unto sin'. (Rom 6:11).'Prayer and fasting' – prayer and self-discipline even from legitimate things.

(d) *Learn to know the will of God in His Word.* The chief means of sanctification that God uses is His Word. God sanctifies through the truth in His Word – therefore get through to the truth in His Word. Do not be content with the letter. *Take time* to get behind the word to the thought – get behind the thought to the spirit in the Word. *Get to know the wide sweep of the truth* – in every part it makes for holiness.

> Holiness in the mind is Light.
> Holiness in the conscience is sensitiveness.
> Holiness in the heart is purity.
> Holiness in the will is power.

Abide in the word of Jesus – live in it – steep your mind in it.

(e) *Study the characters of God's great saints.* They still radiate holiness, Brainard, McCheyne, Mueller, Amy Carmichael.

Group 7

Bible Sermons

THE MYSTERY OF FOLDED WINGS
(Ezek. 1:24)

E zekiel's vision caught sight of 'the land of far distances' and it is small wonder that we so often trip and stumble in our effort to follow him. In few parts of his prophecy do we seem more sightless than in this first chapter, which treats of beings concerning whose nature and mode of existence we know so very little. They are heavenly couriers of the King of Glory that flit across this page of the Sacred Word, and though their mission is so much hid from us, and their activities often beyond our understanding, there is, one ventures to think, one point at least where they touch our human experience, one attitude in which they seem to resemble God's servants here below – it is when they are asked to stand still and let down their wings. The words introduce us to the mystery of folded wings – a mystery whose inner secret is yielded up to God's people only in the purifying furnace of sorrow and suffering.

Let us observe first of all what wings are these that must be folded.

A reading of the chapter will show that the *most active* of wings must be folded. These are messengers whose activity appears boundless and ceaseless: the chapter vibrates with the rustle of their wings as they haste to do their Lord's bidding. They 'ran and returned as the appearance of a flash of lightning'; 'they turned not when they went: they went every one straight forward' – all which tells us theirs is ready, swift, undeviating service.

Yet there comes a time when these active workers are allowed to stand still and let down their wings. Need *we* be surprised, then, that we meet with these perplexing providences in the lives of God's most diligent earthly servants, when God seems to show that He can do without the most active of His workers, when the toiler is laid low, and when, in the midst of his labours, the useful servant is asked to stand still and fold his wings? This, seemingly, is but God's way with all his workers.

But we must note also that the *most graceful* of wings must be folded. Even a cursory reading of the chapter impresses us with the beauty and grace of the service given by these heavenly workers. There is such unity, alacrity, and devotion, each rivalling the other in perfecting obedience to the will of God. The figures employed to describe their appearance would seem to suggest the many-sidedness of their qualifications: every one had four faces – the face of an ox, denoting patience and endurance; the face of a lion, denoting courage and strength; the face of an eagle, denoting vision and keenness; the face of a man, denoting wisdom and intelligence – a combination of all the graces surely.

Yet, such shining service as that had to cease, for there came a time when they were asked to stand still and let down their wings. Little wonder then that the best equipped of God's earthly servants should have a somewhat similar experience. God's providence seems mysterious when it takes toll of the best of workers and places them in situations in which their particular gifts and graces do not seem to find active employment; but it is God's way with all His workers.

And we observe also that the *most successful* of wings must be folded. These workers had all the elements of true success. Theirs was *expressive* service, a service that could be heard and felt, for 'the noise of their wings was like the noise of great waters'. Theirs was *articulate* and *intelligible* service, a service that could be read and understood, for it was 'as the voice of speech'. And best of all, theirs was truly *divine* service, for it was 'as the voice of the Almighty', and when men heard the rustle of their wings they recognised in it the voice of God, which is the perfect ideal of service.

And yet they, whose labour is so God-honouring and truly divine, are asked to stand still and let down their wings. And we have to learn that true success in the service of God does not exempt the earthly worker from visitations by which his work and usefulness seem suddenly to be cut short. In whatever way the willing servant may read the dark providences of God, he is not entitled to see in them the frown of the Master upon his services, for success is often met with the command to stand still and let down the wings of our effort.

All this will inevitably raise the question: why should the wings of the busy worker have to be folded?

What is God's wise purpose in it all? May it not be, *that we need rest?* It may well be that heavenly beings do not need rest in our conception of it, but the Bible makes it abundantly clear that it is a principle with God that none of His servants should be overdriven. How forcibly God taught this to His ancient people when they came into the new territory of Canaan, where they were to have rest, not only one day in seven, but one year in seven, a year in which the very soil should get rest that it might yield of its best. So with God's toiling servants: Elijah, fretted and disappointed on Mount Horeb, is cast into a deep sleep; our Lord's disciples are often taken aside into a desert place that they may rest awhile; and by many strange experiences God's weary people are given an opportunity to rest and be refreshed. Let us therefore not rebel against the providence of folded wings, since it is the voice of Him who 'knows our frame and remembers we are dust'.

But there may be another reason for folded wings – it is *that we may learn*. It is significant concerning the heavenly workers that 'there was a voice from the firmament that was over their heads when they stood and had let down their wings'. In the stillness of interrupted labour they could hear God's voice and receive His commands. How much more do we, stumbling erring mortals, need to learn, and, if we are His, God gives us the opportunity in ways that may seem to us strange and hard. Wireless operators at sea speak of drawing 'a curtain of silence' – a device by which they can keep in unbroken communication with an endangered vessel. God establishes often a 'curtain of silence' between Himself and His people by means of which He communicates to them messages of truth and comfort that shall be of use to them in after days. The Lord Jesus Christ would seem to have had thirty years of folded wings – years of training and learning and fellowship. When, therefore, the call comes to us to stand still and let down our wings, let us listen for the voice that speaks: there is something that God means us to learn.

And may there not be yet another explanation of folded wings – *that we may obey?* To these well-equipped messengers of God service seemed easy and pleasant: the difficult task would be to 'stand still and let down their wings'. Yet, if they are to be perfected in obedience, they must experience this. And the earthly worker is trained to obedience often in the same way, when in the midst of his labours – strenuous, happy, successful labours – God comes with the stern command to stand still and let down his wings. It is then that one's obedience is really tested and it may take a long sharp discipline to teach the foolish servant that obedience is the heavenliest service, and that 'they also serve who only stand and wait'.

Youth and age, disappointment and failure, affliction and sorrow may be times of folded wings, and may, alike, bring to us a great divine message. Blessed are they who shall respond – 'I will hear what God the Lord will speak: for He will speak peace unto His people'.

THE MASTER AT THE TREASURY
(Mark 12:41)

'And Jesus sat over against the treasury and beheld how the people cast money into the treasury'.

At first glance this may seem a very small incident in the crowded life of our Lord, but when we consider the occasion on which it occurred we begin to wonder that it should have occurred at all. The time of this incident was well in the last week of our Lord's earthly life, with Gethsemane and Calvary rising up before His eye, yet those great personal considerations never for one moment detracted from His interest in the spiritual welfare of His fellows; He could still watch the multitudes that thronged the temple courts as a shepherd watches his sheep or a physician bends over the stricken and diseased. As He sat there in the inner court He could see the thirteen boxes placed on one side to receive the freewill offerings of the people; and we may safely conclude that He was interested in the contributions only as they revealed the contributors: He weighed every soul by its gift, and read every heart by its giving. Under His searching eye things were not what they seemed, and as we read this incident and ponder over it we realise that He saw not as men see, that He commended not as men commend, and that centuries have vindicated that His estimate was not human but Divine.

Here we have, first of all, the Master's Observation. Ever observant, our Lord found souls coming to worship a matter for very special observation; only His observation was quite unlike ours! He did not look at the multitudes that thronged the temple courts; He did not specially watch their contributions to the treasury, but He 'beheld *how* the people cast money into the treasury' – not what they did, but how they did it. He was looking not so much at the people and their money, as at something behind their money, at the motive and impulse behind it, at the reason for giving it. That is something quite peculiar to the Lord Jesus Christ – He is watching *how* men do things, *how* the people cast money into the treasury, *how* the soul and spirit are exercised in the giving. It was so when He was in the house of Simon the Pharisee. Though Simon's table was lavishly spread, there was something missing, there were those acts of courtesy and affection without which the banquet was formal and cold. It was left to a woman 'which was a sinner' to supply those 'extras' that are so precious to the Lord of heaven, and she did it with a sincerity and devotion that won for her not only the Master's defence, but such commendation as Simon's more lavish but less devoted effort failed to win. The Master observed *why* she did it, and as the gift of the sin-forgiven and loving soul it was acceptable to Him.

On a similar occasion the Master sat at a feast in the home in Bethany, and though Martha served with wonted diligence, and Lazarus occupied a seat of honour at the table, to Mary was reserved the deed of love that met with the richest approval: 'Ye have the poor with you always, but Me ye have not always: she did what she could'. In this instance the Master observed *when* she did it, for it proved poignantly true in the experience of the other women who went early to the sepulchre to perform the same deed of affection, and found not the body of the Lord – 'Me ye have not always'(Matt 26:11). It proves solemnly true in the experience of many that there is a time when the opportunity has for ever gone. He has appointed not only a reason why, but a time when we may serve Him.

Believing then that the Master is a close observer of the how, the why, and the when of human effort, that by Him 'actions are weighed' not in the scales of earth, but in the infinitely more sensitive balances of heaven, let us act as under the eye of Him who searches the motive, who has regard to the disposition of heart, and who provides the opportunity for Christian service.

Again we can see here the Master's Commendation. Presiding over the treasury that day was the Lord of the temple, and as He weighed the gifts He sifted and separated them. On the one side He put the gifts of wealth, of formality, of ostentation and show; on the other side, in meagre poverty, two mites, a fraction of a farthing; but in His estimate these two mites were 'more than all'. It is an amazing estimate, so pointed in its comparison, so unqualified in its terms. In the mouth of him who is the True Witness this can be no exaggeration – it is generous praise, but it is also correct estimate. The widow woman gave 'more than they all', and the Lord afterwards let His disciples know something of His standards of measurement. On the one side He placed the big bulky gifts of wealth and affluence, and called them 'abundance' or superfluity. How that word makes them shrivel up! They are merely what is superfluous, what is left over and above personal needs, what is not needed for one's own personal use. On the other side – two mites, yet 'all that she had, even all her living' – what she could not give without feeling the pinch of it, what was almost a necessity to her own comfort, and what she could ill spare. That is still a Divine standard in valuing our gifts; what does our giving mean to us? Is it merely what we can well afford to give without feeling the loss too much? If so he labels it 'superfluity' and it shrivels up under His eye. But the gift that comes out of penury, out of dire necessity, out of blood, is the sterling that is current in the courts of heaven.

Moreover, this commendation has respect not to what the gift was given for so much as what it was given from. How many in Jerusalem, had they been told of the woman's act, would have condemned her for her recklessness and misguided charity. They would hint that the money that went into the treasury was just not too well used; some went to the poor as they seemed, some went to the priests who were well fed and well provided for from other sources! How easy it was to find fault with the widow woman for her extravagant gift! But how little they knew, or could know, the feelings with which she gave it! Deep down in her heart was burning a love to the God of the temple that must find expression; there arose before her memories of blessed hours in that temple when, in the day of sorrow and widowhood and loneliness, she found strength and comfort. At the thought of all this there welled up in her heart a fountain of gratitude, and that stream brought in its train two mites – all she had! Well was it for her that, sitting over against the treasury that day, was One who knew and understood, and who could estimate her gift at its real worth.

We may also observe the Master's Vindication. We said the Master's estimate was accurate and correct when He said concerning these two mites 'more than all'. Now we ask if this commendation was not too high or if it can actually be justified. We declare that the woman's gift was 'more than all' in its *intrinsic worth*. Not only was it more to the woman herself before she cast it in, 'even all her living' – but it was more to her afterwards, and it yielded for her a richer and quicker return than did the gifts of the wealthy. For the rich cast in of their abundance, and thought no more about it; why should they? It was not missed in any way. But the widow woman did think about it, for she felt the pinch of it for many days – it was with a feeling of gratitude to Providence for the privilege He had bestowed upon her, and of prayerfulness to God for the Divine blessing to accompany it. At the same time as it unloaded her heart and unburdened her soul, it stirred up the fountains of love and prayer and joy. She was now a co-worker with God, for He received her gift and would employ it in His service. Oh, the blessedness of such giving! The joy of realising that we may be co-partners with the God of heaven in His glorious work, co-workers with the Holy Ghost in carrying out the Divine purpose. Henceforth His cause is our cause.

The widow's gift was also more in its *moral influence*. Did not that gift produce more for the Kingdom of God than all the rest that day? Think of the dividends that have been coming in from these two mites as they have been trading for God's cause throughout the centuries and yielding their rich return in every age. What inspiration they have been to the poor to give, what warning and direction to the rich how and what to give!

The widow's gift was 'more than all' in its *eternal blessedness* for her. How little the contributors that day knew that they were being watched! How little conscious they were of the eye that penetrated beyond the gift to the motive for giving! Not even the woman knew that her gift was being weighed in the balances of the sanctuary, and our Lord Jesus does not seem to have told her, though He told it to His disciples. I don't suppose she ever knew till they met – she and her mites – in the Master's presence above, and she found that her mites were received in the treasury of heaven, and sent out to trade for the Master. May it not be in some such way as this that the mammon of unrighteousness shall 'receive us into everlasting habitations'(Luke 16:9), where as someone has suggested, the streets of the New Jerusalem are paved with the gold that the saints have given?

> Go break to the needy sweet charity's bread
> For giving is living the Angel said.
> And must I be giving again and again?
> My peevish and pitiless answer came.
> Oh no, said the Angel, piercing me through
> Just give till the Master stops giving to you.

THE OLD AND THE NEW
A Study in Religious Contrasts

When our Lord used the familiar saying 'The old is better', He was not putting the imprimatur of His sanction upon it: rather was His teaching directed to show the falsity and futility of it in all matters of faith and religion. The occasion on which He made use of the saying serves to indicate His mind very clearly. The Pharisees sought to make capital out of the differences between the disciples of Christ and the disciples of John and of the Pharisees themselves with regard to the observance of the religious life. While our Saviour was able to understand the peculiar difficulties of those who, like John's disciples, were clinging to the old order of things, He would nonetheless have them realise the danger and utter futility of it. He warned His hearers particularly of the danger of attempting to mix up the new and the old, the Law and the Gospel. It was as futile as putting a patch of new cloth on to an old threadbare garment – it would prove a misfit, and what was worse, the two pieces would not hold together! Or, it was like putting new wine into old, cracked leather bottles – the new wine, with its powerful ferment, would inevitably burst through the old skins! Thus futile was it to attempt a mixing together of the old religion and the new! And yet He understood why men had a clinging to the old; it was so human! 'No man, having drunk old wine, straightway desireth new; for he saith, The old is better'. But because it was a common human frailty, it was not, therefore, to be judged as permissible or right. That is the spiritual lesson He would have us learn from the two little parables of the Old Garment and the Old Bottles – the folly of our clinging to the old natural religion, imagining that because it is old, it is, therefore, better than the new life of faith in Christ Jesus. Man is naturally religious, and he clings tenaciously to his natural religion. When the Gospel is presented to him, with its new offer, its new demands, and its new promises in Christ Jesus, he falls back on his own religion, saying 'The old is better'. Let us discuss this situation in which multitudes of our fellows find themselves when confronted with the offer of Christ in the Gospel.

I

Let us compare the New and the Old in their presentation of God's demands upon our lives. Religion is something that presses the demands of God upon human lives. Man has all along been feeling instinctively the claims of God, and he has been responding, in his own dark and stumbling way, to the Divine claims. That is Natural Religion. Christianity, as the Supernatural Religion, has come, likewise, to present the demands of God. And wherein do they differ? The Old religion presents God's claims as GIVE, the New as TAKE. The two are irreconcilable, and it should not be difficult to determine which is the better. Natural religion haunts the soul of men with the Divine summons, Give! Undoubtedly there is justice in this demand. If God has made us for Himself, He has the right to demand of us that we should render to Him. Man, even in the darkness of his natural condition, recognises this, and God becomes to him merely One to whom he is bound to give. And God seems so hard to satisfy, an insatiable Being, distant, exacting, implacable! Christianity, on the other hand, presents the demand of God, not as give, but as take! The religion of the New Covenant is a movement, not on man's part to give to God, but on God's part to give to man. It all originates in God, for He it is that planned, and that executes the plan, bringing blessings untold to the children of men, free and unpriced. And His demand of men is that we receive; He treats us as having nothing, and He supplies everything! Its receptiveness is the distinctive thing about the Christian life from beginning to end. It originates in receiving, it thrives in receiving, and it is crowned by receiving. Does this not constitute the good news of the Gospel, when the soul that has struggled painfully and despairingly to give to God, has heard a voice from Heaven saying 'Come unto Me, all ye that labour and are heavy laden, and I will give you rest'? The Christian, who has been taught in happy experience, the distinction between the religion of giving and that of receiving, will not subscribe to the saying, 'The old is better!'.

II

We may, again, compare the New and the Old as means of peace. Religion, whatever its nature, attempts to minister peace to the troubled soul of man. That is its chief function. If man were not a troubled soul, with a sense of fear, and variance and alienation, he would not feel his need of religion. Thus it is that all religions, whatever their origin, claim to minister peace to the inner life, to impart a sense of conciliation with God, and secure harmony with the universe around. Here the Old and the New can be compared and sharply contrasted. The urge of Natural religion as a means to peace is, DO!; the Christian religion brings the peace-giving message DONE! What a world of difference separates the two! The natural religion of man concentrates on self-effort as a means of winning the favour of God, the approval of conscience, and the sense of harmony within and around. And so man's religion sets him adoing: rites, ceremonies, deeds of merit, works of righteousness are all attempted in the effort to secure peace. It is a laborious task , a seemingly endless task, and it proves ultimately a wholly unsatisfying task! The Divine religion, on the other hand, steps into the troubled soul of man with the message: done! The peace we yearn for is made, secured and sealed by the Blood of the Son of God! It is part of the good news of the Gospel that when man was an exile, a fugitive and an outcast, a prey to fear, a creature of sorrow, and a child of wrath, God took in hand to make peace, peace that would satisfy Him and pacify the heart and conscience of man. And by entering into that peace, man shall experience its blessedness, and 'the peace of God, which passeth understanding, shall garrison the heart and mind through Christ Jesus'. To a soul who has once toiled for peace and is now possessed by the peace of God, it can never be true that 'The old is better!'

III

We shall now compare the New and the Old as supplying the motives for obedience and service. Religion is designed to supply the grand underlying motive for spiritual obedience and benevolent service. It is, indeed, acknowledged on all hands that religion is the most fundamental driving force, the most moving thing, in the whole fe of man. It has great deeds of service to its credit. Now Natural Religion says that FEAR is the great motive power, while Christian religion says it is LOVE. Here there is indeed a contrast! Fear is undoubtedly a great compelling power, and the soul of man is specially susceptible to fear: fear of the unseen world, fear of the unknown, fear of the God who rules all! What lengths fear may drive man to! There are many who tell us that fear is the strongest force in the world, and the greatest corrective in life. But Christianity has come to contradict this and to claim that, as a fundamental principle of obedience, it is not fear that operates best but love! Fear looks forward to punishment and sets the soul agoing in awful agitation; love looks backward to forgiveness, and sets the soul agoing with a joyful heart and a glowing purpose. Love is the new wine of the Kingdom, the mighty ferment that bursts through all the natural containers! It is undoubtedly true that love, springing from a sense of Divine forgiveness, has been the mightiest force ever let loose upon the world. And it has been let loose by the Lord Jesus Christ through the Gospel! Fear, as we may see illustrated in the case of the Man with the One Talent, is a barren thing, it paralyses and stultifies, and deadens! But love has the most amazing achievements to its credit. It awakens the mind to think of new channels of service, it stirs the heart to yield its best and its all, and it enables the soul to pour out its full offering freely and joyfully. As the grand motive for obedience and service, few can claim that 'The old is better!'

IV

We may compare the New and the Old, lastly, as a Way of life. Religion, if it is worth the name, supplies man with a way of life; it presents the best known way of planning and laying out the life for our present well-being and our highest destiny. It will not be disputed that Natural Religion presents self-interest as the first great consideration of the human life, while Christianity presents self-sacrifice as the only pathway of the Christian life. What a contrast between the new spirit, and the old! Religion of the old order incites us to take the most out of life, Christianity urges us to put the most into life. Here is a contrast indeed! Man, instinctively and naturally, is an acquisitive creature: he is ever bent on acquiring, on getting as much pleasure and luxury, and possessions out of life as he can. Consequently he is greedingly devouring everything, till he leaves life threadbare and empty. Of how many is it true that, having come to possess all they set out to possess, they now find that life now holds nothing more, it is empty and worthless! That is not Christ's way of life for His followers. He came forward to tell men the astounding news that 'a man's life consisteth not in the abundance of the things which he possesseth'. Things, mere things, don't go to make life! Things don't belong to the stuff that life is made of! Christ came to proclaim that if any man would be His disciple, he must take up his cross, he must be willing to sacrifice, and make self-sacrifice the fundamental principle of his living. Nay more, Christ claimed that it was the man that lost his life that would find life, and paradox as it may seem, it has proved true in the experience of countless men who yielded up their lives on the altar of service and were, at the end of the day, given back their lives enriched a thousand-fold.

It were easy to go on showing by many such arguments that, for our existence in this present life, the old is not better. How much more is this true in dealing with our hope for a life to come! When man, conscious that he is a pilgrim to a world of spirits, gropes for the door of hope and stretches out an empty hand for a staff on which to lean in the last dark valley, it is the 'good hope' in Christ that provides him with light and comfort and assurance on the last lone mile of the road. There most assuredly the Old is not better! There, alas! the Old shall vanish when, all too often, there does not seem time or inclination to embrace the New. And yet in life many find the old religion the most difficult refuge to abandon; it is man's last trench! Therefore men resort to the compromise of which our Lord has warned us in those parables, the attempt to patch the old with the new, to secure the new wine and retain the old bottles! The Master's verdict on this condition is decisive and final; both shall be lost.

THE BARREN FIG-TREE

**'When Jesus came to the fig-tree he found nothing but
leaves, for the time of figs was not yet. And Jesus answered
and said unto it, No man eat fruit of thee hereafter.'**

(Mark 11:13)

This wayside incident in the last journey of our Saviour to Jerusalem has all the forcefulness and pregnant meaning of a parable. The simple occurrences of our Lord's life were at all times fraught with deep and hidden significance but much more so the events that crowded into that last journey, so faithfully and fully recorded by all the evangelists. Even a fruitless fig-tree by the way is made an emblem of a people highly favoured and richly blessed of God, whose profession of allegiance to Him was so deceitful and unreal. In the doom of the barren fig-tree the Lord portrays the doom, first of unbelieving Israel, and then of all whose religion is a profession without practice and a show without substance.

Here we have, first of all, a Delightful Prospect. There were several things about this solitary fig-tree that made it for Christ and His disciples a delightful prospect. There was, for instance, the *conspicuous foliage.* To the eye weary with the endless stretch of dusty road the sight of a tree with overhanging branches and green foliage must have been both soothing and refreshing. It held out at least a prospect of cool shade where the weary traveller may rest a while. As the 'one fig-tree', solitary in its leafy verdure, to the travel-stained Master and disciples, so is the profession of Christ, in a God-forgetting world, to a quickened soul. How refreshing to find a man or woman who has an interest in the things of God, or to receive a mere hand-clasp from a fellow pilgrim Zionwards! Who of us but felt the attractiveness of that solitary soul who bore witness for the Lord when all around seemed unheeding and forgetful? But there was the added attraction here of *seeming fruitfulness.* A fig-tree with the foliage fully developed was likely to have fruit, since, in the case of the fig-tree, the fruit generally comes along with, or even before, the leaf. The Master and His disciples, hungry, thirsty and weary, looked forward to sitting under its shade to be refreshed by its rich and luscious fruit. This, too, is a delightful prospect when we meet one of whom we may expect not only the green leaves of an untarnished profession, but also the abounding fruits of Christian graces in the life and character. To discover the heavenly graces of faith and love, of righteousness and holiness and godly zeal, amidst the barrenness of earth, must seem like the grapes of Eshcol, foretastes and firstfruits of a heavenly land. There was also here the prospect of *early ripeness*. Since 'the time of figs was not yet', it must have been early in the season, and it was pleasant indeed to find here one tree standing out from the rest as obviously bearing fruit. It was the joy of those who are about to gather the first ripe fruits of the season. How delightful a prospect it is for us, as Christian men and Christian workers, when we see reason to expect early fruit! In our homes and congregations early godliness, early love to Christ, early breathings after holiness – what delightful firstfruits they are! It was some such prospect as this that Christ and His disciples had that day.

But we see unfolding here a Bitter Disappointment. We read that when our Lord came to it 'He found nothing but leaves'. Thus was a prospect so delightful turned into a bitter disappointment. Here we meet with that sad disappointment of a *duty undischarged*. The primary duty of a tree is to give fruit, and if it fails in this, it fails altogether, as no amount of leaves or branches or flowers can compensate for lack of fruit. Its growth may be tremendous, its branches far-reaching, its foliage green and conspicuous, and its blossoms large and sweetly scented, but if it lacks fruit it forfeits its place in creation, and is but a cumberer of the ground. With what bitter disappointment we look upon some lives – they seem to have everything but 'the one thing needful'. They are strong and healthy, kind and helpful, but in their duty towards God they have utterly failed. If we are barren towards God, it avails little that we plead the gentleness and goodness of our nature or the generosity and correctness of our conduct. How often has a minister been attracted by outward disposition, only to meet with the galling disappointment of spiritual barrenness. This disappointment appears, too, as that of a *service unrendered*. What a privilege this should have been! The Saviour of the world, the Creator of heaven and earth, was anhungered, and in the hour of His need He came to this tree to satisfy His wants. But alas! It failed to respond: it refused to refresh its Creator as He went forth to lift from the earth its curse. To our human way of thinking what can constitute a more bitter disappointment than God visiting souls that have been under Gospel blessings, demanding the fruits of our faith and service and obedience and finding none? Such a time comes to every man, but most of us know not the day of our visitation – and we may never know it till we hear Him say, 'I was anhungered and ye gave me no meat.' Oh, the tragedy of negative goodness! This is the disappointment of a *promise unfulfilled*. This tree stood out from all the rest with its foliage, its signs of fruit and early maturity; but alas! when the Lord's hand searched it, it was found barren. The distant promise was not fulfilled, the appearance was but an empty show, for 'He found nothing but leaves'. With what bitterness do we look upon those who gave early promise of godliness and an interest in Divine things, but who are now utterly destitute! When we looked for fruit we found only worldliness and greed of gain and secret sin. The world, the flesh and the devil have come in to rob the life of all its fruit and to leave an early promise for ever unfulfilled.

We see depicted here, too, a Fearful Doom. What can be more terrible than the record 'Jesus answered and said unto it, No man eat fruit of thee hereafter for ever'. That was Christ's answer to the barrenness of that leafy fig-tree. In that answer we see the fearful doom of *perpetual barrenness*. 'Let no fruit grow on thee henceforth' were the words Matthew records: as if the Lord said, 'Since thou didst not discharge thy duty, thou hast lost thy opportunity: no longer canst thou discharge it, for, barren in the day of testing, thou shalt be barren forever'. This is truly a fearful doom – to have the Divine visitation, and hereafter be allowed to remain barren for ever. Over how many lives could 'Ichabod' be written, for the glory of their early profession and opportunity and promise is departed and they are left a wilderness for ever. This doom included *gradual withering*, for in the morning as the disciples passed by 'they saw the fig-tree dried up from its roots'. It was no thunderbolt from above that did it, no whirlwind or lightning from the skies that tore it up, but it 'dried up from the roots'. Gently, imperceptibly, the forces of nature were withdrawn, the forces that give sap and growth and sustenance, and soon the glossy leaves grow dull, and the powerful branches drop till eventually it is 'dried up from its roots' and dead. Need one say that this fearfully and graphically portrays the doom of the unfruitful in Christ Jesus in our churches and congregations, when those spiritual forces that make for life and growth and vitality are withdrawn and the whole personality – body, soul, and spirit – withers up under the blight of sin? There remains to be added that this doom brought *final extinction*. This is sure and speedy, for whatever use men may make of a leafy fig-tree, barren though it be, the withered and blasted trunk need only be left alone to fall in pieces to the ground. It is a mercy to cut it away, for it is only a blot on the landscape. Is it not a fitting end to an empty life and a barren profession? 'Cut it down, why cumbereth it the ground?' Justice and mercy alike demand it.

THE WIND OF THE SPIRIT

It was our Lord who most frequently drew attention to the close connection between natural and spiritual law, a connection that was to him inevitable and inescapable since the one God was the Author of both. For that reason He used the most commonplace of natural phenomena to illustrate the most mystical spiritual experiences, and to cast light upon the hidden operations of the Spirit of God. There is, for example, that well-known illustration of His concerning the working of the Spirit of God in the regeneration of the human soul: 'The wind bloweth where it listeth, and thou hearest the sound thereof, but canst not tell whence it cometh and whither it goeth; so is everyone that is born of the Spirit'. Here our Lord clearly teaches that there are attributes of the wind in its operation that are analogous to the workings of the Holy Spirit of God, and He indicates what these are. They are three, and we might do well to take them to heart in these days of spiritual dearth and spiritual unrest, when the minds of earnest Christian people seem to oscillate between despair of any general spiritual revival visiting the land, and a feverish agitation to do something to produce that revival themselves. Taking the wind as the natural agency that guides us to a clearer perception of the operations of the Spirit of God, we note these simple facts.

I

The wind *cannot be controlled, but it can be used.* 'The wind bloweth where it listeth' and so cannot be controlled or interfered with in its course. It is a sovereign influence and none can temper or soften or change it in its course. This quality of the wind has remained unchanged with the passing of the years, and unaffected by the advance of human knowledge.

On the other hand it is equally true that while neither the wise man nor the fool can control the wind, both can use it to their own advantage. If we give obedience to the laws of the wind, we may make it serve us and bless us. We can set our sails to catch the breeze and it drives us either out to sea or into port. Whither the wind drives depends on the set of the sails, and a skilled mariner can sail in the teeth of the wind.

In like manner there are spiritual processes, as our text suggests, that cannot be controlled; but they can be made use of to our lasting good. We are not disposers of our own lot; the Father of spirits has perfect control of those spiritual processes within us that affect us so deeply and may change us so radically. In many an unwilling breast there stirs a movement towards spiritual realities which we cannot control. We may resist and oppose it and try to stem it, but we shall find it as irresistible as the wind, since it is the movings of the life-giving Spirit of God. Let us not try to smother the rising concern within our breasts, lest we be found to resist the Holy Ghost. Rather let us use it to our eventual peace and blessedness. As with individuals so with nations, 'the wind bloweth where it listeth'. In His nation-wide movements the Holy Spirit of God is not subject to man's control. One era He blows softly over Asia, another over Europe, another over America, and yet another over the distant Islands of the Sea. Truly, in all His operations the Holy Spirit is like the wind which 'bloweth where it listeth'. May it be ours to set our sails to catch the first fresh gust of wind that alone produces that 'forward movement' that our human organisation has sought to produce in vain. And even when the wind blows from unexpected quarters, may we be skilled mariners that can sail in the teeth of the wind, and be driven by many strange and apparently harsh providences into havens of spiritual security and peace.

II

The second quality of the wind we note from our text is that *it cannot be seen, though it can be heard*. 'Thou hearest the sound thereof', is our Saviour's comment on the wind. Though heard, it is invisible! There is an element of secrecy about the wind; no one has ever seen it! The keenest eye cannot see it, nor can it become visible through the telescope or under the microscope. But it can be heard; it has a distinctive sound as it rushes through the trees of the forest. We can see the mighty monarchs of the forest under its influence and sometimes break before its gale. Thus the sough of the wind is known to us all; we have heard it whistle to every tune and on every key, while it remains itself invisible. So are the movements of the Spirit of God. Spiritual processes, as a rule, cannot be seen. There is a great secrecy about the Divinest things in life; God's mightiest forces are secret forces; God's greatest works are operations in which the Hand of the Worker is hid. But though God's greatest forces are unseen, they may often be heard; they find expression in language that becomes audible and intelligible. For example the life that is under the regenerating and sanctifying power of the Spirit of God is a life that speaks. Great lives have been known to bend before the breeze and they gave forth an unwonted sound, sometimes they sighed like the wind among the trees of the wood, sometimes they gave forth music like the Aeolian harps of the Black Forest! On the day of Pentecost, when the Holy Spirit came like a rushing wind, every man in the motley crowd heard the Apostles speak in his own tongue. When the Holy Spirit of God is in direct contact with men, we will hear them speak in our own tongue, in a language that our hearts and consciences can understand, the language of conviction, of pardon, of peace and grace. Thus we claim that spiritual processes are secret in their operation, but not in their results. They may not be seen at work, but they will be heard in their effects. They produce lives that speak.

III

From the third quality of the wind that our Lord mentions, we note that *the wind cannot be understood, but it can be experienced.* 'Thou canst not tell whence it cometh or whither it goeth', points to our complete ignorance. The way of the wind is wrapped in mystery, and we are still very ignorant of the laws that govern it. Though we speak in technical terms of 'depressions' and such like, the fact remains that atmospheric movements are very much a mystery to us. Yet though we do not understand the way of the wind, we can experience its blessings. It brings to us the clouds that carry the rain, and the breath that cools the fevered brow. It brings to us the very life that we constantly breathe. Yet we confess that we 'do not understand whence it cometh or whither it goeth'. Shall we not believe in the wind because we do not fully understand it? Shall we cease to use it because we do not comprehend it? Since we do not understand the composition of the atmosphere, or know the origin and destination of the wind, shall we refuse to breathe it? Surely not!

In like manner we do not profess to understand the life -giving processes of the Spirit of God, but we experience them, and therefore, we fully believe them. We are called to believe and to experience many things we do not understand. Though our religion is not unnatural, it is super-natural and it stretches far beyond our present comprehension. There is mystery in our religion before which the spirit of man must stand with bared head and unshod feet. Yet we can live within that mystery and experience its regenerating and sanctifying power. In other words, though there are things in our religion beyond our comprehension, they are not for that reason outside our experience.

There are glorious and profound mysteries in our Gospel which we do not fully understand, yet they are having a profound influence upon our hearts and lives. The central fact of the Gospel message – the Incarnation – is beyond our present powers of comprehension, and it seems to us an event in which, to quote a mystic of last century, nature stood aside to let God pass by. But we are not, for that reason, to question its reality. Indeed, to the Christian heart it has been through the ages the pillar of our hope and the great source of our comfort. Other truths there are in our most holy Faith which we cannot fully understand, but which we can experience in their reality of light and comfort and peace. 'Thou canst not tell' may be written over many of our most deeply cherished articles of faith, but we shall not cease to cherish them for the reason that we have had experience of their truth and their power.

Thus simply stated, these are facts so patent as to be almost self-evident. Yet the holding of them in memory would keep us from those extremes in evangelism which characterise so much of our Christian effort, the extreme, on the one hand, of our despair when we feel our helplessness in face of the task committed to us, and that of a self-confidence bordering on presumption when we recognise the might of the instruments placed in our hands. We need this admonition always, and there can be no surer corrective to black despair or a facile optimism than this consciousness of God's sovereignty in grace. Let us contemplate this sovereignty of the gracious Spirit of God and then by faith take hold of His sovereignty as the only means by which we can wield power with God and with man. Then shall we recognise with gratitude and awe that the movements of the Divine Spirit are like the wind which cannot be controlled but can be used, which cannot be seen but can be heard, which cannot be understood but can be experienced.

BURNING BUT NOT CONSUMED

Of all the symbolic incidents in the Old Testament it is probable that the incident of the Burning Bush, recorded in Exodus, has appealed most to the popular imagination as a symbol of the imperishable life of the Church of God. It is rather a pity that its interpretation has been restricted to what is, after all, only one aspect of its spiritual significance. Viewed in its original setting, it has a much wider reference than a portrayal of the struggle and victory of the Children of Israel. To Moses it was more than a message: it was a revelation. He turned aside to see 'this great sight' with the awe of one who was to see unveiled the most impenetrable and mysterious of Divine realities. It was just an acacia or thorn – bush aflame on the hillside, but it was heaven's fire, and it imparted Heaven's illumination to his soul.

I

Here Moses was given a revelation of the essential nature of God. The world, old in sin, was but young in spiritual knowledge and perception; the children of men were but learning the alphabet of the Divine Revelation that was in the fullness of time to be enshrined in the Book and unveiled in the Person of Emmanuel. But as the most learned of men go back to the alphabet for the building up of their knowledge, so we go back to the symbolic expression of God given to Moses in the Burning Bush as one of the foundation truths of the entire Revelation of God. It was as Moses gazed into the heart of the burning bush that he heard God declare: 'I AM THAT I AM'. The burning bush was the outward unfolding of that mysterious Name. Fire as the source of light, warmth, energy, purification, was a fit symbol of God's Name and had been used of God in His revelation of Himself in earlier times. But here was fire burning continuously without being fed, a bush ablaze without being consumed, an unfolding of the Being of God as the source of all activity, yet Himself underived and dependent on none. He could declare I AM as the only One who had existence in Himself, and he could declare I AM THAT I AM as the only One whose existence continued in being endlessly and unchangeably, able to impart its light and heat, yet deriving nothing from its environment, always burning yet never burning out! However little we are able to comprehend the infinitude of the Eternal One, we are able, at least, to recognise here a symbol of Him who is the source of light and energy to a universe, who pours forth the living stream of His life upon men and angels, and yet is not one whit diminished by all the liberality of His self-giving! In short, here is a worthy symbol of God: a bush aflame but not destroyed, burning but not burnt; a symbol of God ever active, ever living, ever giving, and yet the same God still, owing His existence to none, fed by His own boundless energy and His own unwearied power; the ageless and timeless, the ever – present I AM.

II

Here too was a Revelation of God's incarnation in Jesus Christ, who as 'the Angel of the Lord', delighted to visit His people. The burning bush was a symbol, not, perhaps, so much as of what God was, as of what God was to be. It indicated an act of tremendous condescension. An acacia bush, a bush of dry thorns,was a lowly shrine for heaven's fire, but there in the heart of that thorn – bush dwelt and burnt the sacred flame. Was it not a foreshadowing of that wondrous condescension when God stooped into our nature in the Person of Jesus Christ, and His glory dwelt in a frail tabernacle of clay? That body of ours, marred by sin, abounding in manifold infirmities, was no fit abode for the sacred fire, but 'He abhorred not the virgin's womb', He took upon Him our nature with all its sinless frailties, and was made in all things like unto His brethren. The thorn-bush, dried and bleached in the desert sun, was a fit emblem of the nature that the Son of God took, and in which He wrought out salvation for men. It was in that nature that we had the further unfolding of the Divine 'I AM' by Him who declared: 'I AM the light of the world'; 'I AM the Good Shepherd'; 'I AM the Vine'; 'I AM the bread of life.' And as Moses turned aside 'to see this great sight', a bush burning but not consumed, so men in every age have turned aside to gaze into the mystery of godliness, God manifest in the flesh, of whom they could say, 'He dwelt among us, and we beheld His glory, the glory as of the only-begotten of the Father, full of grace and truth'.

III

Here, doubtless, Moses was given also a vision of God's triumph in His Church. Israel, though chosen and called of God, was in bonds and galling servitude in Egypt. Under the taskmaster's cruel lash Israel groaned and toiled without any appearing to plead its cause. The representatives of the Living God, the chosen people, were apparently to be exterminated and their light for ever extinguished. So Moses might have thought when he raised his hand to strike the Egyptian, the first blow in a forlorn cause! And when God called him to the leadership he stoutly refused to champion so hopeless a cause. But God was to make him see that no trial and no persecution could destroy the chosen race or extinguish the witness committed to their trust. The bush might burn, but the bush would not be consumed! No fire of human hatred or of the devil's kindling could destroy a cause associated with the name and glory of the living God. The fury of men and devils might rage, but God's Church would survive the fiercest storm. How often Moses needed that vision for the troublous days that lay ahead of him! How often Israel in the wilderness, the prey of her own folly and the victim of the world's hate, seemed ready to perish! But through it all she got safe convoy till she crossed the Jordan and entered the Canaan of promise. How often has this same truth been illustrated in the history of the Church of God through the ages! Burned but not consumed! As the Church entered the fires of opposition and persecution, many saw but a dry thorn-bush aflame and ready to be consumed. But in the furnace with the suffering Church there appeared one like unto the Son of Man, and the Church emerged purified and strengthened. Today in many of the countries of Europe, the Church of God is passing through the fire, and many think they have seen the last of the Confessional Church in Germany, and of the Protestant Church in Holland and Norway. But these fires cannot consume the living Church: they will burn themselves out and the cause of God will emerge strengthened and cleansed by the fires of persecution it has passed through. This is truly a vision for these days – burned but not consumed!

IV

We may find here a further revelation of the strength of Divine life in the soul. Let us not be surprised that the glory of God could dwell in the desert thorn-bush! It can dwell in a more unlikely place than that, when it has its abode in the desecrated and ruined temple of man's heart! The life of God in the soul is a spark from Heaven's altar, and it burns with all the intensity of immortality. At times the Divine fire may seem to burn low, and to the eye of man it may appear as if it had been extinguished! But it is a heavenly flame and it cannot burn out: it glows with the Eternity of the Life of God.

'And I give unto them eternal life, and they shall never perish' is the charter of our immortality, and the final pledge that the bush shall not be consumed. Many today are giving expression to alarm lest young

Christians entering the Services may have their Christian life extinguished. As this fire that Moses saw in the humble acacia bush was not fed or sustained by its environment, so the Christian life is not fed from its surroundings or kept alive by its favourable environment. It comes from above, and it is maintained by the power of the life of God. It must burn, but it will never burn out however uncongenial the circumstances under which it has to exist. Let us find courage where Moses found courage, in the perseverance, not of the saints, but of their God!

Here then is an Old Testament figure in which God stoops down to our finite comprehension, and the Angel of the Covenant anticipates the day when He shall tabernacle with men and show unto them the Father. In that revelation is the sheet-anchor of a suffering Church and the security of the tempted soul. We need its illumination and its comfort in these days.

BETWEEN THE BATTLES

Melchizedek is without doubt one of the most mysterious figures of the Old Testament. His person and origin and identity are all shrouded in mystery. He was Priest of the most High God and also King of Salem, thus combining two offices seldom or never brought together in one person. And the reference to him in the New Testament only serves to deepen the mystery; 'without father, without mother, without descent, having neither beginning of days, nor end of life', states the mystery; it does not attempt to solve it. The historical narrative introduces Melchizedek only in the one incident in Abraham's life as he was returning from the slaughter of the kings. He came out of the shadows to meet Abraham and to bless him, and having exercised this ministry he returned into the shadows whence he came. Thus we know Melchizedek only as he crossed Abraham's path, but that one glimpse of the Royal Priest of Salem has become to all the ages a foregleam of the Priestly King who clothed in mystery, stepped from Eternity to time, and, having fulfilled His mission of blessing, stepped back again to His Priestly Throne. David in the Old Testament, and the writer to the Hebrews in the New, both testify that Christ is here, and that the blessing of Melchizedek is fragrant with His heavenly Benediction. Let us consider the incident in that light.

I

The Grace of the Lord Jesus is revealed in this incident in that the blessing was bestowed at a time of very special need in Abraham's life. In fact it was given between two great battles that Abraham waged, the one physical, the other moral and spiritual. The first battle revealed Abraham as a man of no ordinary courage and enterprise. Chedorlaomer, the warlike King of the Elamites, swept down upon the cities of the plain and the Sodomites were overthrown. Sodom was sacked and its men taken off as slaves. Among the captives was Lot, Abraham's nephew, the man who apparently found the gaiety of Sodom more attractive than the fellowship of his spiritually-minded uncle. It is significant that the man who had chosen the life of separateness from the world had now to come to the rescue. Abraham might well have argued that since Lot had been given the first right of choice and had deliberately chosen the rich plains overlooking Sodom, he should now be left to face out the consequences of his choice. But true spiritual separation never argues thus! The man who is set apart for God is set apart that he may more faithfully serve God and bless men. Separation can never mean isolation, and Abraham, recognising his responsibility, hastened to the rescue. And in the encounter with the Elamites, no doubt intoxicated with success and hampered by the extent of their loot, Abraham was eminently successful. Lot and the captive Sodomites with all their goods were delivered. This was Abraham's first battle and it was bravely joined and successfully fought.

The second battle came close on the heels of the first, and it was more perilous because more sinister. When the King of Sodom had heard of Abraham's gallant and successful intervention, he set out to meet him and extend to him a grateful welcome. It was a memorable meeting near Salem, afterwards Jerusalem. Grateful for his timely and courageous help, the King of Sodom offered Abraham all the spoil. It was no small matter for a nomadic shepherd like Abraham – though he was already rich in flocks and herds – to have the spoil of a town of Sodom's luxury. But Abraham's response to the offer affords one of the finest glimpses of the nobility of his soul. He seems to have anticipated this very possibility, to have thought the matter out beforehand, nay, rather to have fought it out in his heart, as his reply indicates: 'I have lift up my hand unto the Lord, the most high God, the possessor of heaven and earth, that I will not take from a thread even to a shoelatchet, and that I will not take anything that is thine, lest thou shouldest say, I have made Abram rich.' It was a truly sublime response revealing that whatever may be said of the descendants of Abraham throughout the ages, no avarice or greed of filthy lucre can be laid to the charge of their great progenitor! Abraham would not soil his hands with the spoil of Sodom. He did not feel his need of it, for his God was the possessor of heaven and earth! That was surely the bigger battle of the two, and Abraham emerged triumphantly.

Now it was between these two battles that Melchizedek appeared. As Abraham was returning from the rout of the kings, the royal priest of Salem came out to meet him with bread and wine. It was no mere act of Eastern hospitality: it was a sacrament of moral encouragement and spiritual refreshment. It was intended to serve the double purpose of reviving and refreshing Abraham after his conflict and of strengthening and encouraging him for the battle that was to come. That it did serve this twofold purpose we cannot doubt, and this act alone would make Melchizedek a fitting prototype of the Lord Jesus Christ, whose sacramental grace serves the double purpose of refreshing and reviving the soul after its fierce battle with the world, the flesh and the devil, and of preparing it to meet the fresh assaults of the kingdom of darkness. Our Lord often meets his weary people with this refreshment between the battles of their spiritual life, and they are encouraged and strengthened to fight on.

II

It is surely pertinent to ask what particular encouragement Abraham did receive from this meeting with the Priest of Salem. Though there may have been something mystical and not open to investigation in the encouragement given by the bread and wine, there accompanied it a revelation of God that was particularly fitted to strengthen the faith of Abraham at this time. In fact Melchizedek had given to Abraham a new name for God, never before revealed in the Bible: 'the Most High God, Possessor of heaven and earth.' That it was appropriate to Abraham's circumstances we cannot doubt, that it made a deep impression on him we know from the fact that he used this very name in his dealings with the King of Sodom. It was a revelation of God that made it easier for Abraham to refuse outright the loot of Sodom. Why should he take ought from man or be debtor to the King of Sodom when his God was the Possessor of heaven and earth! Why should he fear the might of men when he had with him the Most High God! Thus the sacrament of bread and wine was accompanied by a revelation of God's strength and sufficiency that made it easier for the tempted soul to fight on. Is not this what the Lord Jesus Christ in His sacramental grace does for the souls of His people? He gives them a fresh vision of the resources of His grace for them and a fresh revelation of the glory of His Father. We do not seek to empty the Sacrament of its mystic quality, but we do affirm that if it is not accompanied by a fresh revelation of the Lord in His power and grace, it is not the source of strength and encouragement that it was designed to be. But when the Sacrament is accompanied by a vision of the Lord of Grace and Glory, then it is to the tired and battling soul a source of encouragement and refreshment. And the Lord often bestows this blessing in all its fullness between the battles, putting the seal of His approval on our faithfulness in the past, and strengthening our hearts for what is to come. When we are tempted with the bribe of an ungodly world, we shall remember this vision of God in the bounty of His grace. Why should we soil our hands with ill-gotten gains when our God is Possessor of heaven and earth!

III

Abraham's response to this gracious visitation was characteristic of the man, and remains characteristic of the gracious soul in every age. He gave to Melchizedek 'tithes of all'. In this Abraham clearly showed that he recognised the Divine mission of his mysterious host: he made returns that were appropriate only to the service and cause of the living God. The response was spontaneous, the urge of spiritual instincts and perceptions, the expression of the soul's gratitude and sense of indebtedness. It was a material return for spiritual mercies. But who would venture to say that in that transaction Abraham was materially minded in proffering the gifts, or Melchizedek in receiving them? It was all part of the one gracious sacrament: the Divine revelation and the soul's response. Here we come face to face with the demands made upon us by the gracious visitations of our Lord. Though the demand is essentially spiritual, it has its material aspect. Each fresh revelation of the sufficiency of God demands from us renewed faith, trust and devotion, and these graces find immediate expression in the deliberate and intelligent support of God's cause and kingdom in the world. Thus the whole of life comes under the gracious influence of our spiritual experiences, and all is dedicated to the service and glory of the God who has had mercy upon us. The material and the spiritual are absorbed in one burning passion to give glory to God and show forth the riches of His grace to the world. At any rate, those who have had Abraham's experience need no such argument to urge them to give their tithes to the Church of God; it is the spontaneous response of the deepest instincts of the soul.

THE TWO GREAT MARVELS

Only twice is it recorded of our Lord that He marvelled. And the objects of His marvel were strange. Many who came to Jerusalem wondered at the architecture of the Temple and the massive stones that went to its building. Others marvelled at the skill and learning and eloquence of the great teachers of Israel. But He didn't. His wonders were in another world, in another sphere than that of time and sense, in the world of spiritual life and operations. On the one occasion it is recorded that He marvelled at *faith,* on the other at *unbelief.* The faith of the Roman centurion who sent to Him a request for the healing of his sick servant, and the unbelief of the people of Nazareth who said of Him: 'Is not this the carpenter, the son of Mary, the brother of James and Joses and of Judah and Simon?' were alike matters of surprising wonder to Him. It may help to clear away the unrealities of our own world if we can enter His for a brief while and see through His eyes the wonders that are there.

I

The first marvel we note is the Seat of Faith and the Haven of Unbelief.

It is an undoubted wonder where faith is sometimes found. In this case it was found in the breast of a Roman soldier, a man who was not in his youth instructed in the things of God, and whose occupation and training tended to make him rough, unfeeling and unspiritual. Yet in that apparently inhospitable soil there lived and grew a living faith that directed him for help in the hour of need to the healing power of the Lord Jesus and inspired him with the utmost confidence in the efficacy of Christ's word to heal whether at a distance or nigh at hand. It is of that faith that the Master said that He had 'not found so great faith, no, not in Israel'.

It was to the Lord an equally great marvel where unbelief could find a haven and take deep hold. There were the Jews of His day, enlightened by the ministry of priests and prophets through many generations, their Messiah portrayed to them in psalm and prophecy, in rite and sacrifice, a people reputed to possess the most sensitive spiritual nature of all the peoples of the earth, and yet when their Messiah came to them in the fullness of His glory and grace they despised and rejected Him! Even 'in His own country' and 'His own city' of Nazareth, unbelief so built a wall of prejudice between Him and the needy that the hand of His grace was stayed and 'He could there do no mighty work'. Their hostility, their bitter prejudice, their stubborn unbelief caused Him to marvel!

These are still the marvels of the spiritual world: where faith can dwell and thrive; where unbelief can lurk and destroy. In surroundings where one would not expect it, faith is often found living, sturdy, in constant exercise, doing battle against all that could keep the soul in chains. In men whose characters are rough-hewn, whose training and occupation give them little opportunity to become versed in the finer arts of 'good manners', or in the more superficial courtesies of life, there is not infrequently found, if one goes deep enough to look for it, a robust faith in God's power and grace, and a spirit that knows the realities of conflict against what is base and unholy. On the other hand, there are men and women who possess all the advantages of environment and training, with a religious background and religious instruction, with refinement and culture, in whom, on closer contact, we find a hard core of ungodliness and unbelief, of insubmission to the grace of God and unwillingness to become debtors to His mercy.

These are still the marvels of the spiritual world!

II

Another marvel to note is the Hopefulness of Faith and the Despair of Unbelief.

It is most truly a marvel how hopeful faith can be even in the most adverse circumstances. Here was a man who had a valued servant stricken with palsy, not only sick, but 'ready to die'. Here was an advanced case of general paralysis, with the limbs helpless, the nerves shrivelled, the muscles atrophied – a picture of despair! Yet the Roman centurion faces this apparent hopelessness with the confident hope: 'Say a word, and my servant shall be healed.' In the presence of Christ nothing seemed to him hopeless or impossible, for he had the faith that hopeth all things and believeth all things. It was this faith that, in its clinging trust, made Christ marvel.

Equally marvellous is the Despair of Unbelief that shuts its eyes to the light and turns away from the presence of Omnipotence in black despair. Such was the unbelief of Israel in Christ's day! They lived through the ages on the hope of a Messiah, and when Messiah came in fulfilment of every prophecy and promise, hope gave place to despair. Such was the unbelief of the people of Nazareth who stood in the presence of the great Son of God and cried: 'Is not this the Carpenter?'. Through the lowliness of His human guise they could not see the light of His glory and grace, nor could they understand that He Who stood at the carpenter's bench and fashioned from the rough, unhewn block the article of His design and pleasure, could from the base material of life bring, by the transforming power of His grace, lives and characters fashioned to His own heavenly purpose. That which might have led them to hope, only fostered despair, because the light that was in them was darkness!

The Hopefulness of Faith is wonderful! It sees a light in every cloud, and finds a message of encouragement and strength in every situation. This is because faith reaches through to a God with whom nothing is impossible and sees every situation through the unfailing grace of a Saviour. The blessed Lord looks with admiring wonder upon His people who against hope do believe in hope and still put their trust in God. Equally marvellous is the despair of unbelief which shuts its eyes to the light of the noonday sun and says: 'It is night!'. Under the blindness of unbelief the soul cannot see the grace of God even in the full light of Gospel day, and under its promptings the heart gets hard, mechanical, sordid, and lives only for the present day, crying: 'Let us eat and drink, for tomorrow we die'. This is the marvel of unbelief.

III

Another marvel we may consider is the Flights of Faith and the Sinkings of Unbelief.

Faith can soar far above the clouds that hide the face of the sun. For faith uses arguments by which it can rise from the lower levels to the highest of all. Here the Roman centurion made use of his own position and experience to give him an exalted view of the authority and power of the Lord Jesus. As a Roman officer he was given authority over his soldiers; he could 'say to one, Go, and he goeth, and to another, Come, and he cometh'. From this he reasons that there must be authority and discipline in the spiritual world, and that the Lord of all can exercise that authority as and how and when He wills. By such steps does faith rise to the higher levels!

Side by side with this we must place the sinkings of unbelief. The reasoning of unbelief has a downward trend. The citizens of Nazareth knew Jesus from His youth; they knew Him in the intimacy of His home life; they knew all His near relatives. 'Is not this', they said, 'the son of Mary the brother of James and Joses and of Judah and Simon; and are not his sisters here with us?' In these relationships was not His identity as the Son of God very clear? Could they not see how little His glory was derived from his earthly origin! How far removed He was from his earthly connections, from even the best in His earthly family! How reasonable that faith should argue thus! But unbelief argued downwards, despised Him because of His lowly connections, and regarded Him as a deceiver and beside Himself. 'And they were offended at Him'.

Faith is wonderful in that it can soar so high! It makes stepping-stones of its daily experiences and rises from the material to the spiritual, from the earthly to the heavenly. Faith in its pilgrimage upwards steps easily from the natural to the supernatural, as the master so often commanded the disciples to do.

But the sinkings of unbelief are marvellous too. Its reasoning – in so far as it has any – is never upwards! It is a dead weight that drags mind and heart downwards and robs the soul of its all. It takes from us that which we have and leaves us empty and bare. As it robbed the Jews of Nazareth of the healing and grace of the Saviour Who was in their midst, so it makes the Gospel of none effect to men. In this, it is a matter for marvel.

IV

One further marvel we note is the Humility of Faith and the Pride of Unbelief.

In the case of the centurion the humility of faith is striking. 'I am not worthy that Thou shouldst enter under my roof' is the language of a spiritual humility that only faith could produce. As a Roman officer he no doubt had a home that would compare favourably with any in the neighbourhood. But in his own eyes it had a moral and spiritual inadequacy to house the Christ of God! The thought of Christ coming under his roof was overpowering and faith fell prostrate acknowledging its unworthiness. It is wonderful indeed how self-revealing and self-emptying faith can be!

But there is also the Pride of Unbelief. The Jews prided themselves on their knowledge of the Scriptures, their loyalty to Moses, their choice privileges as the elect race, and religious pride blinded their eyes to their need of a Saviour. 'From whence has this man these things? and what wisdom is this that has been given unto Him ?', asked the leaders of the synagogue of Nazareth, and they were offended at Him! Thus does unbelief generate a religious pride that takes offence at the person and work of the Saviour of the world! Is not the offence of the Cross still with us?

The humility of faith is both beautiful and wonderful. In its very nature it cannot be otherwise than humble. For faith is but an outstretched hand, an empty pitcher, a child's cry! It divests the soul of its self-righteousness and is content to appear in garments not its own! It seeks the presence of the Saviour, and yet cries: 'Depart from me, for I am a sinful man, O Lord'.

How proud and self-sufficient unbelief is! It makes a religion of its unbelief and calls it agnosticism, secularism, atheism! It sets up in opposition to the faith, and setting about to establish its own righteousness, it will not submit to the righteousness of God. How wonderful that mere unbelief could be so proud!

If these marvels that stirred the heart of our Saviour to joy or sorrow are not marvels to us, it must surely be because we don't see as he sees, or understand as he understands. Moving on the surface of life, we do not penetrate the depths where the wonders of the spiritual world are to be seen. Let us take up the prayer of the psalmist 'Open thou mine eyes, that I may behold wondrous things out of thy law'.

LOSING AND SAVING

A Law of Nature, of Love, and of Grace

It must have been a matter for surprise, at one time or another, to all readers of the Gospel narrative that our Lord should so often have expressly forbidden His disciples to tell that He was the Christ. Even at Caesarea Philippi He had solicited the disciples' opinion of Him, 'But whom say ye that I am, ?' and Peter had made the great Confession, 'Thou art the Christ, the Son of the living God,' He 'straitly charged them and commanded them to tell no man that thing.' Quite obviously there was the fact – and this does not by any means provide the entire explanation – that He did not wish any man to make His acquaintance merely by hearsay, or rest his faith in the Messiah on the verbal testimony of somebody else. Christianity must have deeper and more solid foundations than that if it is to endure the test that will try every man's faith. For the religion of Christ was to be a stern experience that would shake life to its very foundations and overthrow many of the most deeply cherished principles of human living – 'And He said to them all: if any man will come after Me, let him deny himself, and take up his cross daily and follow Me'. It was then that He laid down the fundamental principle of the Christian life that makes it the very antithesis of all other ways of living and that seems to contradict the basic principle on which every human life is built: 'For whosoever will save his life, shall lose it, but whosoever will lose his life for My sake shall find it'. Radical as this principle is, and challenging as its demands are, it does no violence to our natures, but rather gives outlet to the sanctified emotions of the Christian heart and illustrates the ways of the Grace of God in the lives and destinies of men.

I

We would like to see here, first of all *the Execution of a Law of Nature*.

'Whosoever will save his life shall lose it', strange as its principle may at first sight seem, is but the expression of a law under which we all live, move, and have our being, the law which ensures that what we save by withdrawing from life we lose either the use, or the development, or the enjoyment of it. This principle was inherent in the teaching of the Parable of the Talents inasmuch as the one talent that had not been employed was eventually lost. Looking at life on the plane of everyday living we can, perhaps, single out three negative forces that end in deprivation. They are idleness, indifference and indulgence.

There is a law which ensures that *Idleness* will lead to loss of power, that effort saved is power lost. This holds good everywhere, whether in the physical, the mental or the moral sphere. The limb of the body that is not in constant exercise loses its strength, its muscle, and eventually its place in the functions of the body. Similarly the mind can retain its powers of thinking or remembering only as thought or memory are exercised. Or the moral faculties retain their vitality and authority only as they are employed and obeyed. Thus loss in every sphere of living follows inactivity; if we save effort we inevitably lose the power to make effort!

Then again *Indifference* leads to loss, inasmuch as the failure to put what we have to the test must lead to lack of progress or development. In that respect what we save we dwarf, stunt and starve, and few things so dwarf and starve the life as self-centredness, that indifference to the interests of others that never brings a man beyond himself or his own interests. Unconcern about the needs of others so impoverishes the life that no growth or development is possible. The selfishness of sin has eaten up the lives of countless men. They only think of themselves, they live a cramped and increasingly narrowing existence within their own borders, and they remain small men, dwarfed souls, stunted spirits. They may go on living, or rather existing, but they never grow.

There is also *Indulgence* as a depriving factor in human life. As idleness is loss of power, and indifference loss of development, so indulgence is loss of enjoyment. It is a commonplace observation that those who are bent on gratifying their own selves, their desires, pleasures, and ambitions, soon lose the joy of living. One such person could write in his thirty -sixth year:-

> My days are in the yellow leaf
> The flowers and fruits of love are gone
> The worm, the canker, and the grief
> Are mine alone

Those whose only aim in life is to please themselves, to gratify their own desires, to indulge their own tastes, will, sooner or later, find the honey of life turn into vinegar, and its sweets become bitter.

II

We can see here, also, *the **operation of a Law of Love***.

'He that loseth his life for My sake' points to the central principle around which Christian life and activity operate: it is the love that gives its all for Christ's sake. Love in operation in one constant, willing, unreserved sacrifice.

It may be stated as *the sacrifice of the Apparent for the Real*. Love aims at giving not merely its possessions, but itself, for that is the logical and ultimate act of love, even to lose its life. Christian love that has the Lord Jesus Christ as its object has touched a reality for Whom the apparent good of life can well be sacrificed. For this reason it denies itself what the world might consider essential and entirely legitimate. The Christian has a will of his own, but he does not always follow it; he has desires of his own, but he does not always gratify them; he has hopes of his own, but he does not always seek to realise them; he has interests of his own, but he does not try to advance them. Christian love is thus moving on a plane of its own, guided by laws of its own, and urged by the one controlling, all-absorbing passion, 'for Christ's sake'.

Or we may put it that Christian love *sacrifices the Near for the Distant*. The keen eye of love sees the distant scene, and with that vision in its eye it becomes blind and deaf to much that lies between. The world does not understand this and often wonders why the Christian does not avail himself of an undoubted advantage, why he foregoes his undoubted rights, why he does not press his legitimate claims. It is because he sees beyond them, and so he makes the present the servant of the future, makes what is beside him serve a distant end and move him on to a distant goal. The Christian is thus the child of the future, its glory is ever gleaming in his eye, and for its prize he can afford to let much of the present slip by. For 'Christ has died for our sins that He might redeem us from this *present* evil world' – from the tyranny of things present as well as from the taint of things evil.

To put it somewhat differently, love *sacrifices the Passing for the Permanent*.

The faith that worketh by love is the great valuator of the spiritual life. It was by it that Moses esteemed the reproach of Christ greater riches than the treasures of Egypt. It is the true calculator of real values; it can differentiate between the shadow and the substance, between the passing and the permanent. And having made its evaluation, it sacrifices the passing things of life for the permanent things, the temporal for the spiritual, the shadow for the substance, time for eternity. It considers this sacrifice supremely worthwhile, because it has learned that the things which are seen are temporal, the things which are unseen are eternal. It is losing its life, but it does it in obedience to a higher law, the law that demands that we sacrifice the less for the greater, the transitory and temporal for the spiritual and eternal.

III

We see here, lastly, *the* **Reward of a Law of Grace**.

Grace has its own laws and its own order; it also has its compensations and rewards. This is one of them: 'He that loseth his life shall find it'.

He shall find it *in personal enjoyment,* for there is no doubt that the joy of giving is greater and of a much higher order than the joy of getting. It is frequently pointed out that it is not what we get out of life that gladdens the heart, but what we put into it. The Christian worker knows the deep, abiding joy of losing his life for Christ's sake and the Gospel's, for it satisfies the whole being, gives scope for all the powers of mind and intellect, and stimulates the soul. Nothing else seems so worthy of man, for nothing else employs man so fully, gives such scope for his energies, such employment for his faculties, such exercise for all his powers.

He shall find his life, also, *in final accomplishment.* The lost life is yet to be found, and it will prove a richer, fuller life than had ever been given. The one-talent man would no doubt have reckoned that the ten talents parted with and used in trading were lost, but far from being lost, they were found in greater abundance! So the life that is lost for Christ is found at the end of the day in a fullness never anticipated even by faith. What a return it must be when Christ gives back the life lost in Him and lost for Him! Thus will we find not only joy in its spending, but riches in its return, as each word and deed will yield its own rich harvest.

We believe that the lost life will also be found *in eternal Blessedness.* The recompense of faith is not confined to this life by any means, and the life lost for Christ will doubtlessly be most fully found in the glory beyond where it shall receive its ultimate crown. There it is that the acquitted of the Lord shall 'receive back the things done in the body' and the streets of the new Jerusalem will shine with the gold that the saints have given to their Lord. It is a striking and solemn fact that in His graphic portrayal of the last things, our Lord made the blessedness of His saints contingent upon what they had done for Him and in His name: 'Come ye blessed of my Father, inherit the kingdom prepared for you from the foundation of the world. For I was an hungered and ye gave Me meat; I was thirsty and ye gave Me drink; I was a stranger and ye took Me in; naked and ye clothed Me; I was sick and ye visited Me; I was in prison and ye came unto Me.' So close is the connection between the service and sacrifice of the saints and their capacity for the enjoyment of their eternal felicity!

Thus it is that the great Law that constitutes the operative principle of the Christian's faith and life will be seen to be in entire harmony with the law of the universe and the fulfilment of the immutable will and purpose of the Ever Blessed God.

THE FADING LEAF AND ITS MESSAGE

('We all do fade as a Leaf' – Isa. 64:6)

Whatever we may think of this verse as a text, it is regularly seasonable, and falling leaves bear their own message to us. Each season of the year has its corresponding season in human life; each phase in nature has its corresponding phase in the lives of men; the spring time of sowing, the summer of growth, the autumn of maturity, and final decay, and then the winter of silence and inactivity. One of the most arresting phases of autumn is the fading leaf. Leaves have at all times a wonderful human interest about them: their freshness, their seasonableness, their mystery, attract us! Summer would not be summer without them – and autumn, why, without them it would lose much of its peculiar charm! But the autumn leaves all bear a message to us: it is whispered in every leaf that flutters to the ground; and it is this: 'We all do fade as a leaf'.

Leaves fade silently. So do we! Almost all the vital developments of nature are silent: the seed sprouts in the ground in silence, the bud expands into the full-blown rose in silence. But perhaps nothing is so silent as the fading leaf. It is one of the most noiseless of all nature's processes: one week the leaf seems all green and fair, and the next it has lost its hue, and we realise we are 'at the turn of the leaf'. So it is in human life. We all do fade as a leaf. We were all young and buoyant and life seemed full to overflowing. But silently our ranks got thinned: one after another dropped out as noiselessly as a leaf is carried by a gust of wind! When we pause to think and reflect, the silence of these departures overwhelms us! So it will be with all of us. No awful handwriting will appear on the wall telling us in the midst of our rejoicing, as it told Belshazzer of old, 'Mene, Mene, tekel upharsin'. No solemn message comes to us as it once came to Hezekiah warning him: 'Set thine house in order, for thou shalt die and not live'. Such events as our departure from this life are not heralded by the blare of many trumpets. We all do fade as a leaf, and when we depart some of us leave nothing behind to tell we were there. Some do nothing to keep their memories fresh and green in the hearts of those who knew them. Others leave behind them no mark other than a scar that cannot be healed, a gnarled knot that refuses to be smoothened. Some reach the close abruptly, and they come to the end of life as you would come on a precipice. But in whatever manner it happens, we all do fade as a leaf in late autumn – silently.

Leaves fade differently. So do we! In the spring and summer there may seem a sameness about the leaves of the forest; they all have a fresh and glossy green, so that we classify them all alike as the green and glossy foliage of summer. But when autumn comes they all take on different hues: the oak is different from the ash, and the birch from the beech! Some leaves seem all covered with unsightly black spots, some decay with a colourless drabness, others decay with crimson and gold. Decay, it would seem, brings out their individual character. So it does in human life. We all do fade as a leaf, but we fade differently. In youth men may seem very much alike – full of life and vitality and spirits. But they age differently. Age reveals what the life has been with unfailing accuracy. Some get sour, discontented, querulous, ill-tempered, as they get old. Some show a tenacious grasp of the world and get more earthly-minded with each advancing year. Some complain of Providence and say they had a hard lot and an unjust deal. Some show up the errors and follies of early life, if not always in their faces, most truly in their dispositions. Some grow old under a dark cloud, without one softening shadow. And some, thank God, grow old sweetly and serenely and contentedly. We all do fade as a leaf- but we fade differently.

Leaves fade beautifully. So may we. Can any of us have walked through the fields and forests in autumn without a sense of the glory of this season? With its varying tints and hues of crimson and gold the forest seems lit up by tongues of fire. The rowan tree looks beautiful in spring, and then in flower, and in berry, but nothing can rival its glory in autumn as it begins to decay! Each leaf of the tree seems to borrow all the tints of the sun and to hand them out to us long after the sun has set! Yes, leaves fade beautifully, and so may we! There need be no such thing as an ugly, or useless, or discontented old age. There can be such a thing as a beautiful growing old – an eventide that is rosy with life! As the man of God looks back he sees that goodness and mercy had followed him all his days; as he looks forward he sees the Father's House at the end of the road! And he catches the light of home long before he arrives there, and so he ages beautifully.

Leaves fade hopefully. So should we! At first sight we may imagine that the fall of the leaf indicates only decay. But it is not really decay that makes the leaf fall – it is the new life behind it. Each leaf has a young bud in its socket, and nourishes it with its own expiring life. That young life that it nurses in its bosom contains all the hope of spring and summer. It is the pledge that the tree is not to die in winter, but is to live on into the spring and summer. So should we fade! We are enabled by grace to have in our bosoms that provision for the future that makes us die in hope – in glorious hope. And the more we fade, the more strong should grow the blessed hope of immortality till, finally, we have a desire 'to depart and be with Christ, which is far better'. While our outward man perish, the inner man is renewed day by day. Since we must all fade – let us fade in full possession of a good hope through grace.

'We all do fade as a leaf' – but even the fading leaf carries to us a message of comfort and good cheer.

HOW JESUS ANSWERS PRAYER
(A Study of Three Prayers and their Answers)

It seems an undoubted fact that all kinds and classes of men, religious and irreligious, cultured and uncultured, rich and poor, are *interested* in prayer. There are, of course, those who have tested and proved the reality of prayer till it has become to them the central fact of life, the controlling habit of their daily living. Even they want to learn about prayer, for they must feel that they are but on the outer fringes of a realm of limitless possibilities. There are also those who once prayed and now pray no longer, or at least pray but spasmodically and half-heartedly. They are still interested in prayer, for they are not at all easy- minded about their present condition. It was no emancipation that came to them when they abandoned prayer! There are those who don't pray and think it is no use knocking at God's door – and yet even they are very interested in prayer, and often wonder what is on the other side of that door! For all of us, then, the study of a chapter in the Gospel by Mark should prove interesting, since it throws unusually clear light on two things – the kinds of prayer that men pray, and the kinds of answer that men receive. It is the chapter that records the three incidents of the destruction of the Gadarene swine, the healing of the demoniac among the tombs and the raising of Jairus' daughter. In connection with each of these incidents there is a prayer and its answer that may be regarded as typical of its kind.

I

There meets us first what we may regard as the *Prayer of Evil Desire*, answered in Judgment. This is the prayer of the devils that were in possession of the demented man: 'and all the devils besought him saying, Send us into the swine that we may enter into them. And forthwith Jesus gave them leave.' Here the terms of the prayer were granted, but its real desire was not answered. Its desire was undoubtedly evil. Though we know so little of the spirits of darkness that prowl about the habitations of man, it seems clear from the Scripture that they covet above all things to be in possession of a material body. The lack of a body would appear to restrict their movements and place limits on their contacts with man. For this reason they are ever seeking a human body as the vehicle of their evil designs and their means of entering into the sphere of human activities. And so they had tenanted this unfortunate man, dethroning his reason, demoralising his nature, disintegrating his manhood, till eventually his habitation was among the tombs, his kinship with the dead rather than with the living. But at the behest of our Lord, the legion of devils was dispossessed and the unholy tenants were commanded to depart. They viewed this with distaste, since it would curb their activities and thwart their designs. And so they prayed that if they could not tenant human lives, they might be permitted to tenant the bodies of animals. Christ answered their prayer and gave them leave to enter the herd of swine. But in answering their prayer he thwarted their desire: their tenancy of the swine was short – lived, for their victims rushed headlong into the water and were drowned. Thus the evil spirits were cast out into the emptiness of space, their earthly contacts broken, and their power for evil temporarily checked. Christ answered the prayer but it was in judgment. We believe He so answers prayer still. Men can pray, and do pray with evil design, to be in a position to satisfy and indulge themselves that they may 'consume it upon their lusts'. God may answer the precise terms of the prayer and do it in judgment. Of Israel in the wilderness it is said: 'He gave them their request, but sent leanness into their soul'.

II

The next incident, that of the demoniac now restored, sitting at the feet of Jesus, clothed and in his right mind, contains *the Prayer of Devoted Zeal*. Here the terms of the prayer were declined, but the desire of the prayer was granted. One thing the healed demoniac, now in his right mind, his right state and his right place, seemed to view with apprehension – it was the prospect of severance from his Healer. How could he stand alone and not become a prey again to the spirits of evil that had dragged him so low? How could he manifest his gratitude to the Lord his Healer? And so he prayed 'that he might be with Him'. It was a reasonable prayer, with a pious and proper design, and uttered in true zeal and devotion. But the Lord did not grant the terms of the prayer: 'Go home to thy friends' was the strange reply. But He gave the grateful soul his prayer's desire, for He gave him an opportunity to exercise his devotion among his own folk to whom he should tell 'how great things the Lord had done.... and how He had had compassion'. And in that service for his Lord, would he not have the Master's presence more near, more real, more blessed, than if he had travelled by His side! And so the desire of the prayer was answered; and one day the terms of the prayer would be answered too, when at last the weary servant laid him down to rest and in the breaking light of the morning he saw One standing on the other Shore, and in an ecstasy of recognition he cried 'It is the Lord'. And so he was forever with the Lord! Are there not many experiences where God seems to deny the petition even of devoted zeal and love, but its deepest desire is granted. Our love is often foolish and short-sighted, and He answers with a love wise and clear-sighted. As Paul prays in an agony of soul that the thorn in his flesh may be removed that he may thereby be a more effective servant of the Lord he loves, the petition is refused, the thorn in the flesh remains, but by that very thorn he is made what he prayed to be, a more dedicated and successful servant of his Lord.

III

The third incident, that of the raising of Jairus' daughter, contains *the Prayer of Simple Faith*. This was answered in Grace 'exceeding abundantly above all' he asked or thought. Jairus was a man in whose heart had been awakened a faith in Christ remarkable for its strength and its simplicity. Nothing could be simpler, more artless, and yet more appealing than the prayer with which he approached the Master: 'My little daughter lieth at the point of death; I pray thee, come and lay Thy hands on her, that she may be healed; and she shall live'. These are the words of strong, natural, paternal affection; they are the words also of childlike faith and unquestioning confidence. Jairus was a father to his child, but himself a child in the presence of his Divine Benefactor. Christ accompanied him and answered the prayer by doing a greater thing than Jairus had asked, or would conceive of asking: He brought his little girl back from the dead! And so the clinging, childlike faith of His people meets with abounding grace at the hands of the Lord. Simple faith puts us so in tune with the mind and will of our Lord that we may ask what we will and it shall be given unto us. Christ can thus honour the faith that honours Him. But even simple faith has its discipline leading it from one degree of trust to another: it was so in the case of Jairus. The Lord knew what would happen in the way, the message that would reach him and rend his parental heart: 'Thy daughter is dead; why trouble thou the Master any further?' Even Jairus' simple faith would falter then if the Lord had not been there to reassure him and say 'Be not afraid, only believe'. Faith, though it remain simple, must increase in strength and confidence and assurance, and in the very answer to prayer there may come the discipline that gives it further strength and further simplicity.

Thus we learn that Jesus answers prayer! But as the Heavens are higher than the earth, so is His answer higher than our prayer. Full oft He answers 'by fearful works', in language that may affright and dismay, but it is always an answer suited to our circumstances and often in language that heart can understand and conscience can interpret.

THE PRIEST UPON THE THRONE

Tnere are few things on which we need more clear thinking at the present day than on the Bible's revelation of the Kingdom and reign of Jesus Christ in the world. There is very general agreement among thoughtful people that there is only one cure for the world's ills, only one effective challenge to the power of tyranny and oppression let loose in the world – it is the Kingdom of Jesus Christ. There is, however, as we have indicated, much confusion as to what that Kingdom consists in and how it is to be ushered in. This is not to be wondered at, considering that Christ's Kingdom is not of this world. Even the prophets of old who heralded the King who was to reign in righteousness spoke to a people who utterly failed to catch the true significance of their prophetic message. Zechariah, in his own day, spoke of the New Order, but his words sounded strange to the world rulers of his day. Even his most spiritually minded hearers found it difficult to reconcile his prophecy with their own preconceptions and expectations of the King and His Kingdom. This must have been specially so when Zechariah spoke of One who should 'sit as a priest on His throne', for priesthood and kingship were two offices never combined in Israel. Yet it was an integral part of Zechariah's prophecy that the King should be a Priest upon the Throne. To understand this figure is to grasp something of the true meaning of the reign of Jesus Christ and realise something of the glory and grace of His Kingdom.

Zechariah's figure unveils, first of all, '*the foundations of Christ's Kingdom*'. Christ's right to rule is seen to rest in His priesthood. The great kingdoms of this earth rose and fell in rapid succession because their foundations were built on values that could not stand the test of time – on injustice, tyranny, oppression, and selfishness. The Kingdom of Jesus Christ has survived, and will survive, because it is built upon a priesthood that represents supreme and eternal values, values that have stood every test that can be imposed. In that priesthood Christ performed an act of self-abasement that has linked us to Him in ties which death failed to break and the grave could not dissolve, because they partake of the very essence of eternal things. In that priesthood He paid the price for man's redemption in the currency of His own blood, and that blood will stand supreme in the scale of eternal values and can suffer no depreciation while the character of God remains the standard of spiritual values. In that priesthood He offers a mediation by which men are presented to God and God to men, and no other medium for man's approach to God can ever be found that is suitable for man and is acceptable to God. These, therefore, are supreme and final values. And they are the foundations of Christ's Kingdom. Not on naked power, not on underived authority, does the Kingdom of grace stand, as well it might considering that the King of Grace is also the Eternal Son of God. Rather has He built it on the eternal values of His incarnation, sacrifice and mediation, that shall be acknowledged by the entire rational universe as values that are unchallengeable and supreme. Thus shall the Lamb that is in the midst of the Throne for ever appear 'as it had been slain'.

We have suggested to us here, also, *the nature of Christ's Kingdom.* How does He rule and what are the forces of government that are operative in His Kingdom? Because 'He shall sit as a priest upon His throne', therefore the forces He wields are priestly forces. The King is robed in His priestly vestments when He raises the sceptre of His dominion over His realm. This Isaiah saw when he beheld Him coming from Edom 'with dyed garments from Bozrah, glorious in His apparel, travelling in the greatness of His strength'. This is what the Roman soldiers might have seen in the Praetorium Hall had they eyes to see the true meaning of their mock coronation. When they cast over His shoulder an old discarded robe of royal purple, could they not see that the royal glory of His grace could be seen only when He chose to take upon Him the faded garment of our humanity? When they wove a garment of thorns about His brow for a crown, did they not realise that these thorns were the emblems of earth's curse and the fruit of man's sin, and that in bearing these sins in His own body on the tree He won His crown rights over His dominion? When they placed in His hand a reed for a sceptre, did they not understand that this emblem of weakness and tenderness suited well One who should rule His realms by the tender constraints of His Love? This is what John the Seer saw through the Open door into the glory beyond – 'a Lamb as it had been slain'. Thus there were foregleams in every age, even from the midday darkness of Calvary, that He was a Priest upon His Throne, and that the forces of His rule were priestly forces. He wields dominion by the exercise of His priesthood: by absolution to the sinner, pardon to the guilty, rest to the heavy laden, love to the outcast. These are the portals by which He grants admission to His Kingdom, and these are the forces by which He regulates and controls His Empire. The poet tells us of monarchs who

> Wade through slaughter to a throne
> And shut the gates of mercy on mankind

This Monarch waded through His own blood to His priestly Throne, and thus opened for evermore the gates of mercy for mankind.

We have further suggested to us here *the sphere of Christ's Kingdom.* Where does He rule and what is the seat of His Kingdom? This is what Pilate wondered at when he asked his Prisoner: ' Art thou a king then?' The Roman ruler could not be expected to understand the claim: 'My kingdom is not of this world'. But it is evident that this must be so since 'He sits as a priest upon His throne'. A priest deals with spiritual realities, with the affairs of the inner life, the things of the mind, the conscience, and the heart. It is in these realms that Christ exercises His personal reign as King. He rules in the realm of the mind by the convincing power and light of His truth. The extent and importance of that realm we are only now beginning to grasp with our new insistence upon the power of thought, the dominion of ideas, and the organisation of propaganda. But Christ has been King in that realm throughout the centuries, penetrating the minds of men with the light of His truth and making them behold the light of the knowledge of the glory of God in the face of Jesus Christ. As Christ rules the realm of mind, in like manner He exercises His sovereign authority in the human conscience, where righteousness and judgment, pardon and mercy are His instruments of government. A conscience gripped by the pardon of God and in possession of the peace of Heaven is a conscience under the rule of the Lord Jesus and responsive to His will. Similarly He exercises His priestly reign in the human heart, whose every throb and emotion is brought under the sway of redeeming grace. 'Who loved me and gave Himself for me' is the motive power from which there is no appeal or escape, calling forth a responsive love that makes the soul for evermore the bondslave of Jesus Christ. Thus the whole empire of the human soul-mind, conscience and heart are brought under the sceptre of the royal Priest, and all the forces within that vast domain are coordinated and unified by obedience to His will and exercised in yielding Him loyal service.

Zechariah also gives us a hint as to *the end and goal of His Kingdom*. Why does He rule and what is the grand design and purpose to which His Kingdom moves? Many earthly potentates wield power for power's sake, and often seek dominion to serve their own base and selfish ends. Christ's Kingdom has a definite and predetermined goal: 'even He shall build the temple of the Lord'. Zechariah saw the Kings of Babylon build their magnificent marble temples that were to be monuments of their own glory, but the Prophet sees another Temple yet to be built. It is the Temple of the Lord, the shrine where His glory shall dwell, and where His self-revelation shall be perfect and complete. That Temple will be built by the King who exercises His royal dominion as a Priest, redeeming men and fashioning them as stones meet for the Heavenly Temple. And when that Temple is completed and the whole intelligent universe shall assemble to behold the glory of God in His House and admire Him in His saints, then He who reigned as Priest shall see of the travail of His soul and shall be satisfied. Then shall He deliver up the Kingdom unto the Father, when He shall have put down all rule and all authority and power, that God may be all in all.

In Damascus there stands a mosque which had once been a heathen temple. It had passed into Christian hands and on its portal were engraved the words: 'Thy Kingdom, O Christ, is an everlasting Kingdom'. For twelve centuries that Church has been in the hands of the worshippers of Mohammed. Has the Cross then been eclipsed by the Crescent? No. We believe it was a gracious instinct and a true insight into the permanence of the Cross that made the early followers of Christ engrave in stone this testimony to the permanence and everlastingness of His Kingdom. In this our own day, when the forces of darkness are fiercely assailing the bulwarks of Christ's Kingdom, let us find confidence and comfort in the assurance that He is upon His Priestly Throne and that amidst the upheavals and convulsions of earth He is building the Temple of the Lord with priestly forces against which the gates of hell shall not prevail.

SAVING FAITH

What is faith? To some it will seem almost morbidly introspective to ask such a question.

And yet it is vitally necessary, if only to clear up the confusion in present day thinking about the nature of the faith that saves, and to account for the saddening spectacle of so many who 'believed'and have quickly fallen away. Because it is possible to distinguish between various kinds of faith, it has been found necessary to single out one as 'saving faith'. Here we are examining not a difference in degree, but a difference in kind.

Kinds of Faith

The mind of man can exercise faith in very many directions – so much so that most of our human activities call for the exercise of faith at one stage or another. And yet there is only one kind of faith that saves. Even in the sphere of religion, there is frequently a faith in exercise that is not saving faith. There is, for example, a kind of historical faith towards the truth of the Bible that does not involve the moral and spiritual response that accompanies salvation. The Scriptures may be accepted as implicitly as any facts of history, as trustworthy and true, without any sense of personal involvement. We may have a persuasion of the truths of Christianity, even accompanied by some promptings of conscience, but devoid of moral or spiritual conviction. This kind of faith is grounded mainly in the emotional life, and is only temporary. Closely akin to it, though perhaps more intense, is our faith in the miraculous and the supernatural. Here we see the mechanics, as it were, of Faith Healing, some of which is doubtlessly accredited as genuine. But beyond what healing ensues to mind or body, it is not saving. Often it seems nothing more than merely faith in Faith, and yet it works strangely, and sometimes effectively, in the sub-conscious life, releasing hidden powers within.

Source and Object of Faith

Saving faith is of quite a different order, both as to its source and its object. It has its seat in the spiritual nature of man, and not in his spiritual nature only, but in a work of grace wrought by God in the depth of his being. Faith in the Christian is thus the complement of grace in

God. God's approach to man is by grace, and man's response is by faith. It is the responsive act of a quickened soul. We can, therefore, say that saving faith has its roots in the regenerate life imparted by God to the soul, and is indeed the response of that life to the call of God, as a child's cry is his response to his mother's presence. It is the object of saving faith, however, that causes it to be saving. The special act of saving faith consists in receiving the Lord Jesus Christ and resting upon Him. Of course, there may be progression discernible in this faith. It began, probably, by receiving the Divine revelation given in the Scriptures, and so by accepting the testimony of the word concerning Jesus Christ. But it led to a specific faith in the Living Word to whom the written word pointed. Thus from believing about Christ, the soul is led to believing in Christ, and accepting Him in all that the Scriptures reveal Him to be. We believe that there is no such thing as saving faith making a partial acceptance of Christ, as, for example, accepting Him as Lord to save, but not as Lord to rule. There may be progressive knowledge of the sufficiency of Christ, but the faith that saves accepts a whole Christ.

Nature of Faith

As to the nature of Saving Faith there are intellectual, emotional and volitional elements that are operative, to a greater or lesser degree, in the faith that saves. The intellectual element, involving knowledge, is that of a positive understanding of the truth revealed in the Word of God, extending, at least, to the truths necessary for salvation. This involves more than mere knowledge, it includes understanding and spiritual insight.

There is an emotional element, involving conviction. It is a characteristic of the knowledge that it leads to the conviction by which one is led not only to give an assent to the truth, but to claim a personal interest in it, and this conviction involves feeling. Conviction takes place when knowledge enters the moral nature and is rooted there. Thus it can be said that in understanding we take hold of the truth, but in conviction the truth takes hold of us.

There is a volitional element in Saving Faith, involving a decision of the will and an act of trust. This is the decisive element in faith: when the mind is enlightened, the emotions stirred, then the will is moved to act.

Faith thus takes toll of the entire inner being of man and is an act of the mind, heart, and will by which the entire soul goes out to its object and embraces it. A faith that stops short with assent, or with conviction, falls short of salvation. In the Gospel, saving faith finds its object in Jesus Christ, and by trust accepts and appropriates Him, and in an act of committal rests on Him alone for salvation.

Faith and Assurance

The question is often canvassed whether assurance is of the essence of saving faith, that is, whether a true believer has always the assurance of his salvation, or whether he attains to it in the progress of his spiritual life. The problem is more easily settled if we decide on the kind of assurance we are looking for. There is an objective assurance which has to do with God, with His faithfuness and His power. Every Christian has this assurance, for it is of the very essence of faith. But there is a subjective assurance based on personal experience and the certainty we have of having received grace and salvation. In the one case it is faith resting on the faithfulness of God and finding its certainty and security there. In the other it is the assurance that is based on the enjoyment of the Divine presence and the witness of the Holy Spirit within. The Christian can have both, but at times he may have the first without the second. For the subjective assurance he may have to wait, and the diligent waiting is never unprofitable, as he approaches God again and again with the prayer: 'Say Thou unto my soul, I am thy salvation' (Ps. 35:3).

In the light of these facts, the conclusion we must come to is that saving faith is different in kind, and not merely in degree. It is not too little faith falling short of salvation, but the absence of any saving faith at all. Our Lord enforced this lesson in the case of His disciples when they asked Him: 'Lord, increase our faith.' His reply was: 'If ye had faith, as a grain of mustard seed....' It is therefore not a matter of quantity, but of quality. The weakest faith that rests upon the Lord Jesus Christ is saving faith. Every kind of faith that falls short of Him, whatever miracles it may perform, is not saving faith. It is a qualitative difference we are examining, not a quantitative. And its action is necessarily receptive: it is *the receptive faculty* of the regenerate soul. For that reason it is compared to the eye that sees, the ear that hears, the hand that touches, the mouth that tastes, the realities of our physical experience. After the same manner, faith is the soul's faculty that makes contact with the realities of the spiritual world, and its contacts become the most solid realities of our spiritual experience.

Group 8

The Devil

THE PERSONALITY OF THE DEVIL

1. The word 'Angel', whether in Hebrew or Greek, denotes office rather than nature, denotes 'one sent', a messenger. It has now come to be known as an intelligent spirit.

It is highly probable that the devil was created before man; e.g. in Job 38:4 we read 'Where wast thou when I laid the foundations of the earth?'.

Scripture speaks of elect angels and angels that kept not their first estate. These fallen angels are under the organisation of one who is the master devil. This great fallen spirit has many names and titles –

Satan	= adversary
Diabolos	= traducer, used only of the devil
Abaddon	= perdition
Accuser of the brethren	= Rev. 12 v10
Adversary	=1 Peter 5:8
Angel of the bottomless pit, Apollyon	= Rev. 9:11
Father of lies	= John 8:44
Murderer	=anthropoctonos= man-murderer
Power of darkness	= Col.1:13
Prince of this world	= John 14:30
Prince of the devils	= Matth. 12:24
Prince of the power of the air, the spirit that now worketh in the children of diso- bedience	= Eph. 2:2
Ruler of the darkness of this world	= Eph. 6:12
Serpent	= 2 Cor. 11:3
God of this world	= 2 Cor. 4:4
The wicked one	= Matth. 13:38

This would suffice to prove beyond doubt the devil's personality under whom evil is organised. All this leads us to the conclusion that there is a multitude of spiritual beings actuated towards God and man made in His image. This demoniac host is presided over by a mastermind, a personality who designs their personality, and organises warfare against God and man. Our conflict, therefore, is with principalities and powers.

2. Apostasy of the Devil

The activities of the devil are confined to the invisible. The devil is a created spirit, a rational creature possessing superhuman power and wisdom as well as other angelic attributes, and in his first estate was one of the princes of high angelic order in heaven. The time, cause and manner of his fall are not clearly revealed. We are told a certain section of angels kept not their own principality. This probably happened in ages before the creation of the earth.

Two facts are clear:-

(a)   The first estate of the devil was in the truth . Many expositors take 'I beheld Satan as lightning fall from heaven' (Luke 10:18) as referring to time before Creation. Isaiah refers to 'Lucifer, son of the morning' (Isa. 14:12-14). As to the cause of the downfall of the son of the morning, it can, perhaps, be associated with spiritual pride. It is said of the fallen angels that they left their habitation (Jude v.6), i. e. that they were not satisfied with their sphere of influence that was assigned to them by God.

(b)   The present state of the devil as revealed in Scripture indicates that there are spirits, evil, wicked, with an intellectual knowledge of the truth in which they once stood, and to which they stood in allegiance. They are in chains of darkness, but have access to this present world. Their chains are held in the Sovereign hand of Him to whom angels are subject. They have certain liberties to display their enmity against the Most High. They use the hearts and minds of men to control also men's bodies as an easier means of conflict with the human race, and a more completely disguised form of carrying out their malignant designs. We know that this liberty is only for a time – 'Art thou come to torment us before the time?' (Matt. 8:29). The devil knows that his time is short. The spirits are motivated by feelings of envy, disappointment, frustration, and when the cause of God is operating the devil is especially active.

3. The Powers of the Devil

(a) His power extends over fallen angels. He is energising and directing their movements. Satan has an empire that accepts his authority with slavish submission. That they are great in number is evident. There is organisation and one purpose among them.

(b)   His power extends over man. Man is himself partly spirit and is susceptible to the appeal and influence from that direction. Wiles and devices are attributes of Satan and also depths of strategy (Rev. 2:24). The devil's indwelling is represented as being a strong man armed, garrisoned, and so holding his garrison in peace. The spirits of men are said to be led captive by him at his will, for when the world sinned it went over to the allegiance of the devil. The power of death is attributed to Satan. This does not mean that he has power to kill, but only to bring the bitterness of death and its fear as an enslaving power into the experience of men. The sting of death is sin and the devil uses this sting to our hurt and enslavement.

(c)   The world of evil is the empire over which the devil bears undisputed sway. The order of this visible world is subjected to interference from this invisible realm. He seems also to have access to heavenly places themselves. He is the accuser of the brethren. In Zechariah 3:1,2 we read 'He showed me Joshua the high priest standing before the angel of the Lord, and Satan standing at his right hand to resist him'. We read too in Job 1:6 'When the sons of God came to present themselves before the Lord, and Satan came also among them'. These glimpses of the spiritual world indicate that the devil is possessed of very great authority, perhaps delegated authority, and he is filled with insatiable hatred to the Kingdom of God, but we must remember his authority is not unlimited. He cannot touch the saints but by the will of God. His power is not almighty. He is subservient to the will of Heaven. He is not omniscient, though he and his host go to and fro' throughout the earth, gaining intimate knowledge of human affairs. He is not all-seeing nor all-wise. These are the attributes of the Almighty only.

4. The Activities of Satan

(a)   To the devil is ascribed as agent the apostasy of man. The serpent is said to have beguiled Eve.

(b)   To the devil is ascribed the Crucifixion of Christ. In the wilderness he assaulted the second Adam with identical temptations to the first Adam, but He did not fail. He departed from Christ for a season. He must have come again and again. It was Satan that entered into Judas Iscariot with the urge to betray Christ. It was Satan who planned and got his agents to execute the death of Christ.

(c)   Satan harasses and perplexes the Church. Even when he knows that he cannot destroy it he can do it hurt. The ancient promise ran, 'It shall bruise thy head and thou shalt bruise his heel', and the heel is now being bruised, but yet another promise is given, 'The God of peace shall bruise Satan under your feet shortly' (Rom. 16:20). He is still the arch tempter and is often transformed into an angel of light. It is said he never appears undisguised.

(d)   Satan resists the operations of the Gospel. The eyes of them that believe not are blinded by the god of this world. The parable of the sower unveils the activities of the devil in this field. The superhuman power he exerts over men is appalling though largely inscrutable.

5. The Final Doom of the Devil

Christ has come to destroy the works of the devil (1 John 3:8). Scripture makes clear that God will judge the world and his kingdom. His unlawful possession will not be left in his grasp, and the world shall be wrested out of his hand. There are indications that the devil is operating under a sense of his impending doom. That sentence had been upon him from the fall – 'Enmity between his seed and thy seed'. The place of doom is already in existence – fire prepared for the devil and his angels. When that is effected the devil will be limited and will never invade again God's dominion.

THE KINGDOM HINDERED

The present day trend of world affairs, with its emphasis on material values and its indifference to Christian morality, is evidently disturbing the minds of many who have had a facile conception of the world getting 'better and better', and society moving steadily, if slowly, towards the goal of human happiness and prosperity. Even to thoughtful Christian people, who have been accustomed to regard the progress of the Kingdom of God towards a millennium of spiritual triumph and glory as part and parcel of their most holy faith, the present situation, with its retrogression towards the moral and spiritual standards of a pagan society, is challenging and testing in the extreme. Has the promise failed, or have they been mistaken in their interpretation of the place that the Kingdom of Christ is to occupy in this world? Or may it not be that they have not clearly understood the path by which the Kingdom that is not meat and drink but righteousness and peace and joy in the Holy Ghost is to attain to the place of pre-eminence and supremacy in the world undoubtedly promised by the Word of God?

The teaching of our Lord throughout the Gospels, and more especially in the Parables of the Kingdom, contains clear warning, reiterated with solemn emphasis in His more private intercourse with His disciples, that His Kingdom was to meet with rising antagonism and opposition that should, for a time, hinder its progress and appear to nullify its teaching. So loath have men been to accept this aspect of the progress of the Kingdom of God in the world that much of Christ's teaching has been either set aside or completely misapplied, and parables that were clearly intended to sound this note of warning have been so interpreted as to foster the hope of a cause everywhere triumphant and a Kingdom that should sweep all opposition from its path. There is, in particular, a group of four parables that come into this category. They are the parables of the Sower, the Tares, the Mustard Seed and the Leaven, spoken all at one time, to the multitudes and most evidently intended to impress upon them one great truth concerning the nature and progress of the Kingdom of Heaven in the world. What that truth was it is not difficult to determine if we approach the parables without prejudice or preconceptions as to their interpretation. It is that the Kingdom of Grace was to be hindered in its advancement in the world by the stubbornness of human unbelief, by the subtlety of the Devil's opposition, by the application of human wisdom, and by the self-propagating nature of moral evil. We believe that these forces of opposition, operating with increasing momentum and subtlety, are unveiled in the four parables referred to.

There is, first, the opposition to the Kingdom of God from the stubbornness of unbelief that is so deeply entrenched in the human heart. This is strikingly illustrated in the Parable of the Sower. Of the four soils contemplated in the parable, only one is productive. In the other three the good seed never comes to harvest. The human heart, unprepared by the Spirit of God, is impervious to the Gospel message because of unbelief. The negative relation of unbelief to the Word of God is strikingly suggested by the prepositions *by, upon* and *among*, applied to the reception given to the seed by the *wayside,* the *stony places* and the *thorns* respectively. Here unbelief hinders the entry and progress of the Kingdom of God in the human heart by indifference, insubmission and compromise, three aspects of unbelief that still cry, 'We will not have this Man to rule over us'. This is the first hindrance illustrated by our Lord, that presented by the natural heart of man.

Next, there is the opposition to the Kingdom of God from the malice of the Devil, whose enmity operates in a hidden and subtle form. This finds illustration in the Parable of the Tares. Here it is not the soil that is at the root of the trouble but the fact that *mixed* seed has been sown. Darnel or tares has been introduced into the soil along with the good seed, and it was done 'while men slept'. There was a second sower at work in this field and his identity is revealed by the quality of the grain he has sown – it was grain whose development was calculated to stifle and eventually kill the lawful growth, and whose real nature could not be recognised till the growth was sufficiently advanced to make removal all but impossible. Thus the identity of the sower was clear: 'An enemy has done this.' This parable, therefore, brings us a step further in the unveiling of the opposition to the Kingdom of God in the world – it is not merely the stubborn unbelief of the human heart, but more cunning and more terrible, the malignant Spirit, enemy to God and to man, that fosters and employs human unbelief, the Devil. Here we have our Lord's teaching on the mystery that so often perplexes the human mind, the introduction of moral evil and its development in the world, and, more relevant to our present study, the purpose of moral evil, namely the hindering of the Kingdom of God in the world.

The third in the group of parables spoken to the multitudes illustrates the hindrance to the Kingdom of God from the application of the methods indicated by human wisdom. This we believe to be the teaching of the Parable of the Mustard Seed. The mustard seed is small in itself, and though its growth is rapid and relatively large, it is by nature merely a *herb*, even if 'the greatest among herbs'. In the parable, however, there appears unnatural growth, for the herb 'becometh a tree so that the birds of the air come and lodge in the branches thereof'. In no instance can a herb, under natural conditions, become a tree with spreading branches; that would point rather to forced growth under artificial conditions! And the Kingdom of God, that is the outward expression and manifestation of the principle of grace in the heart, will remain a herb of God's planting tender and fragile in appearance, yet true to its nature and Divine purpose, unless it yields to artificial pressure and assumes a growth and development that are untrue to its real nature. Was this meant to be a solemn warning from the lips of Christ Himself, that His Church would enter into alliance with the world, accept its protection and government, and become 'great' on the level of worldly standards? That this has happened finds impressive illustration in the growth and affluence of the Papacy, and no impartial observer will deny that throughout the ages the unclean birds of the air found – and still find – lodgment in its branches! To some extent at least this prophecy has found fulfilment in all the branches of the Christian Church, and to the extent in which the professing Church has courted and accepted the greatness of the world, it has become the sheltering place of many unclean forces, and has hindered, rather than advanced, the progress of the Kingdom of God in the world.

The remaining parable of the group, that of the Leaven, illustrates the hindrance to the Kingdom of God through the self-propagating nature of the evil that has contaminated the professing Church of God. The first three parables were drawn from the field; the Parable of the Leaven is taken from the home. The 'three measures of meal 'to which frequent reference is made elsewhere in the Scriptures, is never associated with leaven, except in this parable. Rather is it a condition of its use, according to the Divine injunction, that it be not prepared with leaven. But on this occasion a woman surreptitiously took leaven and 'hid it' in the three measures of meal, knowing that she was doing something that was expressly forbidden. It may have been due to her ignorance of the nature of leaven, or to her defiance of the Divine commandment, but, in any case, the leaven did its work and propagated itself in what, after all, was its most natural medium, till the whole of the three measures had been leavened. Does this not teach us that the final and great hindrance to the progress of the Kingdom of God in the world is the nature of sin itself as a self-propagating and contaminating influence. If sin is introduced, deliberately albeit surreptitiously, into the Church and cherished in its membership, it will do its contaminating work till the entire Church in its outward organisation is affected and to that extent crippled for its Divine work in the world. It is its tolerance of sin that, in the last analysis, has maimed the Church for its work and made its witness to the Kingdom of God ineffective and unconvincing. For it is the natural law under which sin operates that its influence cannot be circumscribed or its infection localised once it has been introduced and given shelter in the life of the professing Church of God.

If the four parables that fall into this one group are to be regarded as enforcing several aspects of the one great truth, then the truth they enshrine has its bearing upon our sombre events and upon the duty of Christian men and women towards the Kingdom of their Lord that is being hindered. If the policies of nations are activated by prejudices, fears and suspicions rather than by Christian principles of conduct, if the love of many within the Church be grown cold and their loyalty seem to falter, let our faith find solace and strengthening in the knowledge that the Master has warned us that His Kingdom should suffer violence from within as well as from without. Above all, let us begin where our Lord's teaching in these parables began, at the condition of our own hearts, whose unbelief is the primary, as it is the chief, hindrance to the coming of the Kingdom of God in the world. For only as the Kingdom of Christ is come within our own hearts can we have the true earnest of the promise that it is to come in the world and that

'His large and great dominion shall

From sea to sea extend'.